A Special Issue of
Cognition & Emotion

Associative Learning of Likes and Dislikes

Edited by

Jan de Houwer
Ghent University, Belgium

Frank Baeyens
University of Leuven, Belgium

and

Andy Field
University of Sussex, UK

 Psychology Press
Taylor & Francis Group

HOVE AND NEW YORK

Published in 2005 by Psychology Press Ltd
27 Church Road, Hove, East Sussex BN3 2FA

Simultaneously published in the USA and Canada
by Psychology Press
711 Third Avenue, New York, NY 10017

First issued in paperback 2015

*Psychology Press is an imprint of the Taylor and Francis Group,
an informa business*

British Library Cataloguing in Publication Data
A catalogue record for this book is available from the British Library

ISBN 13: 978-1-138-87795-5 (pbk)
ISBN 13: 978-1-8416-9949-3 (hbk)

ISSN 0269-9931

Typeset DP Photosetting, Aylesbury, Bucks

Contents*

Associative learning of likes and dislikes: Some current controversies and possible ways forward
Jan De Houwer, Frank Baeyens, and Andy P. Field　　161

Evaluative conditioning in social psychology: Facts and speculations
Eva Walther, Benjamin Nagengast, and Claudia Trasselli　　175

Reactance in affective-evaluative learning: Outside of conscious control?
Marianne Hammerl and Eamon P. Fulcher　　197

Dissociating the effects of attention and contingency awareness on evaluative conditioning effects in the visual paradigm
Andy P. Field and Annette C. Moore　　217

Resistance to extinction of human evaluative conditioning using a between-subjects design
E. Díaz, G. Ruiz, and F. Baeyens　　245

No support for dual process accounts of human affective learning in simple Pavlovian conditioning
Ottmar V. Lipp and Helena M. Purkis　　269

Beyond evaluative conditioning? Searching for associative transfer of nonevaluative stimulus properties
Tom Meersmans, Jan De Houwer, Frank Baeyens, Tom Randell, and Paul Eelen　　283

Subject Index　　307

---

* This book is also a special issue of the journal *Cognition & Emotion*, and forms issue 2 of Volume 19 (2005). The page numbers are taken from the journal and so begin with p. 161.

COGNITION AND EMOTION
2005, 19 (2), 161–174

Associative learning of likes and dislikes: Some current controversies and possible ways forward

Jan De Houwer

Ghent University, Belgium

Frank Baeyens

University of Leuven, Belgium

Andy P. Field

University of Sussex, UK

Evaluative conditioning (EC) is one of the terms that is used to refer to associatively induced changes in liking. Many controversies have arisen in the literature on EC. Do associatively induced changes in liking actually exist? Does EC depend on awareness of the fact that stimuli are associated? Is EC resistant to extinction? Does attention help or hinder EC? As an introduction to this special issue, we will discuss the extent to which the papers that are published in this issue help to resolve some of the controversies that surround EC. We also speculate about possible boundary conditions of EC and attempt to reconcile conflicting results on the functional properties of EC.

Preferences are assumed to play a crucial role in many phenomena that are studied in learning psychology (e.g., Martin & Levey, 1978), social psychology (e.g., Zajonc, 1980; also see Walther, Nagengast, & Trasseli, this issue), consumer science (e.g., Stuart, Shimp, & Engle, 1987), emotion research (e.g., Sherer, 1993), and clinical psychology (e.g., Hermans, 1998). Given the pervasive impact that preferences have on behaviour, it is important to know where these likes and dislikes come from. Although some preferences are genetically determined, most stem from learning that took place during the lifetime of the individual (e.g., Rozin, 1982). In this special issue, we focus on one such type of

Correspondence concerning this article should be addressed to Jan De Houwer, Department of Psychology, Ghent University, Henri Dunantlaan 2, B-9000 Ghent, Belgium; e-mail: Jan.DeHouwer@UGent.be

We thank Paul Eelen and the Fund for Scientific Research (Flanders, Belgium) for making possible the special interest meeting on which this special issue was based. We also thank Eva Walther for her critical comments on an earlier draft of this paper.

http://www.tandf.co.uk/journals/pp/02699931.html   DOI:10.1080/02699930441000265

learning: Associative learning of likes and dislikes, that is, changes in liking that are due to the pairing of stimuli.[1]

Various terms, such as evaluative conditioning, evaluative learning, and affective learning, have been used to refer to an observed change in the liking of a stimulus that results from pairing this stimulus with another, liked or disliked stimulus. Because the term "evaluative conditioning" (EC) is the only of these terms that refers to the fact that the induced changes in liking are due to the pairing of stimuli (rather than to other factors, such as the mere repeated presentation of a stimulus), we prefer to use this term. De Houwer, Thomas, and Baeyens (2001; see also Field, in press) recently reviewed the literature on EC. From this review, it became apparent that there are still many controversies about the conditions under which the pairing of stimuli will lead to changes in liking. In an attempt to stimulate the debate about these issues, we organised a special interest meeting on EC which was attended by most researchers who were at the time actively engaged in EC research. This meeting took place in May of 2002 and was sponsored by the Fund for Scientific Research (Flanders, Belgium) as part of the Scientific Research Network "Acquisition, Representation, and Activation of Evaluative Judgements and Emotions". Because many of the papers that were presented during the meeting indeed furthered our knowledge about EC, we decided to put together this special issue on the basis of these papers. As an introduction, we will describe some of the controversies that surrounded research on EC at the time we held the meeting and will discuss to which extent the papers in this special issue help to resolve these controversies. We conclude by discussing possible solutions for the remaining unresolved issues.

CURRENT CONTROVERSIES

Is EC a genuine phenomenon?

Shanks and Dickinson (1990) and Field and Davey (1997, 1998, 1999) convincingly argued and demonstrated that apparent EC effects can be due to an artefact that is related to the stimulus assignment procedure. In several early EC studies (e.g., Baeyens, Crombez, Van den Bergh, & Eelen, 1988), researchers assigned neutral stimuli (conditioned stimuli or CSs) to liked or disliked stimuli (unconditioned stimuli or USs) on the basis of perceptual similarity. If, for

---

[1] Note that when we talk about "associative learning", "conditioning", or "associatively induced changes in behaviour", we do not want to imply that observed changes in behaviour are due to the formation of associative links between representations. We only want to indicate that the changes in behaviour are due to fact that stimuli have been paired (i.e., presented together) in a certain manner. That is, we use "associative learning" to refer to an effect (i.e., a change in behaviour that is due to pairing stimuli) rather than to a theory (i.e., the formation of associations between representations).

instance, a neutral stimulus was perceptually most similar to a liked picture, it was repeatedly presented together with this liked picture during the learning phase. If it was most similar to a disliked picture, it would be paired with that disliked picture. Most often, neutral stimuli that were paired with liked stimuli were afterwards liked more than neutral stimuli that were paired with disliked stimuli. Field and Davey (1999), however, showed that a neutral stimulus that is most similar to a liked stimulus will be liked more during a second rating phase than a neutral stimulus that is most similar to a dislike picture even when the stimuli were not paired or when the stimuli were never presented during the learning phase!

Field and Davey (1997, 1998, 1999) therefore argued that to demonstrate that changes in liking are due to associative learning, EC studies should include between-subject control conditions in which stimuli are not paired. Given that few if any studies included such controls, they raised doubts about the very existence of EC as an associative learning phenomenon. Some have argued that there are many within-subjects studies in which the construction of stimulus pairs was counterbalanced across participants or randomised and that therefore do provide strong evidence for the associative nature of EC (e.g., Baeyens, De Houwer, Vansteenwegen, & Eelen, 1998; De Houwer, Baeyens, Vansteenwe-gen, & Eelen, 2000; De Houwer et al., 2001). Nevertheless, it is good to see that several of the EC experiments that are reported in this special issue did include a between-subjects control condition and still found strong evidence for EC (Díaz, Ruiz, & Baeyens, this issue; Field & Moore, this issue; Hammerl & Fulcher, this issue). This should eliminate all doubts about whether genuine EC effects do exist.

But as is noted by Field and Moore (this issue), EC is certainly not a robust research finding. Field and Davey (1999) and Rozin, Wrzesniewski, and Byrnes (1998) already reported several genuine failures to find EC, that is, failures that were probably not due to a lack of statistical power or to obvious flaws in the design. During our special interest meeting in Belgium, many more reports of unpublished failures to find EC emerged (e.g., Field, Lascelles, & Davey, 2003). Even researchers who were eventually successful in finding replicable EC (e.g., Olson & Fazio, 2001; Walther, 2002) spoke about their lengthy struggle to find the parameters under which EC reliably emerged. It thus appears to be the case that EC is subject to many as yet unidentified boundary conditions.

What are the functional properties of EC?

Given that preferences are such important determinants of behaviour, knowledge about the processes that underlie the formation of preferences can help us understand, control, and predict behavior. Researchers have therefore examined the impact of a number of variables on EC in the hope of gaining insight in the processes that underlie EC. Initial research suggested that, in comparison to other forms of Pavlovian associative learning, EC appeared to have several unusual functional characteristics (see De Houwer et al., 2001, for a review; also see Lipp & Purkis, this issue). For instance, EC does not seem to depend on whether the participants are aware of which stimulus was paired with which other stimulus (i.e., contingency awareness) and is not reduced when the CSs are presented on their own after the learning phase (i.e., no extinction). However, because some of the studies on which these conclusions were based used a flawed (i.e., similarity-based) stimulus-assignment procedure (see above), there was still strong disagreement about whether EC indeed has unique functional properties and thus about the nature of the processes that underlie EC. Moreover, some studies indicated that EC at least sometimes does show the same functional properties as other forms of Pavlovian learning. This special issue includes several papers that provide new important information about the role of awareness, extinction, and attention in EC. We will thus focus on these three functional properties.

Awareness of the stimulus pairings.   Just as there has been an intense debate about the role of awareness in learning in general (e.g., Seger, 1994; Shanks & St. John, 1994; Lovibond & Shanks, 2002), there has been a controversy about whether participants need to be aware of the fact that a stimulus was paired with a positive or negative stimulus to show an associatively induced change in the evaluation of the first stimulus (e.g., Baeyens, De Houwer, & Eelen, 1994; Baeyens, Eelen, & Van den Bergh, 1990; De Houwer, 2001; Field, 2000; Fulcher & Hammerl, 2001; Lovibond & Shanks, 2002). This debate was complicated by the fact that doubts were raised about whether EC is a genuine associative phenomenon: If EC is an artefact of stimulus-assignments rather than based on associative learning, it should come as no surprise that EC does not depend on awareness of the presented associations (e.g., Davey, 1994). The papers of Hammerl and Fulcher (this issue) and Field and Moore (this issue) provide an important additional step toward resolving this controversy. Not only do they provide new evidence for unaware EC, they also included between-subject control conditions that allowed them to conclude that the observed EC effects were based on associative learning.

Lipp and Purkis (this issue), on the other hand, describe one of their earlier studies (Purkis & Lipp, 2001) in which they found EC only in participants who could verbalise the crucial CS-US contingency and only after the moment at which these participants could do so. The results of this study strongly suggest that EC does depend on awareness of the stimulus pairings. Importantly, Purkis and Lipp measured awareness during the learning phase rather than only at the end of the experiment. Their awareness measure was thus probably more sensitive than those that are used in most other studies. This raises doubts about the conclusiveness of other studies in which EC did not appear to depend on contingency awareness. Note, however, that the procedure that is used by Lipp and

Purkis is rather atypical in EC research in that only very few stimuli are presented. We will return to this topic later on.

Is EC sensitive to extinction?   Another intriguing finding in the EC literature is that EC appears to be resistant to extinction (e.g., Baeyens et al., 1988; De Houwer et al., 2000). That is, once a stimulus has acquired a valence as the result of being paired with a liked or disliked stimulus, this acquired valence cannot be changed by repeatedly presenting the stimulus on its own. Although there are other forms of learning that also appear to be resistant to extinction (see Field, in press, for a discussion), typically, conditioned responses do decrease rapidly when the CS is repeatedly presented on its own after the learning phase (e.g., Hamm & Vaitl, 1996). If EC is indeed resistant to extinction, this would have many implications (see Walther et al., this issue, for some of the implications for phenomena in social psychology). But because most of the evidence regarding the lack of extinction in EC came from studies that used a similarity-based stimulus-assignment procedure (see above), doubts were raised about this functional property of EC: If changes in liking are not based on associative learning, then it is not surprising that a removal of the association (i.e., presenting one stimulus on its own) has no effect on these changes (e.g., Davey, 1994; Field & Davey, 1997). The paper by Díaz et al. (this issue) tackles this potential problem by including between-subjects controls in extinction studies. Their results confirm that evaluative conditioning is indeed resistant to extinction.

Lipp and Purkis (this issue), however, describe the results of Lipp, Oughton, and LeLievre (2003) who did find extinction in EC if they asked participants to repeatedly rate the valence of the CS at the time it was presented on its own during the extinction phase. Interestingly, they did not find extinction when they looked only at the ratings that participants gave after the extinction phase. They explained this result as an example of renewal, that is, recovery of a conditioned response after removal of the extinction context. Previous failures to find extinction in EC might therefore have been due to the fact that evaluative ratings were only collected after the extinction phase. But as we will discuss later on, there might be other reasons for the discrepancy between the results that were obtained in the studies of Lipp and colleagues and the results that were obtained at other labs.

Does attention help or hamper EC?   In contrast to the many reported experiments about the impact of contingency awareness and extinction on EC, very little research has looked at the role of attention in EC. Field and Moore (this issue) report two experiments that suggest that EC is reduced when participants engage in an attention demanding secondary task during the learning phase (i.e., counting backwards from 300). Although this finding is in line with many theories of associative learning in general, other results suggest that secondary tasks do not always hamper EC. Field and Moore (this issue) themselves point out that Hammerl and Grabitz (2000) did find significant EC when participants solved arithmetical problems during the learning phase, but argue that the divergent results could be due to differences in the nature of the stimuli that were used. Walther (2002, Experiment 5; also see Walther et al., this issue), however, did use stimuli similar to those of Field and Moore and found that, if anything, the presence of a secondary task (remembering an 8 digit number throughout the learning phase) *strengthened* the EC effect. But the secondary task that Walther used was probably less demanding that the secondary task of Field and Moore. Further studies in which the nature of the secondary task is systematically manipulated could thus shed light on these apparently conflicting results.

POSSIBLE WAYS FORWARD

Although the papers that are reported in this special issue will undoubtably help to resolve some of the controversies surrounding EC, they also make clear that many questions remain unanswered. When reading the special issue, one might, for instance, be puzzled by the fact that Lipp and Purkis (this issue) conclude that EC does depend on contingency awareness and does show extinction whereas Hammerl and Fulcher (this issue) and Field and Moore (this issue) present strong evidence that EC does not depend on awareness and Díaz et al. (this issue) demonstrate that EC is resistant to extinction. Likewise, one might be confused by the fact we highlighted that EC effects are not easy to obtain (also see Field & Moore, this issue) whereas the papers in this special issue actually contain several new and well-controlled demonstrations of EC. In the following section, we will present some ideas that might help clarify these two inconsistencies and that could be helpful in guiding future research.

Possible boundary conditions for EC

In many ways, research on EC is still in its early stages. This is evidenced by the fact that little is known about the conditions under which EC effects will emerge and the fact that there are few if any detailed theories of the processes that underlie EC (see De Houwer et al., 2001). Unfortunately, the one weakness strengthens the other. Because it is not easy to find a paradigm that produces reliable EC effects (see Olson & Fazio, 2001, and Walther, 2002, for some promising exceptions), it is difficult to examine the functional properties of EC and thus the processes that underlie EC. Likewise, because there are no detailed theories of EC, it is difficult to make clear predictions about the conditions under which reliable EC effects will be found. Hence, researchers often use a trial-and-error strategy in their attempts to find EC. This also became apparent during the meeting that led to this special issue. There were no reports of studies in which possible boundary conditions were systematically investigated. But several researchers commented on their failures to obtain EC and speculated about the procedural parameters that need to be in place in order to find EC. The parameter that was mentioned most often was the manner in which participants evaluate the stimuli. Various researchers mentioned that they found EC effects only when participants were strongly encouraged to evaluate the stimuli on the basis of their immediate, spontaneous feelings and were asked not to think too much about their evaluation. In relation to this, it was mentioned that one needs stimuli that participants feel they can evaluate in an intuitive, spontaneous manner.

These suggestions are in line with the idea that EC depends on automatic (i.e., unconscious, unintentional, and/or effortless) processes that produce intuitive, subjectively unjustifiable changes in liking. It is possible that these processes can be immunised by controlled (i.e., conscious, intentional, and/or effortful) processes. Alternatively, the output of the automatic processes might only reveal itself in behavior (e.g., evaluative ratings) when that behavior is not determined by other (controlled) processes. Similar suggestions about the importance of intuitive judgements for measuring automatic processes have been made in the context of implicit learning (e.g., Lewicki, Hill, & Czyzewska, 1997; but see Hendrickx, De Houwer, Baeyens, Eelen, & Van Avermaet, 1997) and automatic affective processing (e.g., Fazio, 1986; Koole, Dijksterhuis, & van Knippenberg, 2001). There is also some evidence that deliberative thought is capable of inhibiting automatic affective responding (see Koole et al., 2001, p. 673). It would thus be worthwhile to test whether EC effects are stronger and more reliable when participants rely on intuition. Note, however, that some researchers have failed to find EC even when participants were encouraged to rely on their intuition and when stimuli were used that should allow for an intuitive evaluation (e.g., Field et al., 2003). It is therefore likely that these factors are not the only ones that determine whether EC will be found. There is thus a clear need for studies that investigate possible boundary conditions of EC in a systematic manner.

EC could be due to different processes

One of the most puzzling aspects of the literature on EC is that there are diametrically opposed results about the functional properties of EC. Whereas some researchers found that EC does not depend on contingency awareness and is not resistant to extinction (see De Houwer et al., 2001, for a review, and Field & Moore, this issue, Hammerl & Fulcher, this issue, and Díaz et al., this issue, for new evidence), Lipp and colleagues found strong evidence that EC does depend on awareness and is resistant to extinction (see Lipp & Purkis, this issue). In our opinion, these conflicting data suggest the EC effects that were observed in the studies of Lipp and colleagues were due to processes different from those that produced EC effects in other studies. If this is true, it should come as no surprise that the EC effects of Lipp and colleagues show different functional properties that other EC effects. In this section, we will first give a conceptual analysis of the term "conditioning" that clarifies that EC and other forms of conditioning can indeed be based on a variety of processes. Next, we will present an hypothesis about the processes that might have operated in the studies of Lipp and colleagues.

For many psychologists, the term "conditioning" still has theoretical implications. When someone says that a certain change in behaviour is due to conditioning, most psychologists will infer that the associatively induced changes in behaviour were due to simple, unconscious, automatic processes (see Brewer, 1974). Research on human conditioning has clearly demonstrated, however, that associatively induced changes in behaviour (i.e., conditioning) can also be (and are perhaps even most often) due to or mediated by consciously controlled processes (see Dawson & Shell, 1987; De Houwer, Vandorpe, & Beckers, in press; Lovibond & Shanks, 2002, for reviews). Eelen (1980) pointed out that rather than abandoning the term "conditioning" on the basis of these findings, it should be used to refer to either a procedure or an effect of this procedure and should be stripped from its theoretical connotations. The term "classical conditioning", for instance, should refer to the fact that stimuli are paired in a certain manner (i.e., a procedure) or to the fact that the pairing of stimuli leads to a change in the reaction toward the stimuli (i.e., an effect that is due to the pairing of stimuli).[2] From this perspective, it becomes clear that conditioning effects can result from a variety of processes, automatic or otherwise. This clear separation between conditioning as a procedure, an effect, and a theory allows one to avoid situations in which the term "conditioning" constrains theorising about the possible processes that could be responsible for the observed conditioning effects. For instance, from this perspective, there is no paradox in saying that conditioning effects are due to conscious, controlled processes such as the deliberate generation and testing of hypotheses about CS-US relations (see De Houwer et al., in press, for a discussion).

We believe that research on EC could also benefit from Eelen's (1980) distinction between procedure, effect, and theory. As a procedure, evaluative conditioning is similar to a classical conditioning procedure in that stimuli are paired in a certain manner. The only unique procedural feature is that one measures changes in liking. As an effect, evaluative conditioning refers to an observed change in the liking of a stimulus that results from pairing that stimulus with another, liked or disliked stimulus. There is no logical reason why

---

[2] We want to emphasise that when a conditioning procedure results in changes in behaviour, one needs to be sure that these changes are due to the pairing of the stimuli before one can refer to these changes as a conditioning effect. That is, one always needs to control for nonassociative effects. This definition of conditioning as an effect is, however, neutral with regard to the nature of the processes that are responsible for the fact that the pairing of stimuli results in a change in behaviour.

evaluative conditioning as an effect could be due to simple automatic processes only, nor is there any reason to believe that only associatively induced changes in liking that are based on simple automatic processes should be regarded as "true" evaluative conditioning. This perspective is liberating in that it allows one to appreciate the possibility that some of the EC effects that have been reported in the literature could be due to conscious controlled processes rather than simple automatic processes.

These considerations led us to some speculative ideas about the processes that might have been involved in the studies of Lipp and colleagues (see Lipp & Purkis, this issue, for a review). In these studies, typically one CS was followed by an aversive US (CS+, where + stands for the presence of the US) whereas another CS was not followed by the aversive US (CS−, where − stands for the absence of the US). Moreover, the CSs were typically abstract geometrical forms that most participants probably found difficult to evaluate in an intuitive manner. Nevertheless, results consistently showed that the CS+ was afterwards liked less than the CS−. This finding corresponds to evaluative conditioning as an effect. However, EC might have been based on the formation of conscious propositional knowledge about the CS-US relation. Participants might have evaluated the CS+ as being more negative than the CS− not because of an intuitive, unjustifiable feeling, but because they had formed conscious knowledge about the fact that the CS+ and not the CS− always preceded the aversive US. That is, they had the conscious propositional knowledge that the CS+ was always followed by the aversive US, which they saw as sufficient justification for disliking the CS+. In other words, they had a justifiable preference: They justified their dislike for the CS+ by referring to the fact that it was a reliable signal for the aversive US. The assumption that preferences can be based on conscious propositional knowledge could seem implausible at first sight to psychologists who are most often focused on introspectively undefined or incorrectly defined sources of preferences. However, the fact that some (and perhaps even most) preferences are unjustifiable (i.e., not based on conscious propositional knowledge about contingencies or events that actually led to the preference) does not exclude the possibility that at least some preferences are justifiable (i.e., based on conscious propositional knowledge about the contingencies or events that actually form the basis of the preference).

The assumption that the EC effects that were observed in the studies of Lipp and colleagues were based on conscious propositional knowledge about the CS-US relations is compatible with the fact that those EC effects depended on contingency awareness and showed extinction. If EC is based on conscious knowledge of the CS-US relation, contingency awareness is of course required. In addition, during the extinction phase, participants can form the additional proposition that the CS+ is no longer followed by the US. Formulating this new proposition will reduce EC during extinction but EC can resurface when participants no longer consider this additional knowledge as relevant for evaluating the CS (i.e., renewal). In fact, because human associative learning most often depends on conscious propositional knowledge (see De Houwer et al., in press, and Lovibond & Shanks, 2002, for reviews), one would expect that in those cases where EC is based on conscious propositional knowledge, it will show all the functional properties that are normally found in human associative learning.

It is also important to realise that justifiable preferences might not only be expressed in direct, explicit measures of valence, such as ratings, but also in implicit measures, such as the affective priming task (e.g., Fazio, Sanbonmatsu, Powell, & Kardess, 1986) and the Implicit Association Test (IAT; e.g., Greenwald, McGee, & Schwartz, 1998). Indeed, there is evidence to support this suggestion. For example, asking people to memorise the (positive or negative) meaning of so-called Turkish words is sufficient to observe affective priming (De Houwer, Hermans, & Eelen, 1998) and IAT effects (Mitchell, Anderson, & Lovibond, 2003) when the Turkish words are used as (prime) stimuli. Likewise, Gregg, Banaji, and Seibt (2004) found that nonsense labels will function as positive or negative concepts in an IAT after merely asking participants to suppose that one label is the name of a group of aggressive people whereas the other label is the name of a group of victims. These findings are reminiscent of earlier findings which showed that merely informing participants that a CS will be followed by a US is sufficient to induce autonomic conditioned responses toward the CS (see Dawson & Shell, 1987, for a review). Although further evidence is needed, it does at least seem plausible that justifiable preferences might indeed be detected also when using implicit measures of valence. Note that this in no way excludes the possibility that implicit measures most often reflect unjustifiable preferences.

If both direct evaluative ratings and implicit measures of valence can reflect either justifiable or unjustifiable preferences, how is one to determine whether a conditioned preference is justifiable? At present, the best option seems to just ask the participant to report the reasons behind his/her evaluation of a particular stimulus. If the participant confidently reports propositional knowledge about the actual CS-US contingency as the reason for his/her preference, one can conclude that the conditioned preference is justified. Note that participants need to be aware of the CS-US contingency before they can use the knowledge of the CS-US contingency as a justification for their preference. However, participants will not necessarily use their conscious knowledge of the contingencies to form an opinion of the CSs. It is thus useful to both examine whether participants are aware of the contingencies and whether participants attribute their preferences to this conscious knowledge. Such an approach will be particularly useful in studies in which contingency awareness is good (e.g., because only few CS-US pairs are presented).

Although we realise that there are problems associated with verbal reports (e.g., Nisbett & Wilson, 1977), one should realise that verbal reports can at least sometimes provide valuable insights (see Smith & Miller, 1978, for an insightful critique of Nisbett & Wilson, 1977). Also note that researchers do already rely heavily on verbal reports when studying the role of contingency awareness in EC. We believe that research on EC could benefit greatly if participants were asked to justify their preferences. It would, for instance, be interesting to see whether participants in studies, such as those of Lipp and colleagues, will report that their evaluation of the CS+ is based on the CS-US contingency. It would also be interesting to examine whether the functional properties of EC are related to whether participants can justify their preferences in an accurate manner. As Meersmans et al. (this issue) point out, one could also manipulate instructions (e.g., about the nature of the CSs and USs) in such a way that they inhibit or promote the use of conscious knowledge of CS-US contingencies as a basis for ratings. Meersmans et al. also found the distinction between justified and unjustified beliefs helpful to interpret their finding that associative transfer of nonevaluative stimulus properties seems to depend on awareness of the contingencies.

Regardless of the merits of our ideas about the processes that were involved in the studies of Lipp and colleagues, it is important to realise that not all EC effects might be based on the same types of processes. Which processes are involved could depend on procedural parameters, such as the number and nature of the stimuli, the number of times that the CS-US pairs are presented, the intensity of the USs, and instructions. From this perspective, it is interesting to note that researchers use many different paradigms for studying EC. In fact, almost every researcher seems to have his or her own paradigm. Given this state of affairs, it is perhaps not surprising that findings from different labs do not always converge. In any case, an important challenge for future research is to clarify which type of processes can produce EC effects and to identify the procedural elements that determine the nature of the processes that are responsible for the observed effects.

CONCLUSION

Despite the many controversies that have plagued research on EC, it remains a fascinating research topic. Research on EC not only has the potential to lead to important new theoretical insights in the processes that underlie learning and memory, it also has immediate implications for our understanding of numerous phenomena in social psychology, consumer science, emotion theory, and clinical psychology (see Walther et al., this issue, for an inspiring discussion of the possible implications of existing EC research for many topics in social psychology, consumer science, and clinical psychology). Moreover, there is the exciting prospect of many intriguing questions that await an answer. We therefore hope that more researchers will join our battle to gain a better understanding of this important phenomenon.

REFERENCES

Baeyens, F., Crombez, G., Van den Bergh, O., & Eelen, P. (1988). Once in contact, always in contact: Evaluative conditioning is resistant to extinction. *Advances in Behaviour Research and Therapy, 10,* 179–199.

Baeyens, F., De Houwer, J., & Eelen, P. (1994). Awareness inflated, evaluative conditioning underestimated. *Behavioral and Brain Sciences, 17,* 396–397.

Baeyens, F., De Houwer, J., Vansteenwegen, D., & Eelen, P. (1998). Evaluative conditioning is a form of associative learning: On the artifactual nature of Field and Davey's (1997) artifactual account of evaluative learning. *Learning and Motivation, 29,* 461–474.

Baeyens, F., Eelen, P. & Van den Bergh, O. (1990). Contingency awareness in evaluative conditioning: A case for unaware affective-evaluative learning. *Cognition and Emotion, 4,* 3–18.

Brewer, W. F. (1974). There is no convincing evidence of conditioning in adult humans. In W. B. Weimer & D. S. Palermo (Eds.), *Cognition and the symbolic processes* (pp. 1–42). Hillsdale, NJ: Erlbaum.

Davey, G. C. L. (1994). Defining the important questions to ask about evaluative conditioning: A reply to Martin and Levey (1994). *Behaviour Research and Therapy, 32,* 307–310.

Dawson, M. E., & Schell, A. M. (1987). Human autonomic and skeletal classical conditioning: The role of conscious cognitive factors. In G. Davey (Ed.), *Cognitive processes and Pavlovian conditioning in humans* (pp. 27–56). Chichester, UK: Wiley.

De Houwer, J. (2001). Contingency awareness and evaluative conditioning: When will it be enough? *Consciousness and Cognition, 10,* 550–558.

De Houwer, J., Baeyens, F., Vansteenwegen, D., & Eelen, P. (2000). Evaluative conditioning in the picture-picture paradigm with random assignment of conditioned stimuli to unconditioned stimuli. *Journal of Experimental Psychology: Animal Behavior Processes, 26,* 237–242.

De Houwer, J., Hermans, D., & Eelen, P. (1998). Affective and identity priming with episodically associated stimuli. *Cognition and Emotion, 12,* 145–169.

De Houwer, J., Thomas, S., & Baeyens, F. (2001) Associative learning of likes and dislikes: A review of 25 years of research on human evaluative conditioning. *Psychological Bulletin, 127,* 853–869.

De Houwer, J., Vandorpe, S., & Beckers, T. (in press). On the role of controlled cognitive processes in human associative learning. In A. Wills (Ed.), *New directions in human associative learning.* Mahwah, NJ: Erlbaum.

Díaz, E., Ruiz, G., & Baeyens, F. (2005). Resistance to extinction of human evaluative conditioning using a between-subjects design. *Cognition and Emotion, 19,* 245–268.

Eelen, P. (1980). Klassieke conditioning: Klassiek en toch modern [Classical conditioning: Classic but nevertheless modern]. In Liber Amicorum Prof. J.R. Nuttin, *Gedrag, dynamische relatie en betekeniswereld [Behaviour, dynamic relation, and world of meaning]* (pp. 321–343), Leuven, Belgium: Universitaire Pers Leuven.

Fazio, R. H. (1986). How do attitudes guide behavior? In R. M. Sorrentine & E. T. Higgins (Eds.), *The handbook of motivation and cognition: Foundations of social behavior* (pp. 204–243). New York: Guilford Press.

Fazio, R. H., Sanbonmatsu, D. M., Powell, M. C., & Kardes, F. R. (1986). On the automatic activation of attitudes. *Journal of Personality and Social Psychology, 50,* 229–238.

Field, A. P. (2000). I like it, but I'm not sure why: Can evaluative conditioning occur without conscious awareness? *Consciousness and Cognition, 9,* 13–36.

Field, A. P. (in press). Learning to like (or dislike): Associative learning of preferences. In A. J. Wills (Ed.), *New directions in human associative learning.* Mahwah, NJ: Erlbaum.

Field, A. P., & Davey, G. C. L. (1997). Conceptual conditioning: evidence for an artifactual account of evaluative learning. *Learning and Motivation, 28,* 446–464.

Field, A. P., & Davey, G. C. L. (1998). Evaluative conditioning: Arti-fact or -fiction? A reply to Baeyens, De Houwer, Vansteenwegen, and Eelen. *Learning and Motivation, 29,* 475–491.

Field, A. P., & Davey, G. C. L. (1999). Reevaluating evaluative conditioning: A nonassociative explanation of conditioning effects in the visual evaluative conditioning paradigm. *Journal of Experimental Psychology: Animal Behaviour Processes*, *25*, 211–224.

Field, A. P., Lascelles, K. R. R., & Davey, G. C. L. (2003). *Evaluative conditioning: Missing presumed dead.* Unpublished manuscript.

Field, A. P., & Moore, A. C. (2005). Dissociating the effects of attention and contingency awareness on the evaluative conditioning effects in the visual paradigm. *Cognition and Emotion*, *19*, 217–243.

Fulcher, E. P., & Hammerl, M. (2001). When all is revealed: A dissociation between evaluative learning and contingency awareness. *Consciousness and Cognition*, *10*, 524–549.

Greenwald, A. G., McGhee, D. E., & Schwartz, J. L. K. (1998). Measuring individual differences in implicit cognition: The Implicit Association Test. *Journal of Personality and Social Psychology*, *74*, 1464–1480.

Gregg, A. P., Banaji, M. R., & Seibt, B. (2004). *Easier made than undone: The asymmetric malleability of automatic preferences.* Manuscript submitted for publication.

Hamm, A. O., & Vaitl, D. (1996). Affective learning and aversion. *Psychophsyiology*, *33*, 698–710.

Hammerl, M., & Fulcher, E. P. (2005). Reactance in affective-evaluative learning: Outside of conscious control? *Cognition and Emotion*, *19*, 197–216.

Hammerl, M., & Grabitz, H.-J. (2000). Affective-evaluative learning in humans: A form of associative learning or only an artifact? *Learning and Motivation*, *31*, 345–363.

Hendrickx, H., De Houwer, J., Baeyens, F., Eelen, P., & Van Avermaet, E. (1997). Hidden Covariation Detection: hide-and-seek. *Journal of Experimental Psychology: Learning, Memory, and Cognition*, *23*, 229–231.

Hermans, D. (Ed.). (1998). Evaluative conditioning [Special Issue]. *Gedragstherapie, 31.*

Koole, S. K., Dijksterhuis, A., & van Knippenberg, A. (2001). What's in a name: Implicit self-esteem and the automatic self. *Journal of Personality and Social Psychology*, *80*, 669–685.

Lewicki, P., Hill, T., & Czyzewska, M. (1997). Hidden covariation detection: A fundamental and ubiquitous phenomenon. *Journal of Experimental Psychology: Learning, Memory, and Cognition*, *23*, 221–228.

Lipp, O. V., Oughton, N., & LeLievre, J. (2003). Evaluative learning in human Pavlovian conditioning: Extinct, but still there? *Learning and Motivation*, *34*, 219–239.

Lipp, O. V., & Purkis, H. M. (2005). No support for dual process accounts of human affective learning to simple Pavlovian conditioning. *Cognition and Emotion*, *19*, 269–282.

Lovibond, P. F., & Shanks, D. R. (2002). The role of awareness in Pavlovian Conditioning: Empirical evidence and theoretical implications. *Journal of Experimental Psychology: Animal Behavior Processes*, *28*, 3–26.

Martin, I., & Levey, A. B. (1978). Evaluative conditioning. *Advances in Behaviour Research and Therapy*, *1*, 57–102.

Meersmans, T., De Houwer, J., Baeyens, F., Randell, T., & Eelen, P. (2005). Beyond evaluative conditioning? Searching for associative transfer of nonevaluative stimulus properties. *Cognition and Emotion*, *19*, 283–306.

Mitchell, C. J., Anderson, N. E., & Lovibond, P. F. (2003). Measuring evaluative conditioning using the implicit association test. *Learning and Motivation*, *34*, 203–217.

Nisbett, R. E., & Wilson, T. D. (1977). Telling more than we can know: Verbal reports on mental processes. *Psychological Review*, *35*, 613–624.

Olson, M. A., & Fazio, R. H. (2001). Implicit attitude formation through classical conditioning. *Psychological Science*, *12*, 413–417.

Purkis, H. M., & Lipp, O. V. (2001). Does affective learning exist in the absence of contingency awareness? *Learning and Motivation*, *32*, 84–99.

Rozin, P. (1982). Human food selection: the interaction of biology, culture and individual experience. In L. M. Barker (Ed.), *The psychobiology of human food selection* (pp. 225–254). Westport, CT: AVI.

Rozin, P., Wrzesniewski, A., & Byrnes, D. (1998). The elusiveness of evaluative conditioning. *Learning and Motivation, 29,* 397–415.

Seger, C. A. (1994). Implicit learning. *Psychological Bulletin, 115,* 163–196.

Shanks, D. R., & Dickinson, A. (1990). Contingency awareness in evaluative conditioning: A comment on Baeyens, Eelen, and van den Bergh. *Cognition and Emotion, 4,* 19–30.

Shanks, D. R., & St. John, M. F. (1994). Characteristics of dissociable human learning systems. *Behavioral and Brain Sciences, 17,* 367–447.

Sherer, K. R. (1993). Neuroscience projections to current debates in emotion psychology. *Cognition and Emotion, 7,* 1–42.

Smith, E. R., & Miller, F. D. (1978). Limits on perception of cognitive processes: A reply to Nisbett and Wilson. *Psychological Review, 85,* 355–362.

Stuart, E. W., Shimp, T. A., & Engle, R. W. (1987). Classical conditioning of consumer attitudes: Four experiments in an advertising context. *Journal of Consumer Research, 14,* 334–351.

Walther, E. (2002). Guilty by mere association: Evaluative conditioning and the spreading attitude effect. *Journal of Personality and Social Psychology, 82,* 919–934.

Walther, E., Nagengast, B., & Trasselli, C. (2005). Evaluative conditioning in social psychology: Facts and speculations. *Cognition and Emotion, 19,* 175–196.

Zajonc, R. B. (1980). Feeling and thinking. Preferences need no inferences. *American Psychologist, 35,* 151–175.

COGNITION AND EMOTION
2005, 19 (2), 175–196

Evaluative conditioning in social psychology: Facts and speculations

Eva Walther, Benjamin Nagengast, and Claudia Trasselli

University of Heidelberg, Germany

The aim of the present paper is to examine the contribution of evaluative conditioning (EC) to attitude formation theory in social psychology. This aim is pursued on two fronts. First, evaluative conditioning is analysed for its relevance to social psychological research. We show that conditioned attitudes can be acquired through simple co-occurrences of a neutral and a valenced stimulus. Moreover, we argue that conditioned attitudes are not confined to direct contact with a valenced stimulus, but can be formed and dynamically reformed indirectly, through association chains. Second, social research is examined in an effort to identify evaluative learning mechanisms. We suggest that several important phenomena in social psychology (e.g., ingroup favouritism, prejudice, name letter effect) are at least partly due to simple mechanisms of evaluative learning. The implications for attitude formation theory and for applied settings are discussed.

Social psychology is replete with attitude research. While a vast amount of empirical work and a high degree of theoretical elaboration have been devoted to the topic of attitude activation (Bargh, Chaiken, Raymond, & Hymes, 1996; Fazio, 2001; Greenwald, McGhee, & Schwartz, 1998) social psychology is comparatively silent on the question of where likes and dislikes of objects, individuals, and events initially come from. All varieties of attitude activation are extensively reported in textbooks and articles, yet surprisingly little has been written on the question of how attitudes are formed or acquired in the first place.

If textbooks mention anything at all, they refer to classical conditioning as a mechanism that leads to attitude formation (Eagly & Chaiken, 1993). The old

Correspondence concerning this article should be addressed to Eva Walther, Department of Psychology, University of Heidelberg, Hauptstrasse 47–51, 69117 Heidelberg, Germany; e-mail: Eva.Walther@psychologie.uni-heidelberg.de

This research was supported by a grant from the Deutsche Forschungsgemeinschaft. We are grateful to Tina Langer, M. W. Utzi, and Joerg Wolter for their constructive comments on an earlier draft of this article. Thanks are also due to John Bargh, who directed our attention to the close relationship between evaluative conditioning and balance theory.

http://www.tandf.co.uk/journals/pp/02699931.html   DOI:10.1080/02699930441000274

Pavlovian bell-food paradigm is often cited as a prototypical example of how attitudes are acquired. A closer examination, however, reveals that the bell-food paradigm is not at all suitable for explaining the origin of attitudes. In modern learning theories, the bell-food example is considered an instance of signal learning, that is to say, a higher order cognitive learning mechanism that allows the organism to make predictions about significant events in the environment (Mackintosh, 1983; Rescorla & Wagner, 1972). What the organism learns within this signal learning paradigm is an if-then relationship between the bell (conditioned stimulus; CS) and the food (unconditioned stimulus; US)—in other words, the organism acquires an expectancy that the food will follow if the bell rings.

However, attitudinal processes typically do not refer to the prediction of events (Cacioppo, Marshall-Goodell, Tassinary, & Petty, 1992). Rather, attitude formation processes refer to the affective or cognitive meaning attitudinal objects acquire in the context of pleasant or unpleasant experiences. A paradigm that addresses this attitude formation processes is evaluative conditioning (EC). EC can be described as the learning of likes and dislikes, that is, as the acquisition of preferences. More specifically, EC refers to the transfer of affect from a US to a CS as the result of a learning procedure. In the prototypical EC paradigm, the picture-picture paradigm, a subjectively neutral picture of a human face (CS) is presented repeatedly with a subjectively liked or disliked human face (US). The result is a substantial valence shift in the previously neutral face (e.g., Baeyens, Eelen, Crombez, & Van den Berg, 1992a). Different from classical conditioning studies, the formerly neutral picture (i.e., the CS) in an EC paradigm does not acquire a predictive value, but merely attains the affective qualities of the liked or disliked face (i.e., the US). Thus, after conditioning the formerly neutral face is judged more positively (or negatively) due to the simple co-occurrence with the positively (negatively) evaluated US. This conditioning effect is usually explained by the formation of an association between the cognitive representation of the CS and the US. Although EC is a well-known paradigm in learning psychology and has received much attention in the last few years, the implications of this paradigm for social psychology have been largely neglected.

The aim of the present review is to examine the contribution of EC to attitude formation theory in social psychology (for a comprehensive synopsis of EC research in general, see De Houwer, Thomas, & Baeyens, 2001). This aim is pursued on two fronts. First, we describe the functional characteristics of conditioned attitudes and analyse these characteristics with respect to their relevance for social psychological research. Second, we (re)examine social research in order to identify evaluative learning processes. A basic assumption is that a simple learning mechanism may provide what is often a simple alternative explanation for a number of well-known phenomena in social psychology.

FUNCTIONAL CHARACTERISTICS OF CONDITIONED ATTITUDES

There are six characteristics that are typical of conditioned attitudes and that render the EC paradigm particularly important for attitude research: awareness, contingency, extinction, sensory preconditioning, counterconditioning, and unconditioned stimulus revaluation.

Awareness. First, in contrast to signal learning, EC is presumably not dependent on the awareness of the contingencies between the CS and the US. Although there has been some debate about this aspect (see Lovibond & Shanks, 2002, for an extensive discussion of this issue), there is evidence that evaluative conditioning may also occur in the absence of awareness of the contingencies between the CS and US (e.g., De Houwer, 2001; De Houwer et al., 2001). This means that participants in the standard picture-picture paradigm usually do not know why they like or dislike a particular face after conditioning. In more general terms, this implies that people form attitudes towards objects, individuals, and events without noticing the source of valence that led to the specific (dis)likes.

Evidence that attitudes can be formed without focusing on CS or US has come from recent studies carried out by Olson and Fazio (2001). The authors presented participants with various Pokemon figures among several other pictures and words on a computer screen. The explicit task given to the participants was to press a response key as quickly as possible when a particular Pokemon character (which was not used as a CS) appeared. In fact, however, an EC procedure was administered, in which evaluatively neutral Pokemons were accompanied by negatively evaluated words or pictures. The results indicated that participants acquired a negative attitude towards the formerly neutral Pokemons, although participants did not focus on but were actually distracted from the CS-US contingency. Olson and Fazio thus demonstrated that the formation of attitudes can occur without conscious control, which is similar to what occurs in the social world, where multiple attitudes are formed and changed without an explicit focus on the attitudinal stimuli.

Evidence for nonconscious EC also came from Krosnick and colleagues (Krosnick, Betz, Jussim, & Lynn, 1992), who provided evidence for attitude formation in a paradigm in which the CS was preceded by a subliminally presented affect-arousing picture (see also Niedenthal, 1990, for a similar procedure). However, the fact that the US preceded the CS, along with other methodological issues (e.g., lack of neutral control group, absence of baseline condition), makes it hard to distinguish this result from the effects of affective priming, in which already existing attitudes are activated.

Contingency. Second, EC does not depend on the statistical CS-US contingency to the same degree as signal learning does. Recognising the statistical correlation between the CS and US is a necessary precondition for predicting an event. Affective learning, however, seems to be sensitive to contiguity, that is, to mere spatiotemporal CS-US co-occurrences (De Houwer et al., 2001). Thus, weakening the contingency in an EC paradigm by single CS or US presentations in the acquisition phase does not appear to have much effect on conditioning (Baeyens, Hermans, & Eelen, 1993). One reason why signal learning has been rarely applied to social psychology is that strict contingency between the CS and US hardly ever occurs in the real world, where individuals usually encounter other people in different compositions and settings. Since EC is not restricted to strong CS-US contingencies it increases the range of situations in which evaluative learning can be applied.

Extinction. Third, after successful evaluative learning, unreinforced (i.e., single) CS presentations by themselves do not alter the valence of the stimulus, that is, evaluative conditioning is resistant to extinction. Several studies supported the notion that the acquired valence of the CS remained even when the CS was presented several times without US reinforcement (De Houwer et al., 2001; Walther, 2002). If, for instance, a neutral individual Paul (the CS) is associated with a negatively evaluated outgroup member Marc (the US), this bad company decreases Paul's likeability. Resistance to extinction means that the acquired negative attitude towards Paul through association with Marc does not fade away if Paul shows up alone after the association occurred. Thus, the negative evaluation of Paul, once acquired through EC, is stable and not dependent on further co-occurrences with a negatively evaluated experience.

Counterconditioning. Fourth, attitudes can be changed, not by simple exposure, as the above paragraph suggested, but by postexperimental pairings with an US of the opposite than the acquired valence. Baeyens and colleagues (Baeyens, Eelen, & Van den Berg, 1989), for instance, demonstrated that the conditioned positive valence of a CS can be eliminated or even changed into a negative evaluation due to a counterconditioning procedure, in which the CS was paired with an aversive US. Counterconditioning implies that affective attitudes are not inextinguishable but can be changed through a subsequent conversely valenced affective experience. The acquired negative evaluation of Paul can be effectively altered by presenting Paul in a positive context, for instance, in the context of a highly positively evaluated ingroup member Mary. Thus, the notion of counterconditioning indicates that EC is not confined to the acquisition of attitudes but is also an expedient procedure for changing already existing attitudes.

Sensory preconditioning. Fifth, EC is relevant not only because of the aforementioned qualities, but also because this paradigm reflects the indirect nature of attitude acquisition in the social world. In many social situations, attitudes are formed without the direct experience of a valued event. In terms of EC this means that the evaluatively conditioned attitude may spread to other stimuli pre-associated with the CS ("spreading attitude effect", Walther, 2002). The learning mechanism that mediates the spreading attitude effect is sensory preconditioning. Sensory preconditioning means that the affective value of the CS is transferred (or spreads) to objects or events that are pre-associated with this stimulus due to prior experimental learning (Hammerl & Grabitz, 1996). Although sensory preconditioning is a well-established phenomenon in classical conditioning (Barnet, Grahame, & Miller, 1991; Razran, 1971; Rizley & Rescorla, 1972), the implications of this phenomenon for attitude formation and attitude change in social psychology have been widely neglected. This may be partly due to the fact that sensory preconditioning has been rarely examined in the paradigm of evaluative conditioning (for an exception see Hammerl & Grabitz, 1996), but has been confined predominantly to signal (animal) learning studies.

The spreading attitude effect mediated by sensory preconditioning implies that EC is not restricted to situations in which there is *direct* contact between a neutral and a valued event. There is empirical evidence that evaluative learning might also occur under the complete absence of any kind of valued (conscious or unconscious) experience (Hammerl & Grabitz, 1996). Using the picture-picture paradigm, Walther (2002) presented participants with pairs of evaluatively neutral male faces. In the subsequent evaluative conditioning phase, one of the neutral pictures (the CS) was paired with a negatively evaluated face (the US). The author found that the EC procedure not only affected the evaluation of the CS, but that the evaluation "spreads" to the face that was only pre-associated with the CS: both previously neutral faces were evaluated more negatively, although only one of them (the CS) was in direct contact with the aversive event.

Transferred to real-life settings, the spreading attitude effect implies that a person's bad company not only affects his own reputation, but also that of people associated with him or her, such as family members, friends, or work colleagues. If, for instance, the German foreign minister Joschka Fischer had been seen in a press picture in the company of (the former dictator) Saddam Hussein during one of his visits to the Middle East, this co-occurrence would affect not only the foreign minister's own standing, but also the evaluation of his party, the Greens. According to EC, this devaluation effect might occur irrespective of the foreign minister's intentions and his own critical attitude toward the dictator. Reassuringly, Walther (2002) found that *positive* evaluation may also spread to pre-associated stimuli (experiment 1). Accordingly, Joschka Fischer could improve his reputation by seeking out the company of positively evaluated individuals. Basking in the reflected glory of Nobel Prize winner Daniel Kahneman during festivities may enhance not only Joschka Fischer's popularity, but also that of his Green colleagues in the cabinet, Jürgen Trittin (environment minister) and Renate Künast (agricultural minister).

The mechanism that underlies this extraordinary effect is presumably as follows: The contiguous presentation of the two neutral stimuli, say, Jürgen Trittin and Joschka Fischer, during co-occurrences develops an association in memory between the two. In the conditioning phase, one of the formerly neutral stimuli, for instance, Joschka Fischer, serves as CS and acquires a negative (positive) valence through his co-occurrence with an aversively or favourably evaluated person (Saddam Hussein or Daniel Kahneman). The acquired affective tone of the CS, Joschka Fischer, influences other (pre)associated stimuli that are connected with this stimulus in memory (e.g., Jürgen Trittin).

The spreading attitude effect opens up a wide range of possible applications in several areas of social and applied psychology. The implications of the spreading attitude effect for attitude formation in social psychology are clear: Attitudes are not always based on a direct appetitive or aversive experience. Many prejudiced people have never encountered the objects of their antipathy. Instead, attitudes are often based on prior experiences with similar attitudinal objects, on second-hand information, or on mere pre-associations. The blame that attaches to a family for the crime of a family member, or the devaluation of an individual due to the bad reputation of her ingroup, are only the most blatant examples of the spreading attitude effect.

It is important to note, however, that EC does not affect each and every person, but only those highly specific individuals who are actually associated with the CS through prior experience. However, it can be speculated that interpersonal similarity as a result, for instance, of perceived outgroup homogeneity may enhance the impact of spreading attitudes due to stimulus generalisation. According to general principles of learning theory (Guttman & Kalish, 1956), it is not implausible that perceived similarity provides an ideal precondition for the occurrence of spreading attitude effects. The presumably stronger impact of spreading attitudes in the (similar) outgroup than in the (dissimilar) ingroup is of particular social relevance in the context of the acquisition of negative attitudes like prejudice or derogative processes. This is also important because spreading attitudes, similar to simple EC effects, are not dependent on conscious, deliberate attention, but turn out to be even stronger when participants are distracted from these processes (Walther, 2002, experiment 5; Walther & Trasselli, 2003).

US revaluation. Six, although the concept of EC may provide a parsimonious explanation for many social phenomena, the impact of this account in social psychology presumably depends on the degree to which the underlying learning mechanisms that result in attitude formation can be made clear. In contrast to the early EC theorists Martin and Levy (1987), who explained evaluative conditioning as the result of a "holistic representation" that represents elements of the CS and US as well as the evaluative nature of the US, the spreading attitude effect mediated by sensory preconditioning provides supporting evidence that an association builds the basic structure of the subsequent transfer of valence.

More conclusive evidence for the associative account comes from the US revaluation paradigm. US revaluation means that the valence of the US is experimentally changed into the opposite valence after standard EC has occurred (Baeyens, Eelen, Van den Berg, & Crombez, 1992b). For instance, Baeyens et al. (1992b) postconditionally presented positive USs with negative adjectives and negative USs with evaluatively positive adjectives. As a result of this revaluation, it was not only the valence of the USs that changed: Interestingly and most importantly, the affective meaning of the CSs also changed in the direction of the revaluated USs. In recent studies, Walther and Wernado (2004) replicated US revaluation effects in the context of consumer attitudes. They found that US revaluation effects are not confined to CSs that are similar to the US (e.g., in the face-face paradigm, Baeyens et al., 1992a), but can also be obtained with products as CSs and faces as USs.

Because the US revaluation effects can hardly be explained in any other way than by an associative account, they have important implications for EC theory formation. Moreover, the notion of US revaluation has intriguing implications for attitude formation in social and applied settings. If the spreading attitude effect implies loss of control of attitude formation processes in the social world because the bad company of associated individuals can backfire and affect one's own reputation, this is even more true of US revaluation. An association with positively evaluated individuals, like highly respected experts or admired stars, has a positive impact on one's own image only as long as these positive eva-luations of the associated other persist. If the associated individual loses his/her prestige as a result of an episode of negative behaviour, this slip also affects one's own evaluative judgement.

Similar consequences from US revaluation pertain in the area of advertising. In order to produce positive evaluations of products due to conditioning, it is a common advertising strategy to present products (e.g., AOL, Nutella) along with celebrities (e.g., Boris Becker). Many examples like that of Boris Becker (who cheated on his wife) suggest that this advertising strategy may be risky, at best. Within the logic of US revaluation, the loss of Boris Becker's positive image in public opinion due to unethical behaviour has dramatic consequences for the products associated with him. Although the US revaluation logic is not restricted to evaluatively positive cases of revaluation, there is some evidence in social psychology that social judgement is asymmetric in such a way that negative behaviour is given greater weight than positive behaviour (Reeder & Brewer, 1979). Thus, one can speculate that US revaluation works better in the negative than in the positive direction, an effect that is supported by recent studies (Walther, Blank, Gawronski, & Langer, 2004).

It is precisely these distinctive qualities (independence of awareness and of contingency, resistance to extinction, sensitivity to counterconditioning, sensory preconditioning, and US revaluation) that render the paradigm of EC an extremely fruitful model of attitude acquisition and open the field for social psychology. We often (dis)like people, objects, and events without knowing why. EC can explain why a few co-occurrences between a valued (e.g., prejudiced) person and a neutral person may lead to substantial and stable attitude change not only towards the previously "innocent" individual but also towards other pre-associated individuals. Although a few instances of (pre)conditioning are sufficient to establish evaluative meaning, EC effects are by no means transient in nature. There is ample evidence from basic and applied research that conditioned attitudes are particularly stable and resistant to extinction (see Stevenson, Boakes, Wilson, 2000, for a discussion). Notwithstanding the robustness of conditioned attitudes, there are also experimentally established ways of change. An affective attitude, once acquired can be changed by experiences of the opposite valence. The US revaluation paradigm indicates that revaluating the source of valence also effectively alters the valence of associated stimuli. The spreading attitude effect as well as the US revaluation paradigm support the notion that the acquisition of social attitudes is not restricted to a direct contact with a US, but may be formed and dynamically reformed through association chains and pre-associated stimuli.

Compared to several other influential attitude models, such as affective priming (Fazio, 2001) or evaluative generalisation (Tursky, Lodge, Foley, Reeder, & Foley, 1976), which refer to the activation of already existing attitudes, EC is of critical importance for attitude research because it is one of the few experimental models that explains how likes and dislikes are created (Rozin, Wrzesniewski, & Byrnes 1998). As well as the various examples that EC has strong and straightforward implications for social psychology, there is also evidence for EC in traditional social psychological accounts. Given the prominence and importance of attitudes in social psychology, it is surprising that the paradigm of EC has not received more attention in contemporary social psychological research.

MANIFESTATIONS OF EC

Effects of EC in social psychology, although manifold, are most apparent in the area of *persuasion*. It is well described in persuasion research how simple evaluative features of the source, such as the attractiveness (Petty & Cacioppo, 1984), credibility, or likeability of the communicator (Petty, Cacioppo, & Goldman, 1981), serve as potent persuasion cues particularly in situations in which participants are distracted, low in motivation, or in need of cognition. What this means is that individuals who are unable or unwilling to think about reasons for their attitudes base their attitude on evaluative cues associated with the message. In terms of EC, the message within this persuasion paradigm can be considered the CS, and the characteristics of the communicator the US.

Similar to EC effects, the transfer of valence from the US to the CS can occur unconsciously, that is, the audience usually does not know why they suddenly like one message better than the other. It is also typical for EC-like phenomena that these communicator effects are not reduced but, if anything, enhanced when people are distracted or not motivated to deeply process the information (Walther, 2002; Walther & Trasselli, 2003).

Elements of EC are also involved in the famous *"kill-the-messenger effect"*. This describes the phenomenon whereby transmitters are inevitably associated with the valence of the message they have to convey (Manis, Cornell, Moore, & Jeffrey, 1974). Whereas in persuasion, a neutral message (CS) usually experiences a revaluation through its co-occurrence with an evaluated communicator (US), the opposite mechanism occurs in the kill-the-messenger effect: The messenger (CS) experiences a revaluation by being associated with bad news (US). Similar association-based effects were obtained in a series of intriguing studies by Skowronski, Carlston, Mae, and Crawford (1998), who demonstrated that communicators become involuntarily associated with their verbal description of others. Thus, backbiting about a nasty colleague may have unwelcome negative consequences for the detractor. Although descriptions of other people are (psycho)logically independent of the communicator, simple associative processes nevertheless link these two events together and produce such boomerang-like phenomena.

That conditioning theory may also contribute to research on *stigmatisation* was evident in recent studies by Hebl and Mannix (2003). The authors tested the influence of the company of a stigmatised (i.e., obese) person on the evaluation of associated individuals. The results obtained in paper-and-pencil as well as in real-life settings indicated that job applicants were judged more negatively when they were accompanied by an obese female instead of a female of average weight. The mere co-occurrence of the applicant with an overweight woman was sufficient to cause the applicant to be judged more negatively than a control person on several job-relevant scales. Characteristically for EC processes, this stigmatisation was independent of high level (controlled) cognitive factors, such as knowledge about the relationship of the applicant to his/her companion, an existing explicit anti-fat attitude, or other compensating information.

If transfer of stigmatisation is similar to conditioning, these effects can be expected to be enduring and hard to change. Evidence for the particular stability of conditioned affective attitudes has come from recent studies by Sherman and Kim (2002). The authors demonstrated in a series of studies that the affective preferences for objects persevered even if the cognition that gave rise to the affect ceased to be valid. In the first phase of their studies, participants learned the positive or negative meaning of Chinese ideographs. In a subsequent correction phase, they were informed that these meanings were incorrect. Interestingly, the affective meaning associated with the Chinese ideographs persisted even though this meaning was invalidated—a phenomenon the authors called *"affective perseverance"*. In terms of EC, affective perseverance might be due to the fact that the CS evaluation is preserved when the meaning of the US is cognitively discounted (Baeyens et al., 1992a). Similar to findings in the EC area, Sherman and Kim (2002) found that a counterconditioning procedure was successful in changing the affective meaning of the ideographs. Counter-conditioning implies that a new association of the CS with a US of the opposite valence is established. Taking into account these studies as well as the US revaluation effect, one might argue that evaluatively conditioned attitudes are relatively resistant to cognitive change strategies like discounting, but can be effectively changed by means of affective revaluation.

Apart from these examples, the significance of EC for social psychology depends on the degree to which the comparatively simple valence-driven mechanisms of EC are compatible with or integrated into other kinds of socially relevant information, such as category information (e.g., ingroups/outgroups) or sentiments (e.g., relations). As a matter of fact, many social situations consist not only of the valence of individuals, but also of a variety of other information that determine the social life of an individual. In addition to basic likeability impressions, the relation to other individuals may, for example, strongly determine social judgements. A theoretical approach that aims at covering social attitude formation must take into account both the multiple facets of the social network and the valence of the individual. A theoretical account that meets this criterion is balance theory.

Similarly to EC theory, Heider (1958) suggested that many attitudes are not derived from direct experience. Rather, most interpersonal attitudes are inferred from the valence of and relationship between individuals. Taking only valence information into account, the predictions of balance theory are congruent with those of EC: An individual (CS) associated with a liked or disliked person (US) will be judged similar to this evaluated person. The spreading attitude effect suggests that an individual pre-associated with a conditioned stimulus will be judged to be similar to the formerly neutral partner. In terms of balance theory, this process is called *unit formation*. Unit formation means that the attitude towards an individual is based on the evaluation of the persons associated with him/her. Although balance theory belongs to the standard canon of psychological theories, the mechanisms that underlie unit formation have never been subjected to intensive theoretical investigation. Not only can EC theory explain the when and how of unit formation, it may also have something to say about the associative mechanism underlying affective attitude formation.

In addition to the evaluation of a person, the relationship between individuals may be of critical importance in social situations. Different from EC, balance theory also makes predictions concerning this so-called *sentiment relation* between individuals. Liking someone who is liked by a friend might be easy, but liking someone who is liked by a nasty colleague might be a different thing. In such cases, balance theory predicts that people strive for a state that is called a *balanced sentiment triad.* Generally, a balanced sentiment triad implies that people who are liked by friends are liked, while individuals who are disliked by friends are disliked. In a similar vein, people often exhibit negative attitudes to persons who are liked by individuals they personally dislike, but they show positive attitudes to persons who are disliked by individuals they personally dislike.

Interestingly, unit formation and balanced sentiment triads may have contradictory implications for particular conditions. Let us assume Joschka Fischer meets Saddam Hussein, and Saddam Hussein has a negative attitude toward Fischer. Unit formation should lead to a negative attitude toward Fischer because of his association with a disliked person. Balanced sentiment triad, however, implies a positive attitude toward Fischer because he is disliked by an aversive person. These contradictory implications of EC-like unit formation and balanced sentiment triads in the formation of interpersonal attitudes were investigated in a series of studies by Gawronski, Walther, and Blank (in press). The authors examined under which conditions the conglomerate of (a priori) attitudes and observed sentiment relations results in a balanced sentiment triad, and under which conditions interpersonal attitude formation is dominated by EC. Based on empirical evidence obtained in the EC paradigm, it was hypothesised that unit formation can be considered the result of the mere spatio-temporal co-occurrence between two stimuli—in other words, the result of EC. Hence, evaluations implied by unit formation may reflect simple associative processes (Olson & Fazio, 2001, 2002; Walther, 2002). Balanced sentiment triads, in contrast, may require higher order cognitive processes, such as inferring a positive evaluation of someone who is disliked by a negative person.

Gawronski et al. (in press) tested these assumptions in a series of studies in which participants formed an attitude about two persons through EC and also learned about the relationship between the two individuals through additional verbal information (e.g., "X (dis)likes Y"). The result of this manipulation was assessed with direct (i.e., likeability ratings) as well as indirect attitudes measurements (affective priming task). The findings suggested that balanced sentiment triads were built when participants first formed an attitude about one person, and then learned about this person's sentiment relationship to another individual. Interestingly, these balanced sentiment effects were obtained for directly as well as indirectly assessed attitudes.

However, the conglomerate of interpersonal attitudes does not result in a balanced sentiment triad when participants first learn about the sentiment relation between two neutral individuals, and then receive evaluative information about one of the two targets. In this case, attitude measurements were affected only by the sentiment relation, but not by the valence of the stimuli. This means that balanced sentiment triads emerge only when perceivers already have a positive or negative attitude toward a given individual at the time they learn about his/her sentiment relation to another target. In other words, the process of balance is instigated by the presence of a valenced experience (US), but not when only evaluatively neutral stimuli (CSs) are present.

A possible explanation for this finding is that the existence of an a priori attitude at the time perceivers learn about the sentiment relation between two individuals is a necessary precondition for the application of the balanced sentiment schema. If perceivers have an a priori attitude toward one of two related individuals, the balanced sentiment schema may be activated when perceivers learn about the sentiment relation between the two individuals (Insko, 1984). If, however, perceivers have neutral attitudes toward two individuals at the time they learn about their sentiment relation, the sentiment relation itself obviously has no clear-cut balanced sentiment implications.

The present paradigm indicates that EC and the spreading attitude effect can be fruitfully applied to other accounts of importance in social psychology, such as balance theory. On the one hand, taking EC theory into account may shed some light on the mechanisms underlying simple unit formation processes within balance theory, and may help to identify the preconditions of higher order, balanced sentiment triads. Thus, EC may contribute to the explanation of attitude formation processes that are not yet covered by other theories. On the other hand, the combination of EC with other well-known social psychology paradigms may also speak to the boundary conditions of EC. For instance, balanced sentiment triads are only formed when stimuli already have affective relevance, but not if affectively neutral stimuli are presented.

As well as the valence of and the relation between individuals, a further important source of interpersonal attitudes is self-evaluation (cf. Greenwald & Banaji, 1995). There is multiple evidence for the effect that the (normally positive) self-evaluation may influence the evaluation of objects, individuals, and events. The *mere ownership effect* (Feys, 1995), for instance, states that people have a preference for objects belonging to the self. Giving people an object (e.g., a pen) leads to a more favourable attitude towards this object compared with a not-owned object (Beggan, 1992).

That people exhibit a preference for aspects associated with the self is also supported by the *name letter effect,* which describes the phenomenon that people like letters that are part of their own names better than other letters (Nutin, 1985; see also Koole, Dijksterhuis, & Van Knippenberg, 2001). This effect occurs for all of the letters in people's names, but it is apparently particularly pronounced for people's first and last name initials. Pelham, Mirenberg, and Jones (2002) showed that the name letter preference might even affect major life decisions. The authors found a contingency between people's initials and decisions, such as whom to marry, where to live, and what career to choose.

Although there are several demonstrations that the evaluation of the self plays a crucial role in evaluating other objects and events, the mechanisms that lead to these attitude formation processes are not entirely clear. We argue that most of these effects can be explained with simple EC. In terms of EC, self-evaluation can be conceptualised as a US and other individuals or objects as CSs. According to evaluative learning theory (cf. De Houwer et al., 2001), the mere spatiotemporal CS-US co-occurrence is a sufficient condition for the transfer of valence from the US to the CS (Martin & Levey, 1978). Given that self-evaluation is predominantly positive, associating an object or event with the self may therefore lead to a favourable attitude towards this object or event.

Stapel and Koomen noted in a recent paper that "people use others to evaluate themselves" (2000, p. 1068). The present EC account, however, suggests that the opposite may also be true: People use themselves to evaluate others. Drawing on an EC account (De Houwer et al., 2001; Walther, 2002), we assume that the valence of the self serves as a source (a US) of interpersonal attitudes. In contrast to self-anchoring (Cadinu & Rothbart, 1996) or self-projection (Krueger, 2000) approaches, which conceptualise the self as a cognitive heuristic used in judging others, we suggest that a simple affective mechanism, the transfer of valence from the self to another individual, may be involved in interpersonal (dis)liking.

The idea that self-evaluation may serve as a (unconscious) source of interpersonal attitudes was examined in recent studies by Walther and Trasselli (2003). The authors hypothesised that if the idea of the self-as-US is correct, the mere association of the positively or negatively evaluated self with another, otherwise unrelated and neutral target should lead to self-other evaluative similarity. They tested this hypothesis in a study in which self-evaluation was manipulated by means of false feedback. In a subsequent learning phase, participants were asked to imagine certain individuals, including the self, encountering other persons (e.g., a person named "Eliza"). The idea behind this task was that the act of imagining the encountered individuals would lead to association and a subsequent transfer of valence from the self to the target (i.e., the individuals "associated with the self").

The results indicated that the target was indeed evaluated more similarly to the self than a control person who did not co-occur with the self during the learning phase. However, this effect was only obtained in the negative feedback but not in the positive feedback condition. In the positive feedback condition, an unpredicted self/other dissimilarity took place: The "encountered" individual was judged more negatively than the self. It was obviously the case that mechanisms other than simple associative learning were at work in this group. In order to explain these findings, the authors assumed that a consciously driven dissociation process took place in the positive feedback group. It was speculated that participants tried to enhance their positive self-evaluation by means of a dissimilarity testing process (see Mussweiler, 2003).

This interpretation was examined in a subsequent study (Walther & Trasselli, 2003, experiment 2) that was similar to the previous experiment, except that participants were prevented from engaging in hypothesis-testing by a secondary distracter task. If the dissociation effects were due to cognitive resource-consuming comparison processes, self/other similarity should be eliminated in both conditions as a function of resource allocation. The results confirmed this assumption and provided further support for the EC account. If a second task prevented participants from social comparison processes, conditioning effects took place in both feedback conditions. Generally, these findings provided additional evidence for the idea that evaluative learning is a process that is hindered rather than enhanced by cognitive mechanisms (Betsch, Plessner, & Schallies, 2004; Betsch, Plessner, Schwieren, & Gütig, 2001; De Houwer et al., 2001; Fulcher & Hammerl, 2001; Olson & Fazio, 2001; Walther, 2002).

Taken together, these studies supported the notion that self-evaluation can serve as a source of interpersonal evaluative attitudes. At the same time, however, we obtained boundary conditions of simple evaluative learning effects in interpersonal judgements. Thus, these findings challenge the evaluative learning account insofar as they point to the limits of so-called primitive learning mechanisms within interpersonal attitude formation. Existing evaluative learning approaches strongly rely on association effects but do not cover dissociative contrast-like phenomena.

The basic notion that self-evaluation guides evaluation of others is shared by several social psychologists. Starting from a usually positively evaluated self, Greenwald and Banaji (1995, see also Greenwald et al., 2002) noted "that novel objects that are invested with an association to self should be positively evaluated" (p. 10). Similar to our account, Greenwald and Banaji assumed that this effect reflects associative processes rather than deliberative mechanisms. That means the attitude formation process should work only when the actor is not actually focused on the attitude—a hypothesis that was also supported by our data (Walther & Trasselli, 2003).

That self-evaluation can not only serve as a source (US) but a also as an object (CS) of attitude formation was recently demonstrated by Dijksterhuis (2004). In a series of intriguing studies, Dijksterhuis presented participants with evaluatively positive words preceded by the word "I". Relative to a control condition, this procedure enhanced (implicit) self-evaluation even if both words were presented subliminally, a technique that effectively ruled out demand effects. It is important to note, however, that these studies addressed not the formation of attitudes but rather the *enhancement* of already existing attitudes. Although the difference between two processes is sometimes hard to define, one can suspect that there is a fundamental differences between instigating a concept-evaluation association or activating it.

Conceptualising the self as a source of interpersonal attitudes can also provide alternative explanations for several phenomena in social psychology. A prominent example to which our account could contribute is *ingroup favouritism* in the minimal-group paradigm (Tajfel, Billig, Bundy, & Flament, 1972). While recent studies have shown that ingroups are automatically associated with positive affect, the underlying mechanisms remain unclear (Otten & Wentura,

1999, 2001). Confirming evidence that our EC account explains ingroup biases comes from Perdue, Dovidio, and Gurtman (1990). The authors found that the use of words referring to ingroup or outgroup status, such as "us" or "them", may unconsciously serve as a source of evaluation. In one of their studies, nonsense syllables unobtrusively paired with "ingroup" designating pronouns (e.g., "we") were rated as more pleasant than syllables paired with "outgroup" designators (e.g., "they").

We supposed that this automatic positive evaluation of the ingroup may be due to simple affective learning mechanisms, in which the own person serves as a positive US and the associated group as CS. As speculative as this idea may seem, the implications can be put to a simple empirical test: given that depressive individuals, by definition, posses a negative self-image, the minimal group effect should at least be reduced if a depressive group is tested for its reaction to the ingroup.

EC IN APPLIED SETTINGS

The last example suggests that effects of self-evaluation also play a crucial role in clinical psychology (Fulcher, Mathews, Macintosh, & Law, 2001). If negative self-evaluation is a symptom of depression, and if this negative self-attitude affects other individuals, particularly those closely related to the self, a negative cascade could be started that may aggravate the disease.

Another prominent example is phobias and aversions. Many social or animal phobias involve inappropriate dislikes that are highly resistant to therapeutic intervention and seem to be acquired without contingency awareness (Baeyens et al., 1992a). Because a direct contiguity of CSs and USs is not necessary for EC (cf. the spreading attitude effect), patients may not be aware of the connections between the stimuli. However, subjects may also falsely "remember" the covariation between environmental stimuli. For instance, phobic patients as well as normal subjects tend to overestimate the covariation between spider images and aversive events, such as shock (De Jong & Merckelbach, 2000; Oehman & Mineka, 2003). That means that phobic reactions may be falsely attributed to unrelated events, whereas the real contingencies remain undetected. As a result of EC, phobic objects themselves often elicit an aversive reaction without signalling a negative event. Extinguishing the contingencies between a spider and a phobic reaction may therefore not alter the negative attitude towards a spider. Accordingly, several therapists have applied counter-conditioning with positive US, such as music, to change the intrinsic negative attitude towards the phobic object (Eifert, Craill, Carey, & O'Connor, 1988).

One implication of the spreading attitude effect within EC is that a negative or positive attitude towards an individual or event does not presuppose a direct evaluative experience. Hardly anybody who is afraid of flying has been actually hurt in an aviation accident. More evidence for the indirect effect of evaluative learning comes from a series of intriguing studies conducted by Rozin, Markwith, and McCauley (1994), who demonstrated that the aversion towards a person with AIDS is generalised to objects associated with this person (e.g., a sweater, car, or bed), although it was made clear that the objects were not infected.

Another field of application for EC is advertising and consumer research (Shimp, Stuart, & Engle, 1991). Although the "conditioning of attitudes towards products and brands has become generally accepted and has developed into a unique research stream within consumer behavior" (Till & Priluck, 2000, p. 57), there is surprisingly little empirical work reflecting the contemporary theoretical innovations in this area. EC may be of particular interest for consumer research because this type of learning is not dependent on conscious, deliberate attention, but turns out to be even stronger when participants are distracted (cf. Walther, 2002). Since most advertisements pass by without receiving much attention, using an attitude formation technique that actually profits from this phenomenon may be of critical importance. However, most advertising does not rely on the effects of EC alone. Instead, it combines the impact of several attitude-influencing methods. One of the most prominent influential methods in this context is mood induction. The mood-congruency hypothesis (Bower, 1981) states that consumers are biased in the direction of the prevailing mood, that is, happy consumers will judge the product more favourably than will sad consumers. Likewise, sad mood is believed to have negative influences on product evaluation. With reference to EC, mood-congruency would imply that happy people are more prone to acquire positive (i.e., appetitive) qualities of a CS, whereas individuals in a sad mood would show a predisposition to acquiring the negative (i.e., aversive) meaning of a CS. However, beside this valence-related function, mood may also influence information processing in more general ways. For instance, Schwarz (1990) suggested that mood states inform the organism about the current psychological situation (Schwarz, 1990). In terms of Schwarz's model, happy mood serves as a security cue, signalling that the organism can rely on already acquired (concept) information. Thus, the organism's attention in happy mood is turned to inner psychological states and concepts (e.g., schemas, hypotheses, expectancies). In contrast, sad mood informs the organism that something is going wrong. In sad mood, individuals turn their attention to stimuli from the environment in order to analyse (pre)conditions for the prevailing negative mood state (see Forgas, 2002). Given that associative learning profits more from bottom-up information encoding than from concept-driven information processes (cf. Walther, 2002), the implication is that sad mood rather than happy mood will enhance the acquisition of product evaluation. Transferred to the EC paradigm, this implies that sad mood would improve environmental learning, whereas happy mood would generally decrease the acquisition of new information, independent of the stimuli's valence. Given that mood is intentionally or unintentionally involved in many advertisements and commercials, and that mood is a well-known subject of interest in consumer research as well as in social psychology, it is surprising that the impact of mood has never been examined for its effect on conditioning.

Walther and Grigoriadis (2004) investigated the influence of mood on the EC of consumer attitudes. The results confirmed the notion that consumer attitudes can be formed through simple EC effects. Consistent with previous research, the findings indicated that only a small number of CS-US pairings were sufficient to induce affective attitudes towards a certain product within an EC paradigm (De Houwer et al., 2001; Walther, 2002). Moreover, the results showed that participants in a *sad mood* were more prone to EC than participants in a happy mood. Interestingly, and in contrast to widespread advertising practice, sad mood is not necessarily bad in its effect on attitude formation. To the contrary, our data support the notion that even the acquisition of the *appetitive* meaning of the stimuli was enhanced under bad mood. This is because sad mood increases the likelihood of bottom-up environmental learning and therefore increases the impact of EC.

The special notion of spreading attitudes may also be of relevance in consumer research. For example, the concept of brand extension can only work if the positive attitude towards the brand is extended to other products associated with the brand. While there is a vast amount of research pertaining to this topic (Barone, Miniard, & Romeo, 2000; Flaherty & Pappas, 2000; Lane, 2000; Till & Priluck, 2000), the underlying mechanisms of the how-and-when of brand extensions remain unclear. Thus, a theoretical account is needed to explain whether or not brand extension may be profitable. The spreading attitude effect as a result of evaluative preconditioning provides such an account.

CONCLUSION

In the present overview we have tried to argue that affective attitudes can be formed through simple learning mechanisms. Most interestingly, affective attitude formation is apparently not dependent on the (conscious or unconscious) experience of a valued event, and can work through associative chains as realised in paradigms, such as attitude spread and US revaluation (Baeyens et al., 1992b; Walther, 2002).

Moreover, we have tried to argue that simple learning mechanisms are involved in many social phenomena that are usually explained by cognitive or motivational mechanisms. This is not to say that these higher order processes, such as intentions, hypothesis testing, and deductive reasoning, do not play a role in all of theses paradigms. Without denying the contribution of higher cognitive processes in explaining these phenomena, our argument merely states that simple learning mechanisms may also be involved and may help to explain the origin of attitudes towards individuals and groups.

One of the most fascinating results to emerge from EC research is that simple learning effects may be counteracted by higher cognitive processes, but only under certain conditions (Walther & Trasselli, 2003). Thus, our findings challenge the evaluative learning account insofar as they point to the limits of so-called primitive learning mechanisms within interpersonal attitude formation. Thus, the paradigm of EC provides not only a framework within which these attitude formation processes can be investigated under experimentally controlled conditions, but also a precise terminology and a relatively parsimonious set of theoretical assumptions that might help to distinguish different attitudinal processes.

It is important to note, however, that all these conclusions may be premature with respect to one point. All measurements that address effects of EC assess in one way or another only the *expression* of learning, but not learning itself. It remains unclear whether the acquired attitudes can be actually influenced by mechanisms like revaluation or counterconditioning, or whether these techniques affect only the expression of these attitudes. The application of indirect measurements of EC, such as the affective priming task (Fazio & Olson 2003), provide no solution to this problem, because they, too, assess only a response transformed from an attitude but not the attitude itself. Thus, despite the overwhelming empirical evidence supporting the notion of EC, there are also theoretical as well as empirical problems that remain unresolved.

A further issue is whether EC is restricted in a sense that there are conditions that limit the transfer of valence from the CS to the US. Although the paradigm is standardised, and works with different designs and stimulus material, there are occasional null-findings that are hard to explain (De Houwer et al., 2001). That is, EC is in fact robust but sometimes fails to appear. This later aspect speaks to the notion that CS-US contiguity is a necessary but presumably not a sufficient condition for EC to occur. As mentioned above, this apparent unreliability may also be caused by the measurement of EC. Thus, it might be the case that EC is in fact unrestricted (as many other associative phenomenon are), but that the expression (or application) of evaluative conditioned attitudes is restricted.

On a more general level, one could ask whether EC-like effects are confined to the evaluative dimension or whether similar effect could also obtained with other stimulus properties. If this were the case, it would have strong implication for affective attitude theory formation. Meersman and De Houwer (2004) put this question to an empirical test. The results over an extended series of different attributes like age, brightness, or gender, supported the notion that EC is exclusively an evaluative phenomenon that could not be transferred to the nonevaluative area.

Despite these questions and remaining issues, we believe in the theoretical potential of EC to explain socially relevant phenomena. In summarising the major advantages of the EC paradigm, one must mention its simplicity, on the one hand, and its scope, on the other hand. Moreover, EC highlights the indirect and dynamic nature of attitude formation processes. Applying the EC logic to social psychology is fruitful, because both domains complement each other superbly. Taking EC into account contributes to our understanding of attitude formation driven by basic learning mechanisms that often receive little attention in social psychology, and that are not covered by other current theories. Conversely, applying EC to the social area speaks to the boundary conditions of so-called primitive learning principles and therefore stimulates theory formation in this area.

REFERENCES

Baeyens, F., Eelen, P., Crombez, G., & Van den Bergh, O. (1992a). Human evaluative conditioning: Acquisition trials, presentation schedule, evaluative style and contingency awareness. *Behaviour Research and Therapy, 30,* 133–142.

Baeyens, F., Eelen, P., & Van den Berg, O. (1989). Acquired affective evaluative value: Conservative but not unchangeable. *Behaviour Research and Therapy, 27,* 279–287.

Baeyens, F., Eelen, P., Van den Bergh, O., & Crombez, G. (1992b). The content of learning in human evaluative conditioning: Acquired valence is sensitive to US revaluation. *Learning and Motivation, 23,* 200–224.

Baeyens, F., Hermans, D., & Eelen, P. (1993). The role of CS-US contingency in human evaluative conditioning. *Behaviour Research and Therapy, 31,* 731–737.

Bargh, J. A., Chaiken, S., Raymond, P., & Hymes, C. (1996). The automatic evaluation effect: Unconditional automatic attitude activation with a pronunciation task. *Journal of Experimental Social Psychology, 32,* 185–210

Barnet, R. C., Grahame, N. J., & Miller, R. E. (1991). Comparing the magnitude of second-order conditioning and sensory preconditioning effects. *Bulletin of the Psychonomic Society, 29,* 133–135.

Barone, M. J., Miniard, P. W., & Romeo, J. B. (2000). The influence of positive mood on brand extension evaluations. *Journal of Consumer Research, 26,* 386–400.

Beggan, J. K. (1992). On the social nature of nonsocial perception: The mere ownership effect. *Journal of Personality and Social Psychology, 62,* 229–237.

Betsch, T., Plessner, H., & Schallies, E. (2004). The value-account model of attitude formation. In G. Haddock & G. R. Maio (Eds.), *Contemporary perspectives on the psychology of attitudes.* Hove, UK: Psychology Press.

Betsch, T., Plessner, H., Schwieren, C., & Gütig, R. (2001). I like it but I don't know why: A value-account approach to implicit attitude formation. *Personality and Social Psychology Bulletin, 27,* 242–253.

Bower, G. H. (1981). Mood and memory. *American Psychologist, 36,* 129–148.

Cacioppo, J. T., Marshall-Goodell, B. S., Tassinary, L. G., & Petty, R. E. (1992). Rudimentary determinants of attitudes: Classical conditioning is more effective when prior knowledge about the attitude stimulus is low than high. *Journal of Experimental Social Psychology, 28,* 207–233.

Cadinu, M. R., & Rothbart, M. (1996). Self-anchoring and differentiation processes in the minimal group setting. *Journal of Personality and Social Psychology, 70,* 661–677.

De Houwer, J. (2001). Contingency awareness and evaluative conditioning: When will it be enough? *Consciousness and Cognition, 10,* 550–558.

De Houwer, J., Thomas, S., & Baeyens, F. (2001). Associative learning of likes and dislikes: A review of 25 years of research on human evaluative conditioning. *Psychological Bulletin, 127,* 853–869.

De Jong, P. J., & Merckelbach, H. (2000). Phobia-relevant illusory correlations: The role of phobic responsivity. *Journal of Abnormal Psychology, 109,* 597–60.

Dijksterhuis, A. (2004). I like myself but I don't know why: Enhancing implicit self-esteem by subliminal evaluative conditioning. *Journal of Personality and Social Psychology, 86,* 345–355.

Eagly, A. H., & Chaiken, S. (1993). *The psychology of attitudes.* Fort Worth, TX: Harcourt.

Eifert, G. H., Craill, L., Carey, E., & O'Connor, C. (1988). Affect modification through evaluative conditioning with music. *Behaviour Research and Therapy, 26,* 321–330.

Fazio, R. H. (2001). On the automatic activation of associated evaluations: An overview [special issue]. *Cognition and Emotion, 15,* 115–141.

Fazio, R. H., & Olson, M. A. (2003). Implicit measures in social cognition research: Their meaning and use. *Annual Review of Psychology, 54,* 297–327.

Feys, J. (1995). Mere ownership: Affective self-bias or evaluative conditioning? *European Journal of Social Psychology, 25,* 559–575.

Flaherty, K., & Pappas, J. M. (2000). Implicit personality theory in evaluation of brand extensions. *Psychological Reports, 86,* 807–818.

Forgas, J. P. (2002). Toward understanding the role of affect in social thinking and behavior. *Psychological Inquiry, 13,* 90–102.

Fulcher, E. P., & Hammerl, M. (2001). When all is revealed: A dissociation between evaluative learning and contingency awareness. *Consciousness and Cognition, 10,* 524–549.

Fulcher, E. P., Mathews, A., Mackintosh, B., & Law, S. (2001). Evaluative learning and the allocation of attention to emotional stimuli. *Cognitive Therapy and Research, 25,* 261–280.

Gawronski, B., Walther, E., & Blank, H. (in press). Cognitive consistency and the formation of interpersonal attitudes: Cognitive balance affects the encoding of social information. *Journal of Experimental Social Psychology.*

Greenwald, A. G., & Banaji, M. R. (1995). Implicit social cognition: Attitudes, self-esteem, and stereotypes. *Psychological Review, 102,* 4–27.

Greenwald, A. G., Banaji, M. R., Rudman, L. A., Farnham, S. D., Nosek, B. A., & Mellott, D. S. (2002). A unified theory of implicit attitudes, stereotypes, self-esteem, and self-concept. *Psychological Review, 109,* 3–25.

Greenwald, A. G., McGhee, D. E., & Schwartz, J. L. K. (1998). Measuring individual differences in implicit cognition: The implicit association test. *Journal of Personality and Social Psychology, 74,* 1464–1480.

Guttman, N., & Kalish, H. I. (1956). Discriminability and stimulus generalization. *Journal of Experimental Psychology, 51,* 79–88.

Hammerl, M., & Grabitz, H.-J. (1996). Human evaluative conditioning without experiencing a valued event. *Learning and Motivation, 27,* 278–293.

Hebl, M. R., & Mannix, L. M. (2003). The weight of obesity in evaluation others: A mere proximity effect. *Personality and Social Psychology Bulletin, 29,* 28–39.

Heider, F. (1958). *The psychology of interpersonal relations.* New York: Wiley.

Insko, C. A. (1984). Balance theory, the Jordan paradigm, and the Wiest tetrahedron. In L. Berkowitz (Ed.), *Advances in experimental social psychology* (Vol. 18, pp. 89–140). San Diego, CA: Academic Press.

Koole, S. L., Dijksterhuis, A., & Van Knippenberg, A. (2001). What's in a name: Implicit self-esteem and the automatic self. *Journal of Personality and Social Psychology, 80,* 669–685.

Krosnick, J. A., Betz, A. L., Jussim, L. L., & Lynn, A. R. (1992). Subliminal conditioning of attitudes. *Personality and Social Psychology Bulletin, 18,* 152–162.

Krueger, K. (2000). The projective perception of the social world: A building block of social comparison processes. In J. Suls & L. Wheeler (Eds.), *Handbook of social comparison: Theory and research* (pp. 323–351). New York: Plenum/Kluwer.

Lane, V. (2000). The impact on repetition and and content on consumer perceptions of incongruent extension. *Journal of Marketing, 64,* 80–91.

Lovibond, P. F., & Shanks, D. R. (2002). The role of awareness in Pavlovian conditioning: Empirical evidence and theoretical implications. *Journal of Experimental Psychology. Animal Behavior Processes, 28,* 3–26.

Mackintosh, N. J. (1983). *Conditioning and associative learning.* Oxford, UK: Clarendon.

Manis, M., Cornell, S. D., Moore, J. C., & Jeffrey, C. (1974). Transmission of attitude relevant information through a communication chain. *Journal of Personality and Social Psychology, 30,* 81–94.

Martin, I., & Levey, A. B. (1978). Evaluative conditioning. *Advances in Behaviour Research and Therapy, 1,* 57–101.

Martin, I., & Levey, A. B. (1987). Learning will happen next: Conditioning, evaluation, and cognitive processes. In G. Davey (Ed.), *Cognitive processes and Pavlovian conditioning in humans* (pp. 57–81). Chichester, UK: Wiley.

Meersman, T., & De Houwer, J. (2004). *Associative transfer of non-evaluative stimulus properties.* Unpublished research. University of Leuven.

Mussweiler, T. (2003). Comparison processes in social judgment: Mechanisms and consequences. *Psychological Review, 110,* 472–489.

Niedenthal, P. M. (1990). Implicit perception of affective information. *Journal of Experimental Social Psychology, 26,* 505–527.

Nutin, J. M. Jr. (1985). Narcissism beyond Gestalt and awareness: The name letter effect. *European Journal of Social Psychology, 15,* 353–361.

Oehman, A., & Mineka, S. (2003). The malicious serpent: Snakes as a prototypical stimulus for an evolved module of fear. *Current Directions in Psychological Science, 12,* 5–9.

Olson, M., & Fazio, R. (2001). Implicit attitude formation through classical conditioning. *Psychological Science, 5,* 413–417.

Olson, M. A., & Fazio, R. H. (2002). Implicit acquisition and manifestation of classically conditioned attitudes. *Social Cognition, 20,* 89–103.

Otten, S., & Wentura, D. (1999). About the impact of automaticity in the minimal group paradigm: Evidence from an affective priming task. *Journal of Experimental Social Psychology, 29,* 1049–1072.

Otten, S., & Wentura, D. (2001). Self-anchoring and ingroup favoritism: An individual profiles analysis. *Journal of Experimental Social Psychology, 37,* 525–532.

Pelham, B. W., Mirenberg, M. C., & Jones, J. T. (2002). Why Susi sells seashells by the seashore: implicit egotism and major life decisions. *Journal of Personality and Social Psychology, 82,* 469–487.

Petty, R. E., & Cacioppo, J. T. (1984). The effects of involvement on responses to argument quantity and quality: Central and peripheral routes to persuasion. *Journal of Personality and Social Psychology, 46,* 69–81.

Petty, R. E., & Cacioppo, J. T., & Goldman, R. (1981). Personal involvement as a determinant of argument-based persuasion. *Journal of Personality and Social Psychology, 41,* 847–855.

Perdue, C. W., & Dovidio, J. F., & Gurtman, M. (1990). Us and them: Social categorization and the process of intergroup bias. *Journal of Personality and Social Psychology, 59,* 475–486.

Razran, G. (1971). *Mind in evolution.* Boston: Houghton Mifflin.

Reeder G. D., & Brewer M. B. (1979). A schematic model of dispositional attribution in interpersonal perception. *Psychological Review, 86,* 61–79.

Rescorla, R. A., & Wagner, A. R. (1972). A theory of Pavlovian conditioning: Variations in the effectiveness of reinforcement and nonreinforcement. In A. H. Black, & W. F. Prokasy (Eds.), *Classical conditioning* (Vol. II, pp. 64–99). New York: Appleton-Century-Crofts.

Rizley, R. C., & Rescorla, R. A. (1972). Associations in second-order conditioning and sensory preconditioning. *Journal of Comparative and Physiological Psychology, 81,* 1–11.

Rozin, P., Markwith, M., & McCauley, C. (1994). Sensitivity to indirect contacts with other person: AIDS aversion as a composite of aversion to strangers, infection, moral taint, and misfortune. *Journal of Abnormal Psychology, 103,* 495–504.

Rozin, P., Wrzesniewski, A., & Byrnes, D. (1998). The elusiveness of evaluative conditioning. *Learning and Motivation, 29,* 397–415.

Schwarz, (1990). *Stimmung als Information* [Mood as information]. Heidelberg, Germany: Springer.

Sherman, D. K., & Kim, H. S. (2002). Affective perseverance: The resistance of affect to cognitive invalidation. *Personality and Social Psychology Bulletin, 28*, 224–237.

Shimp, T. A., Stuart, E. W., & Engle, R. W. (1991). A program of classical conditioning experiments testing variations in the conditioned stimulus and context. *Journal of Consumer Research, 18*, 1–12.

Skowronski, J. J., Carlston, D. E., Mae, L., & Crawford, M. T. (1998). Spontaneous trait transference: Communicators take on the qualities they describe others. *Journal of Personality and Social Psychology, 74*, 837–848.

Stapel, D. A., & Koomen, W. (2000). Distinctness of others, mutability of the selves: Their impact on self-evaluation. *Journal of Personality and Social Psychology, 6*, 1068–1078.

Stevenson, R. J., Boakes, R. A., & Wilson, J. P. (2000). Resistance to extinction of conditioned odor perceptions: Evaluative conditioning is not unique. Journal of *Experimental Psychology. Learning, Memory, and Cognition, 26*, 423–444.

Tajfel, H., Billig, M. G., Bundy, R. P., & Flament, C. (1971). Social categorization and ingroup behavior. *European Journal of Social Psychology, 1*, 149–178.

Till, B. D., & Priluck, R. L. (2000). Stimulus generalization in classical conditioning: an initial investigation and extension. *Psychology and Marketing, 17*, 55–72.

Tursky, B., Lodge, M., Foley, M. A., Reeder, R., & Foley, H. (1976). Evaluation of the cognitive component of political issues by use of classical conditioning. *Journal of Personality and Social Psychology, 34*, 865–873.

Walther, E. (2002). Guilty by mere association: Evaluative conditioning and the spreading attitude effect. *Journal of Personality and Social Psychology, 82*, 919–934.

Walther, E., Blank., H., Gawronski, B., & Langer, T. (2004). *The enigmatic US revaluation effect.* Unpublished manuscript, University of Heidelberg.

Walther, E., & Grigoriadis, S. (2003). Why sad people like shoes better: The influence of mood on the evaluative conditioning of consumer attitudes. *Psychology & Marketing, 10*, 755–775.

Walther, E., & Trasselli, C. (2003). I like him, because I like me. Self-evaluation as a source of interpersonal attitudes. *Experimental Psychology, 50*, 239–246.

Walther, E., & Wernado, I. (2004). *Why sex is bad for your spread. US revaluation in the conditioning of consumer attitudes.* Unpublished manuscript, University of Heidelberg.

COGNITION AND EMOTION
2005, 19 (2), 197–216

Reactance in affective-evaluative learning: Outside of conscious control?

Marianne Hammerl

University of Regensburg, Germany

Eamon P. Fulcher

University College Worcester, UK

Recent studies have shown that the basic evaluative conditioning (EC) effect (originally neutral stimuli acquiring an affective value congruent with the valence of the affective stimulus they were paired with) seems to be limited to participants who are unaware of the stimulus pairings. If participants are aware of the pairings, reactance effects occur (i.e., changes in the opposite direction of the valence of the affective stimulus). To examine whether these reactance effects are due to processes of conscious countercontrol or whether the ratings reflect intrinsic feelings towards the stimuli, a new procedure was developed that included a bogus-pipeline condition. In this procedure, which was adapted from attitude research, participants were connected to bogus lie detector equipment leading them to believe that their "true" affective-evaluative responses were being observed. In Experiment 1, reactance effects occurred also in this procedure, suggesting that the effect is spontaneous and not due to processes of conscious countercontrol. In Experiment 2, these effects were replicated using a between-subjects design in addition to the standard within-subjects control condition.

Affective-evaluative learning refers to the phenomenon that the evaluation of a subjectively neutral stimulus can be altered by presenting it in close temporal proximity with an affective stimulus. The positive or negative valence of the affective stimulus determines the direction in which this change occurs. Empirical evidence stems from the early experiments of Razran (1940), who used the term *luncheon technique* to refer to the positive effects of a delicious lunch, and the *attitude conditioning* experiments of Staats and Staats (1958). In

Correspondence concerning this article should be addressed to Marianne Hammerl, University of Regensburg, Department of Psychology, 93040 Regensburg, Germany;
e-mail: marianne.hammerl@psychologie.uni-regensburg.de

The experiments were conducted at the Heinrich-Heine-University Düsseldorf, which was the affiliation of the first author at time of the study. Thanks are due to Frank Baeyens and two anonymous reviewers for their thoughtful comments.

http://www.tandf.co.uk/journals/pp/02699931.html   DOI:10.1080/02699930441000283

recent years, affective-evaluative learning is studied within the paradigm of *evaluative conditioning* (EC), which was first described by Martin and Levey (1978; Levey & Martin, 1975) and developed further by Baeyens and colleagues (e.g., Baeyens, Eelen, & Van den Bergh, 1990). This paradigm consists of three sequential phases. In the first phase (baseline phase), the participants are requested to rate the entire stimulus set in terms of degree of subjective (dis)-liking. On the basis of these ratings, for each participant the stimuli most liked and most disliked are identified as well as stimuli that received a neutral rating. In the second phase (learning phase), the neutral stimuli are paired with either a strongly liked or strongly disliked stimulus. Additionally, control stimulus pairs consisting of two neutral stimuli are presented. In the third phase (test phase), the stimuli are rated a second time with the result that now the previously neutral stimuli that were paired with (dis)liked stimuli are rated more negatively or positively than the neutral stimuli of the control stimulus pairs.

At the procedural level, the EC paradigm strongly resembles other paradigms of human classical conditioning. However, the results obtained in EC experiments are often contrary to what is known from these experiments (see De Houwer, Thomas, & Baeyens, 2001, for a review). Specifically, the finding that EC does not seem to require explicit awareness of the stimulus contingencies is at odds with the dominant view of human classical conditioning that learning only occurs when participants have knowledge of the relevant stimulus pairings. Therefore, it is not surprising that this finding was and still is under intense discussion (as examples, see the recent exchanges of arguments between Fulcher & Hammerl, 2001a, 2001b; De Houwer, 2001; and Field, 2001; as well as between Field, 2000a, 2000b; and Hammerl, 2000).

In order to show that EC does not require awareness of the stimulus contingencies, some experimental efforts are necessary. For instance, the evidence is much stronger when the unawareness of the participants is not only measured post hoc but manipulated throughout the EC experiment by presenting the stimuli subliminally (De Houwer, Hendrickx, & Baeyens, 1997) or by employing a distracter task that occupies participants' attention (Hammerl & Grabitz, 2000). Another improvement comes from more indirect and unobtrusive measurements of the evaluative response by using the Implicit Association Test (Mitchell, Anderson, & Lovibond, 2003) or an affective priming procedure (Hermans, Vansteenwegen, Crombez, Baeyens, & Eelen, 2002). These measurements especially avoid the problem of demand awareness.

In these attempts to test an implicit learning hypothesis, the role of conscious processes seems to have been neglected. One reason for this might be the assumption that the results of unconscious and conscious learning are the same. At least, this is the common argument *against* the existence of learning without awareness; namely, that conscious processes are responsible for certain learning effects but were simply not discovered by the experimenter who thus falsely attributed learning to unconscious processes (e.g., Field, 2000a; Shanks &

St. John, 1994). However, recent findings show that conscious and unconscious processes might lead to different learning outcomes. In three experiments, using different stimulus materials (haptic or visual stimulus materials), different experimental paradigms (EC or priming paradigms), and different techniques to reduce awareness (distracter task or subliminal presentation of the stimuli) and to induce awareness (unveiling the EC effect or requiring the participants to discount the influence of the affective stimuli), Fulcher and Hammerl (2001a) demonstrated that affective-evaluative learning occurred when awareness was *reduced* but not when awareness was induced. Moreover, an effect in the opposite direction to that normally observed in EC experiments emerged when participants were aware. These findings expand observations occasionally reported in previous EC studies (e.g., Baeyens, Heremans, Eelen, & Crombez, 1993; Fulcher, 2002; Hammerl & Grabitz, 2000; Walther, 2001). Thus, the argument mentioned above can be refuted: Rather than *facilitating* evaluative learning, contingency awareness can *inhibit* it.

What was seen in these experiments when participants were aware of the stimulus pairings were evaluative changes of previously neutral stimuli in the opposite direction of the intended experimental manipulation. These findings looked like the boomerang effects well-known from experiments on *psychological reactance* (Brehm, 1966). The purpose of the present study was to examine the mechanism of this reactance effect. It might be a kind of conscious countercontrol (Kihlstrom, 1987) in the sense that participants try to resist against the experimental manipulation resulting in a behaviour in the opposite direction of the presumed intention of the manipulation. This could occur not only in the context of psychological experiments but also in everyday life situation of course. The other possibilty is that the ratings reflect how the participants intrinsically feel toward the stimuli and that these are their "true" spontaneous responses. To distinguish between these two alternatives, a method commonly used in social psychology to improve the validity of self-reports was employed. It is called *bogus pipeline* (BPL) and was introduced by Jones and Sigall (1971) in an attempt to obtain a far closer approximation of what participants really feel and think than it may be with traditional paper-and-pencil questionnaires. By convincing participants that a physiological measurement apparatus is capable of recording their genuine attitudes and opinions, the BPL is effective not only in reducing social desirability but also in resolving usual problems associated with self-report data (demand characteristics, impression management, careless responding), as a meta-analysis after 20 years of BPL research revealed (Roese & Jamieson, 1993). Because of the deception involved in this paradigm, ethical concerns are worth considering. However, as observations of participants in BPL experiments (e.g., Jones & Sigall, 1973) and evaluations of BPL studies by potential participants (Aguinis & Henle, 2001) showed, the BPL method is not perceived as unethical or harmful.

In the present study, a BPL paradigm was employed to examine whether the reactance effect observed in participants aware of the stimulus contingencies is a form of conscious countercontrol or whether it reflects the true feelings toward the stimuli. If the reactance effect is based on conscious countercontrol, then it should disappear in a BPL paradigm. If it is automatically mediated because participants really feel in such way, then the reactance effect is expected to remain.

EXPERIMENT 1

In Experiment 1, a BPL paradigm was used with original lie detector equipment produced by C. H. Stoelting Company (Chicago) connected with an Atari® computer and monitor to intensify the scientific character of the apparatus. Participants were attached by means of finger electrodes (measuring the galvanic skin reponse) whenever the evaluative response was measured (BPL group). In a second group, no such device was present (non-BPL group). In both groups, the standard EC procedure with a within-subject design was employed. As with previous experiments where reactance effects had been observed (Fulcher & Hammerl, 2001a; Hammerl & Grabitz, 2000, experiment 3), we used haptic stimuli and a procedure to increase awareness of the stimulus contingencies. The non-BPL group was an exact replication of the awareness induction group of Experiment 2 of Fulcher and Hammerl (2001a).

Method

Participants

A total of 24 students (12 male, 12 female) of the Heinrich-Heine-University Düsseldorf majoring in subjects other than psychology were recruited as unpaid volunteers. All participants were right-handed and ranged in age from 18 to 29 years ($M = 23.04$, $SD = 2.52$). Participants were randomly assigned to one of the two groups, with gender balanced across groups. The participants were tested individually. Test duration was about 40 minutes. No participants reported any previous experience with psychological research.

Stimuli

The stimulus set consisted of 40 different haptic stimuli. These were pieces (21 cm wide × 29 cm long) of different textures (e.g., linen, wood, fur, silk, and sandpaper). The participants touched these stimuli only with the fingertips of one (i.e., right) hand. The stimuli were presented without additional visual or auditory information.

Apparatus

Each participant was seated in a chair in front of a big black box (120 cm wide × 50 cm long × 70 cm high). In the middle of the box, there was a gap with a textile tube leading into the box. The participant was requested to pass his/her right hand through the tube into the box. Thus, the participant could not see the stimulus that was presented inside the box by the experimenter, who was sitting on the opposite side. Because some of the stimuli produced a scratch or rustle when being touched, the participant had to wear sound-absorbing headphones.

At eye level, a rating scale was attached, which was 52.5 cm wide × 5 cm high and consisted of 21 categories, 2.5 cm each. The categories were labelled −10, −9, ..., 0, ..., +9, +10. In addition, the scale was labelled *disliked* on the left, *neutral* in the middle, and *liked* on the right.

For participants of the BPL group, there was at the left side of the black box the lie detector (Stoelting Company, Chicago) set up with an Atari® computer and monitor faced to the experimenter, not to the participant.

Procedure

The experiment consisted of three sequential phases: baseline phase, learning phase, and test phase.

Baseline phase.   A sheet of paper containing the cover story and the instructions for the experiment was given to the participant, who was led to believe that the purpose of the study was to simulate an everyday life situation. The text for participants of the BPL group was as follows (translated from the German):

> Welcome! Thank you very much for taking part in our study.
>
> We are interested in the influence of haptic stimuli (i.e., stimuli that we perceive via our sense of touch) in our everyday life. Different stimuli will be presented. After touching them, please rate each stimulus according to your first, immediate, spontaneous reaction by means of the scale in front of you. The scale ranges from −10 (*disliked*) through 0 (*neutral*) to +10 (*liked*).
>
> We are especially interested in examining whether your verbal ratings correspond with your physiological responses.
>
> So that you can concentrate better, please wear the headphones lying in front of you. Do you have any questions?

In the non-BPL group, the third paragraph containing the hint at the correspondence between verbal and physiological responses was omitted. Participants of the BPL group were attached to the lie detector via finger electrodes producing an impressive deviation of the needle when the recorder was turned on. After that demonstration, participants had no further sight on their physiological responses. Then, in both groups, the baseline rating of the stimuli began. Each stimulus was presented for 3 seconds and rated immediately by the participant by means of the 21-category scale described above. The ratings given at this stage were the first evaluative responses (ER1). Then, the participant was preoccupied with a filler task. The participant was led to believe that a measurement of his/her current mood was necessary. Therefore, a questionnaire containing 123 adjectives, which described different feelings (Janke & Debus, 1978), was given to the participant. Participants of the BPL group were disconnected from the apparatus so that they could fill out the questionnaire without strain. Meanwhile, the experimenter selected the stimuli that acted subsequently as neutral or liked stimuli. As in previous studies, no disliked stimuli were selected because most of these stimuli were very rough and irritating the fingertips to such an extent that a repeated presentation might have damaged the skin and caused discomfort. A total of six stimuli from the categories -2, -1, 0, $+1$, or $+2$ were selected to act as neutral stimuli, and the two stimuli with the highest rating were used as liked stimuli. If there were more than six stimuli with a rating between -2 and $+2$, the stimuli were selected randomly. The assignment of the neutral stimuli to the liked stimuli and to the neutral stimuli of the control stimulus pairs was also done on a random basis. In this manner, two different N-L pairs and two different N-N pairs were arranged for each participant.

Learning phase.   Prior to the learning phase, all participants were given the following written instructions (translated from the German):

> In order to simulate an everyday life situation (e.g., while going shopping, you may touch some textures several times), we will present some of the stimuli more than once. These stimuli will be textures that you have rated positively or neutrally. The stimuli will be paired; that means, each time two stimuli will be presented shortly one after another. These pairs consist of either two neutrally rated stimuli or one neutrally and one positively rated stimulus. Please note which textures are paired.

Each of the four stimulus pairs was presented six times consecutively. As in Fulcher and Hammerl (2001a, experiment 2), a block-wise presentation order rather than a randomised order was chosen, because it facilitates the acquisition of verbalisable knowledge of the stimulus pairings without causing stronger or faster evaluative learning (Baeyens, Eelen, Crombez, & Van den Bergh, 1992a). However, the order of the presentation of the four blocks was randomised for each participant. The presentation of each stimulus pair was as follows: The first stimulus of a pair was displayed for 2 s, followed by a 3 s trace interval, followed by the second stimulus of the pair also displayed for 2 s. After 8 s, the next trial with the presentation of the same stimulus pair or (after six times) a different stimulus pair began.

Test phase. For participants of the BPL group, the test phase began with connecting them to the lie detector again. The rest of the test phase was identical in both groups. All stimuli that had been used in the learning phase were rated a second time. Therefore, each stimulus was presented for 3 s, and the participant was requested to rate each stimulus by means of the 21-category scale used for the baseline rating. The participant was reminded to rely on his/her first, immediate, spontaneous reaction at this moment. The ratings given at this stage were the second evaluative responses (ER2). Finally, the participant was interviewed to determine his/her awareness of the stimulus pairings. The awareness assessment used was similar to the procedure developed by Baeyens et al. (1990). The first stimulus of each of the four stimulus pairs was presented, and the experimenter asked the participant to recall the contingent stimulus. The participant was told that the question referred to the phase of the experiment in which he/she had touched all the stimuli repeatedly (i.e., the learning phase). Then the participant was asked whether the contingent stimulus of the pair was a liked, a disliked, or a neutral stimulus. A participant merely had to indicate the affective value of the contingent stimulus to be classified as contingency aware of this stimulus pair. In the BPL group, there was a postexperimental manipulation check to examine participants' confidence in the lie detector equipment. This manipulation check consisted of four questions beginning with two rather unspecific questions (translated from the German):

1. What was your first impression when introduced to the lie detector equipment?
2. Did you have any concerns? If so, in which respect?
3. Do you think the apparatus you were connected to was able to provide valid measures with respect to your verbal ratings?
4. Do you want to know whether your verbal ratings corresponded with your physiological responses?

Data analysis

To analyse intergroup comparisons concerning the baseline ratings, Mann-Whitney *U*-tests (two-tailed) were conducted. Intragroup comparisons were tested statistically using Wilcoxon signed-rank tests, one-tailed in the non-BPL group and two-tailed in the BPL group because for that group only a non-directional hypothesis had been stated. For all tests, a *p*-value of .05 or less was accepted as significant.

Results

Awareness data

As described above, a participant merely had to indicate the affective value of the contingent stimulus to be classified as contingency aware of this stimulus pair. However, most participants classified as aware of a given stimulus pair

could also describe the contingent stimulus in terms of the stimulus characteristics (e.g., soft, rough, smooth). As the stimulus set consisted of textures and not
of concrete objects, it was not expected that the participants would recall real
entities. And, indeed, no such associations were reported.

In the non-BPL group, 10 of the 12 participants were classified as aware of all
of the four contingencies and the remaining 2 participants as aware of three of
the four contingencies. The pattern of data described below was the same
whether all 12 participants were considered aware or only the 10 participants
aware of all four contingencies. Therefore, the subgroup "aware" of the non-
BLP group contained all 12 participants.

In the BPL group, 9 of the 12 participants were classified as aware of all of
the four contingencies and 1 participant as aware of three of the four contingencies. As the pattern of data described below was the same whether only
the 9 participants were considered aware or whether also the participant aware of
three of the four contingencies was included in the analysis, the subgroup
"aware" of the BLP group consisted of 10 participants. The remaining 2 participants of the BPL group were aware of only one of the four contingencies.
These participants were classified as unaware.

Evaluative response data

Initial mean evaluative responses to the haptic stimuli selected to act as
neutral or liked stimuli did not differ significantly between the two groups.
Moreover, the ratings were quite similar to the ratings known from previous
experiments with these kinds of stimulus materials (Fulcher & Hammerl, 2001a,
experiments 1 and 2; Hammerl & Grabitz, 2000). The mean ratings of the
stimuli later used as liked stimuli were 7.38 (SD = 1.86) in the non-BPL group
and 7.50 (SD = 2.01) in the BPL group. The stimuli selected to act as neutral
stimuli were rated around zero (see Table 1).

In order to analyse evaluative changes from baseline to test phase ratings,
difference scores (ER2 minus ER1) were calculated. Positive values represent
increases in liking, while negative values show decreases in liking. Table 1
shows that in the non-BPL group, the difference scores for the N-L stimuli
(neutral stimuli that had been paired with liked stimuli) were lower than the
difference scores for the N-N stimuli (neutral stimuli of the control stimulus
pairs). The ratings differed significantly ($p < .025$); thus, a reactance effect was
obtained in this group, in which all participants were classified as aware (see
Figure 1).

Also in the BPL group (total group), the ratings of the N-L stimuli were
significantly lower than the difference scores for the N-N stimuli ($p < .04$); thus,
also in a BPL paradigm, a reactance effect was obtained. However, the subgroup
analysis revealed that this reactance effect was only seen in participants classified as aware, whereas participants considered to be unaware showed the basic

TABLE 1
Experiment 1: Descriptive statistics for evaluative response data in baseline (ER1) and test phase (ER2)

Group	Type of stimulus					
	N-L			N-N		
	ER1	ER2	D	ER1	ER2	D
Non-BPL group						
Total group (*n* = 12)						
M	−0.29	−1.79	−1.50	0.00	−0.25	−0.25
(SD)	(0.54)	(2.15)	(2.07)	(0.67)	(0.94)	(0.72)
BPL group						
Total group (*n* = 12)						
M	−0.17	−2.46	−2.29	−0.21	−0.63	−0.42
(SD)	(0.89)	(1.99)	(2.50)	(0.54)	(2.54)	(2.60)
Subgroup "aware" (*n* = 10)						
M	−0.05	−3.00	−2.95	−0.25	−0.40	−0.15
(SD)	(0.86)	(1.70)	(2.17)	(0.59)	(2.62)	(2.67)
Subgroup "unaware" (*n* = 2)						
M	−0.75	0.25	1.00	0.00	−1.75	−1.75
(SD)	(1.06)	(0.35)	(0.71)	(0.00)	(2.47)	(2.47)

Note: N-L and N-N stimuli were previously neutral stimuli paired either with liked (L) or neutral (N) stimuli. D, difference score (D = ER2 minus ER1).

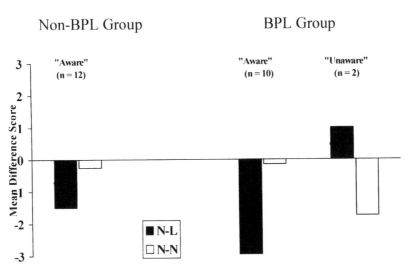

Figure 1. Experiment 1: Mean difference scores (ER2 minus ER1) for evaluative responses to previously neutral stimuli paired either with liked (N-L) or neutral (N-N) stimuli. BPL, bogus pipeline.

EC effect (see Figure 1). The reactance effect in the subgroup "aware" was statistically reliable: The difference scores for the N-L stimuli were significantly lower than the difference scores for the N-N stimuli ($p < .0074$). It was not possible to conduct a test for the subgroup "unaware" because of its small size.

Discussion

The results of Experiment 1 show that a reactance effect occurred in both groups, thus replicating previous findings that indicated reactance effects in participants aware of the stimulus contingencies (Fulcher & Hammerl, 2001a; Hammerl & Grabitz, 2000, experiment 3) and moreover demonstrating that the reactance effect seems to occur automatically. Also in a BPL paradigm where participants were led to believe that their "true" evaluations could be measured, evaluative changes in the opposite direction of the intended experimental manipulation were seen. One could argue, however, that participants might have been suspicious about the supposed purpose of the apparatus because they have shown the same reactance effect as participants who evaluated the stimuli without the BPL paradigm. Participants' spontaneous comments as well as their answers in the postexperimental manipulation check revealed, however, that they were convinced of the device. All participants, for example, were anxious to obtain feedback regarding the correspondence between their own verbal and physiological responses. Furthermore, in the present experiment, the guidelines and instructions that had been effectual in previous studies (see Roese & Jamieson, 1993, for a review) were followed. Thus, we can safely conclude that the BPL method was indeed convincing and that the ratings were an accurate measure of how the participants genuinely felt toward the stimuli.

As this experiment was the first attempt using a BPL preparation within an EC experiment, we need to know that the present finding is a reliable one. Therefore, we attempted to replicate the effect in an additional experiment using a between-subjects design instead of merely using within-control conditions.

EXPERIMENT 2

The standard control conditions in EC experiments are the N-N stimulus pairs (i.e., pairs consisting of two neutral stimuli), thus representing a within-subject control design. The lack of independent control groups in EC experiments was criticised by Davey (1994), Field and Davey (1997, 1998, 1999), and Shanks and Dickinson (1990). In this context, Field and Davey (1997) proposed two independent control groups: a no-treatment control group and a block/sub-block (BSB) control group. In the no-treatment control group, there is no stimulus presentation during the learning phase. The purpose of this group is to control participants' experimental expectancies and the effects of the general procedure, especially the stimulus selection practice and the repetition of the evaluation procedure. This group does not control effects that are due to stimulus exposure.

That is, the purpose of the BSB control group, in which all experimental stimuli shown in the standard EC group are presented, but to ensure that no stimulus associations are built, the stimuli are presented unpaired in two blocks (one block containing each first stimulus of a stimulus pair and one block containing each second stimulus of a stimulus pair) and in a randomised order within each block.

Concerning the basic EC effect, this between-subjects design was successfully employed (Hammerl & Grabitz, 2000) demonstrating affective-evaluative learning only in the standard EC group, whereas in the two control groups, no conditioning-like effects occurred. In the present context, it is necessary to stress that participants' attention had been occupied by a distracter task so that most of the participants were classifiable as unaware. Those who were not classified as unaware showed evaluative changes in the opposite direction. This was the starting point of looking closer at differential effects that awareness and a lack of awareness might have on affective-evaluative responses. As the reactance effect in participants classified as aware is a newly observed phenomenon, it is necessary, in addition to the attempts of replication, to consider methodological artifacts. The nonassociative effects described above (e.g., repetition of the evaluation procedure, mere stimulus exposure) could apply to the reactance effect, too. Therefore, in Experiment 2, not only the BPL group of Experiment 1 was replicated as experimental group (paired group) but also the two independent control groups described above were realised within the BPL paradigm. Thus, in Experiment 2, a design with three independent groups was realised.

Another critical point recently formulated by Lovibond and Shanks (2002) and originally made in Fulcher and Cocks (1997) deals with the lack of immediacy of the awareness measurement. In most studies, the awareness of the stimulus contingencies is measured in the test phase *after* the stimuli have been rated a second time (ER2); that is, immediately after the learning phase where the stimulus contingencies are experienced. Contingency awareness is more critical at the moment in time when the stimuli are being re-evaluated than at some time later in the procedure. Thus, following the recommendation of Lovibond and Shanks to measure awareness as soon as possible, the usual order of measuring ER2 and awareness was reversed.

Method

Participants

A total of 48 students (24 male, 24 female) of the Heinrich-Heine-University Düsseldorf majoring in subjects other than psychology were recruited as unpaid volunteers. All participants were right-handed and ranged in age from 19 to 35 years ($M = 24.13$, $SD = 3.95$). Participants were randomly assigned to one of the three groups, with gender balanced across groups. The participants were tested individually. Test duration was about 40 minutes. No participants reported any previous experience with psychological research.

Stimuli, apparatus, and procedure

The stimulus materials and apparatus for all three groups were the same as for Experiment 1. Concerning the procedure, the three groups differed as follows.

Paired group. This group was a replication of the BPL group of Experiment 1 with the only exception that in the test phase, the order of measuring ER2 and awareness of the stimulus contingencies was reversed.

BSB group. The BSB group differed from the paired group only during the learning phase. The stimuli selected and paired according to the same criteria as in the paired group were, however, not presented in pairs but separated and presented in two isolated blocks. Within these blocks, the number of presentations of each stimulus and the presentation parameters (i.e., stimulus duration, trace and intertrial intervals) were identical to those of the paired group. Thus, a stimulus was presented for 2 s, followed by a 3 s trace interval without stimulation, followed by the same stimulus for 2 s, followed by an 8 s intertrial interval, and so on, until that stimulus had been presented six times (i.e., the same number of presentations as in the paired group). Then, the next stimulus followed. There were two blocks of stimuli: Block A containing four neutral stimuli (i.e., each first stimulus of the four stimulus pairs) and Block B containing two liked and two neutral stimuli (i.e., each second stimulus of the four stimulus pairs). The order of the two blocks was counterbalanced so that half of the participants ($n = 8$) began with Block A, while the other half began with Block B. Within the blocks, the order of stimulus presentations was randomised for each participant. Prior to the learning phase, participants of the BSB group were given the following instructions (translated from the German):

> In order to simulate an everyday life situation (e.g., while going shopping, you may touch some textures several times), we will present some of the stimuli more than once. A total of eight textures will be presented six times consecutively.

Immediately after the learning phase, awareness was measured the same way as in the paired group. However, to be classified as aware, participants in the BSB group could mention as contingent stimulus the given stimulus itself (because each stimulus was presented six times consecutively) or, indeed, the next one that followed the given stimulus. As in the paired group, it was not necessary to recall a particular stimulus. A participant merely had to indicate the affective value of the contingent stimulus to be classified as aware.

No-treatment group. The same number and kind of stimuli were selected and paired as in the paired and BSB groups. However, there was no stimulus presentation at all during the learning phase. Thus, also the awareness measurement was omitted. As the purpose of this control group was to examine the effects of mere repetition of the evaluation procedure, participants were attached to the lie detector, requested for ER1, disconnected from the lie detector to perform the filler task, attached to the lie detector again, and finally requested for ER2.

Data analysis

To analyse intergroup comparisons concerning the baseline ratings, Mann-Whitney U-tests (two-tailed) were conducted. All intragroup comparisons were tested statistically using Wilcoxon signed-rank tests (one-tailed). To analyse intergroup comparisons concerning evaluative changes, Mann-Whitney U-tests (one-tailed) were conducted between the subgroups "aware" of the paired and BSB groups and the subgroups "unaware", respectively. For all tests, a p-value of .05 or less was accepted as significant.

Results

Awareness data

As in Experiment 1, most of the participants classified as aware of a given stimulus pair were able to indicate the affective value of the contingent stimulus *and* to describe its main characteristic.

In the paired group, 9 of the 16 participants were classified as aware of all of the four contingencies and 1 participant as aware of three of the four contingencies. As the pattern of data described below was the same whether only the 9 participants were considered aware or whether also the participant aware of three of the four contingencies was included in the analysis, the subgroup "aware" of the paired group consisted of 10 participants. Of the remaining 6 participants of the paired group, 4 participants were aware of only one of the four contingencies and 2 were aware of two of the four contingencies. As the pattern of data described below was the same whether only the 4 participants that were aware of only one of the four contingencies were considered unaware or whether also the 2 participants aware of two of the four contingencies were included in the analysis, the subgroup "unaware" of the paired group consisted of 6 participants.

In the BSB group, 8 of the 16 participants were classified as aware of all of the four contingencies and 1 participant as aware of three of the four contingencies. As the pattern of data described below was the same whether only the 8 participants were considered aware or whether also the participant aware of three of the four contingencies was included in the analysis, the subgroup "aware" of the BSB group consisted of 9 participants. Of the remaining 7 participants of the BSB group, 4 participants were aware of only one of the four contingencies and 3 were aware of two of the four contingencies. As the pattern of data described below was the same whether only the 4 participants that were aware of only one of the four contingencies were considered unaware or whether also the 3 participants aware of two of the four contingencies were included in the analysis, the subgroup "unaware" of the BSB group consisted of 7 participants.

In the no-treatment group, the awareness measurement was omitted, because there was no stimulus presentation during the learning phase.

Evaluative response data

Initial mean evaluative responses to the haptic stimuli selected to act as neutral or liked stimuli did not differ significantly between the three groups. Moreover, the ratings were quite similar to the ratings in Experiment 1. The mean ratings of the stimuli later used as liked stimuli were 7.34 (SD = 2.14) in the paired group, 7.15 (SD = 1.96) in the BSB group, and 7.25 (SD = 1.91) in the no-treatment group. The stimuli selected to act as neutral stimuli were rated around zero (see Table 2).

As in Experiment 1, difference scores (ER2 minus ER1) were calculated to analyse evaluative changes. Table 2 shows that in all three groups (total groups), the difference scores for the N-L stimuli did not differ very much from the ratings of the N-N stimuli. This was also seen in the Wilcoxon signed-rank tests which showed no significant differences between the ratings of these two kinds of stimuli. Analysing the subgroups (see Figure 2) revealed, however, differences in both subgroups of the paired group, whereas the subgroups of the BSB

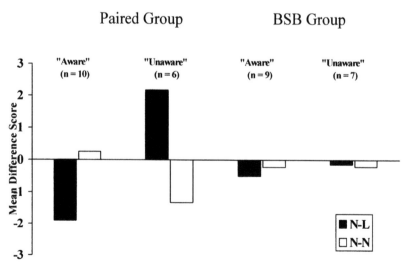

Figure 2. Experiment 2: Mean difference scores (ER2 minus ER1) for evaluative responses to previously neutral stimuli paired either with liked (N-L) or neutral (N-N) stimuli BSB, block/sub-block.

TABLE 2
Experiment 2: Descriptive statistics for evaluative response data in baseline (ER1)
and test phase (ER2)

| | Type of stimulus | | | | | |
| | N-L | | | N-N | | |
Group	ER1	ER2	D	ER1	ER2	D
Paired group						
Total group (*n* = 16)						
M	−0.22	−0.59	−0.37	−0.16	−0.50	−0.34
(SD)	(0.48)	(2.51)	(2.60)	(0.83)	(2.36)	(2.04)
Subgroup "aware" (*n* = 10)						
M	−0.20	−2.10	−1.90	−0.10	0.15	0.25
(SD)	(0.54)	(1.76)	(1.84)	(0.74)	(1.93)	(1.93)
Subgroup "unaware" (*n* = 6)						
M	−0.25	1.92	2.17	−0.25	−1.58	−1.33
(SD)	(0.42)	(1.11)	(1.33)	(1.04)	(2.78)	(1.97)
BSB group						
Total group (*n* = 16)						
M	−0.19	−0.53	−0.34	0.03	−0.19	−0.22
(SD)	(0.68)	(2.11)	(1.87)	(0.53)	(1.99)	(1.91)
Subgroup "aware" (*n* = 9)						
M	−0.22	−0.72	−0.50	0.00	−0.22	−0.22
(SD)	(0.83)	(2.50)	(2.25)	(0.50)	(2.28)	(2.05)
Subgroup "unaware" (*n* = 7)						
M	−0.14	−0.28	−0.14	0.07	−0.14	−0.21
(SD)	(0.48)	(1.63)	(1.41)	(0.61)	(1.73)	(1.87)
No-treatment group						
Total group (*n* = 16)						
M	−0.12	0.22	0.34	−0.03	0.34	0.37
(SD)	(0.72)	(2.22)	(1.96)	(0.90)	(3.32)	(3.01)

Note: N-L and N-N stimuli were previously neutral stimuli paired either with liked (L) or neutral (N) stimuli. D, difference score (D = ER2 minus ER1).

group showed again no differences. The differences in the subgroups of the paired group were statistically reliable: In the subgroup "aware", the difference scores for the N-L stimuli were significantly lower than the difference scores for the N-N stimuli ($p < .004$); in the subgroup "unaware", the difference scores for the N-L stimuli were significantly higher than the difference scores for the N-N stimuli ($p < .01$). The intragroup comparisons concerning the subgroups of the BSB group did not show statistically significant differences between the ratings of the different stimuli.

Intergroup comparisons revealed that the difference scores for the N-L stimuli were significantly lower in the subgroup "aware" of the paired group than in the subgroup "aware" of the BSB group ($p < .05$); whereas in the subgroup "unaware" of the paired group, the difference scores for the N-L stimuli were significantly higher than in the subgroup "unaware" of the BSB group ($p < .01$).

Discussion

The results of Experiment 2 show that the reactance effect in the BPL paradigm is a reliable phenomenon in participants aware of the stimulus contingencies. Moreover, it has been demonstrated in a between-subjects design: In the two control groups proposed by Field and Davey (1997), no such effects occurred. What was not expected was the large number of participants classified as unaware in the paired group ($n = 6$) as well as in the BSB group ($n = 7$). This is surprising as the purpose of Experiment 2 was also to improve the results of the awareness measurement. Therefore, the order of the measurements of ER2 and contingency awareness had been reversed with the unintended consequence that now fewer participants were classified as aware than before. In Experiment 1, 83% of the participants of the BPL group were aware of the stimulus contingencies; whereas in the present experiment, only 62.5% of the participants of the paired group (an exact replication of the BPL group with the exception of the reversed order) could be classified as aware. Nevertheless, participants of the paired group classified as unaware showed the basic EC effect in intra- as well as intergroup comparisons. This shows that the basic EC effect is also demonstrable in a BPL paradigm with a between-subjects design.

GENERAL DISCUSSION

Taken together, the results of the present experiments show that the reactance effect (i.e., evaluative changes in the opposite direction of the intended manipulation) is: (a) a reliable phenomenon as it was replicable (the non-BPL group of Experiment 1 is equivalent to the awareness induction group of Experiment 2 of Fulcher & Hammerl, 2001a); (b) seems to occur automatically as it was also seen in a BPL paradigm; (c) is replicable within the BPL paradigm (the paired group of Experiment 2 is equivalent to the BPL group of Experiment 1 with the exception of the reversed order); and (d) is also demonstrable in a between-subject design. An unexpected finding is the outcome of the reversed measurement order. Assessing contingency awareness directly after the learning phase leads to a decrease of the number of participants classifiable as aware. Thereby, however, a subgroup of participants classifiable as unaware emerged which does not show a reactance effect but the basic EC effect as known from previous experiments when participants were unaware of the stimulus contingencies (Fulcher & Cocks, 1997; Fulcher & Hammerl, 2001a; Fulcher, Mathews, Mackintosh, & Law, 2001; Hammerl & Grabitz, 2000). As the total group (and with that the subgroup, too) was realised in a BPL paradigm within a between-subjects design, the finding extends the scope of the effect.

The results show that conscious and unconscious processes might lead to different behaviours and that the debate of whether EC can be "truly" unconscious should be broadened. Effects due to unconscious processes are seemingly not just a miniature version of the outcomes of conscious processes. These differential consequences of the kind of the underlying process are seen not only in EC studies (Baeyens et al., 1993; Fulcher, 2002; Fulcher & Hammerl, 2001a; Hammerl & Grabitz, 2000; Walther, 2001) but also in studies on impression formation (Dijksterhuis, Spears, & Lépinasse, 2001; Strack, Schwarz, Bless, Kübler, & Wänke, 1993), affective priming (Murphy & Zajonc, 1993), and perception (Merikle, Smilek, & Eastwood, 2001). The present results suggest that at least in the EC paradigm, these effects are occurring automatically in the sense that participants genuinely feel different toward the stimuli when they know the circumstances than when they do not. It would be interesting to examine whether a BPL paradigm would show similar results in the experimental paradigms mentioned above.

Another interesting line of future research would be whether the reactance effect in affective-evaluative learning is as resistant to extinction as the basic EC effect (Baeyens, Crombez, Van den Bergh, & Eelen, 1988; Fulcher & Cocks, 1997; Levey & Martin, 1975; Stevenson, Boakes, & Wilson, 2000) and whether such complex associative learning structures are involved as seen in EC that is sensitive to postconditioning revaluation (Baeyens, Eelen, Van den Bergh, & Crombez, 1992b; Hammerl, Bloch, & Silverthorne, 1997) and sensory preconditioning (Hammerl & Grabitz, 1996; Walther, 2002). Looking closer at reactance effects could also shed some light on the elusiveness of the EC effect because sometimes EC experiments result in unexpected failures (Rozin, Wrzesniewski, & Byrnes, 1998). Also theoretical models of EC, such as the conceptual-categorisation account (Davey, 1994), the holistic account (Martin & Levey, 1994), or the referential account (Baeyens & De Houwer, 1995; Baeyens, Eelen, & Crombez, 1995) might get a broader scope of explanation when considering evaluative changes in the opposite direction to the basic EC effect. The connectionist account of Fulcher (2002) supposes that a discounting mechanism is employed when participants are aware of the stimulus contingencies. This mechanism becomes more active as awareness increases and serves to isolate the effects of the affective stimulus on the neutral stimulus. However, since participants may often not be fully aware of the precise evaluational influence of the affective stimulus, and since nonconscious evaluative learning mechanisms may still operate, they may overestimate this influence rather than merely discount it. Hence, the result is a contrast effect rather than a null effect.

What was not expected was the outcome of the reversed measurement order in Experiment 2 (awareness measurement prior to the measurement of the evaluative response). Apparently, requesting participants to evaluate the stimuli does not interfere with the subsequent task to verbalise the knowledge of the learning phase but instead seems to facilitate it. It appears as if the presentation of the stimuli (for the purpose of their evaluation) activates some associative structures that have an influence not only on the kind of evaluation (changed or unchanged and if changed then in the direction or opposite direction of the value of the affective stimulus) but also on the subsequent verbalisation of the circumstances of the stimulus presentations. Without that prior activation, the questions concerning these circumstances seem to be more difficult. These are only speculations that have to be tested in further experiments, in which the manipulation of the measurement order should occur in the same experiment (the present speculations are based only on a between-experiment comparison without statistical reliability).

The strength of this research is in trying to prise apart the relationship between learning and awareness and the present expected and unexpected findings are in line with a recent statement by Frensch and Rünger (2003) who wrote (p. 16): "...the question of how exactly awareness and learning might be interrelated has only recently begun to be addressed empirically".

REFERENCES

Aguinis, H., & Henle, C. A. (2001). Empirical assessment of the ethics of the bogus pipeline. *Journal of Applied Social Psychology, 31*, 352–375.

Baeyens, F., Crombez, G., Van den Bergh, O., & Eelen, P. (1988). Once in contact always in contact: Evaluative conditioning is resistant to extinction. *Advances in Behaviour Research and Therapy, 10*, 179–199.

Baeyens, F., & De Houwer, J. (1995). Evaluative conditioning is a qualitatively distinct form of classical conditioning: A reply to Davey (1994). *Behaviour Research and Therapy, 33*, 825–831.

Baeyens, F., Eelen, P., & Crombez, G. (1995). Pavlovian associations are forever: On classical conditioning and extinction. *Journal of Psychophysiology, 9*, 127–141.

Baeyens, F., Eelen, P., Crombez, G., & Van den Bergh, O. (1992a). Human evaluative conditioning: Acquisition trials, presentation schedule, evaluative style and contingency awareness. *Behaviour Research and Therapy, 30*, 133–142.

Baeyens, F., Eelen, P., & Van den Bergh, O. (1990). Contingency awareness in evaluative conditioning: A case for unaware affective-evaluative learning. *Cognition and Emotion, 4*, 3–18.

Baeyens, F., Eelen, P., Van den Bergh, O., & Crombez, G. (1992b). The content of learning in human evaluative conditioning: Acquired valence is sensitive to US-revaluation. *Learning and Motivation, 23*, 200–224.

Baeyens, F., Heremans, R., Eelen, P., & Crombez, G. (1993). Hidden-covariation detection and imagery ability. *European Journal of Cognitive Psychology, 5*, 435–456.

Brehm, J. W. (1966). *A theory of psychological reactance*. New York: Academic Press.

Davey, G. C. L. (1994). Is evaluative conditioning a qualitatively distinct form of classical conditioning? *Behaviour Research and Therapy, 32*, 291–299.

De Houwer, J. (2001). Contingency awareness and evaluative conditioning: When will it be enough? *Consciousness and Cognition, 10*, 550–558.

De Houwer, J., Hendrickx, H., & Baeyens, F. (1997). Evaluative learning with "subliminally" presented stimuli. *Consciousness and Cognition, 6*, 87–107.

De Houwer, J., Thomas, S., & Baeyens, F. (2001). Associative learning of likes and dislikes: A review of 25 years of research on human evaluative conditioning. *Psychological Bulletin, 127*, 853–869.

Dijksterhuis, A., Spears, R., & Lépinasse, V. (2001). Reflecting and deflecting stereotypes: Assimilation and contrast in impression formation and automatic behavior. *Journal of Experimental Social Psychology, 37*, 286–299.

Field, A. P. (2000a). I like it, but I'm not sure why: Can evaluative conditioning occur without conscious awareness? *Consciousness and Cognition, 9*, 13–36.

Field, A. P. (2000b). Evaluative conditioning is Pavlovian conditioning: Issues of definition, measurement, and the theoretical importance of contingency awareness. *Consciousness and Cognition, 9*, 41–49.

Field, A. P. (2001). When all is still concealed: Are we closer to understanding the mechanisms underlying evaluative conditioning? *Consciousness and Cognition, 10*, 559–566.

Field, A. P., & Davey, G. C. L. (1997). Conceptual conditioning: Evidence for an artifactual account of evaluative conditioning. *Learning and Motivation, 28*, 446–464.

Field, A. P., & Davey, G. C. L. (1998). Evaluative conditioning: Arti-fact or -fiction? A reply to Baeyens, De Houwer, Vansteenwegen, and Eelen (1998). *Learning and Motivation, 29*, 475–491.

Field, A. P., & Davey, G. C. L. (1999). Reevaluating evaluative conditioning: A nonassociative explanation of conditioning effects in the visual evaluative conditioning paradigm. *Journal of Experimental Psychology: Animal Behavior Processes, 25*, 211–224.

Frensch, P. A., & Rünger, D. (2003). Implicit learning. *Current Directions in Psychological Science, 12*, 13–18.

Fulcher, E. P. (2002). Neurons with attitudes: A connectionist account of human evaluative learning. In S. Moore & M. Oaksford (Eds.), *Emotional cognition: From brain to behaviour* (pp. 75–109). Amsterdam: John Benjamins.

Fulcher, E. P., & Cocks, R. P. (1997). Dissociative storage systems in human evaluative conditioning. *Behaviour Research and Therapy, 35*, 1–10.

Fulcher, E. P., & Hammerl, M. (2001a). When all is revealed: A dissociation between evaluative learning and contingency awareness. *Consciousness and Cognition, 10*, 524–549.

Fulcher, E. P., & Hammerl, M. (2001b). When all is considered: Evaluative learning does not require contingency awareness. *Consciousness and Cognition, 10*, 567–573.

Fulcher, E. P., Mathews, A., Mackintosh, B., & Law, S. (2001). Evaluative learning and the allocation of attention to emotional stimuli. *Cognitive Therapy and Research, 25*, 261–280.

Hammerl, M. (2000). I like it, but only when I'm not sure why: Evaluative conditioning and the awareness issue. *Consciousness and Cognition, 9*, 37–40.

Hammerl, M., Bloch, M., & Silverthorne, C. P. (1997). Effects of US-alone presentations on human evaluative conditioning. *Learning and Motivation, 28*, 491–509.

Hammerl, M., & Grabitz, H.-J. (1996). Human evaluative conditioning without experiencing a valued event. *Learning and Motivation, 27*, 278–293.

Hammerl, M., & Grabitz, H.-J. (2000). Affective-evaluative learning in humans: A form of associative learning or only an artifact? *Learning and Motivation, 31*, 345–363.

Hermans, D., Vansteenwegen, D., Crombez, G., Baeyens, F., & Eelen, P. (2002). Expectancy learning and evaluative learning in human classical conditioning: Affective priming as an indirect and unobtrusive measure of conditioned stimulus valence. *Behaviour Research and Therapy, 40*, 217–234.

Janke, W., & Debus, G. (1978). *Die Eigenschaftswörterliste (EWL)* [The adjective check list (EWL)]. Göttingen: Hogrefe.

Jones, E. E., & Sigall, H. (1971). The bogus pipeline: A new paradigm for measuring affect and attitude. *Psychological Bulletin, 76*, 349–364.

Jones, E. E., & Sigall, H. (1973). Where there is ignis, there may be fire. *Psychological Bulletin, 79*, 260–262.

Kihlstrom, J. F. (1987). The cognitive unconscious. *Science, 237*, 1445–1452.

Levey, A. B., & Martin, I. (1975). Classical conditioning of human "evaluative" responses. *Behaviour Research and Therapy, 13*, 221–226.

Lovibond, P. F., & Shanks, D. R. (2002). The role of awareness in Pavlovian conditioning: Empirical evidence and theoretical implications. *Journal of Experimental Psychology. Animal Behavior Processes, 28*, 3–26.

Martin, I., & Levey, A. B. (1978). Evaluative conditioning. *Advances in Behaviour Research and Therapy, 1*, 57–101.

Martin, I. & Levey, A. B. (1994). The evaluative response: Primitive but necessary. *Behaviour Research and Therapy, 32*, 301–305.

Merikle, P. M., Smilek, D., & Eastwood, J. D. (2001). Perception without awareness: Perspectives from cognitive psychology. *Cognition, 79*, 115–134.

Mitchell, C. J., Anderson, N. E., & Lovibond, P. F. (2003). Measuring evaluative conditioning using the Implicit Association Test. *Learning and Motivation, 34*, 203–217.

Murphy, S. T., & Zajonc, R. B. (1993). Affect, cognition, and awareness: Affective priming with optimal and suboptimal stimulus exposures. *Journal of Personality and Social Psychology, 64*, 723–739.

Razran, G. H. S. (1940). Conditioned response changes in rating and appraising sociopolitical slogans. *Psychological Bulletin, 37*, 481.

Roese, N. J., & Jamieson, D. W. (1993). Twenty years of bogus pipeline research: A critical review and meta-analysis. *Psychological Bulletin, 114*, 363–375.

Rozin, P., Wrzesniewski, A., & Byrnes, D. (1998). The elusiveness of evaluative conditioning. *Learning and Motivation, 29*, 397–415.

Shanks, D. R., & Dickinson, A. (1990). Contingency awareness in evaluative conditioning: A comment on Baeyens, Eelen, and Van den Bergh. *Cognition and Emotion, 4*, 19–30.

Shanks, D. R., & St. John, M. F. (1994). Characteristics of dissociable human learning systems. *Behavioral and Brain Sciences, 17*, 367–447.

Staats, A. W., & Staats, C. K. (1958). Attitudes established by classical conditioning. *Journal of Abnormal and Social Psychology, 57*, 37–40.

Stevenson, R. J., Boakes, R. A., & Wilson, J. P. (2000). Resistance to extinction of conditioned odor perceptions: Evaluative conditioning is not unique. *Journal of Experimental Psychology. Learning, Memory, and Cognition, 26*, 423–440.

Strack, F., Schwarz, N., Bless, H., Kübler, A., & Wänke, M. (1993). Awareness of the influence as a determinant of assimilation versus contrast. *European Journal of Social Psychology, 23*, 53–62.

Walther, E. (2001). *Guilty by mere association: Evaluative conditioning and the spreading attitude effect.* Oral paper presented at the 43rd Annual German Experimental Psychology Meeting, Regensburg.

Walther, E. (2002). Guilty by mere association: Evaluative conditioning and the spreading attitude effect. *Journal of Personality and Social Psychology, 82*, 919–934.

COGNITION AND EMOTION
2005, 19 (2), 217–243

Dissociating the effects of attention and contingency awareness on evaluative conditioning effects in the visual paradigm

Andy P. Field and Annette C. Moore

University of Sussex, Brighton, UK

Two experiments are described that investigate the effects of attention in moderating evaluative conditioning (EC) effects in a picture-picture paradigm in which previously discovered experimental artifacts (e.g., Field & Davey, 1999) were overcome by counterbalancing conditioned stimuli (CSs) and unconditioned stimuli (USs) across participants. Conditioned responses for individuals who had attention enhanced were compared against a control group and groups for whom attention was impeded using a distracter task. In a second experiment the effects of attention were dissociated from those of contingency awareness by using backward-masked US presentations. The results of these experiments indicate that although associative EC effects may not be disrupted by a lack of contingency awareness, attention is an important factor in establishing conditioning. These results shed some light onto the possible boundary conditions that could explain past inconsistencies in obtaining EC effects in the visual paradigm.

Evaluative conditioning (EC) is a process by which neutral stimuli acquire affect through contiguous pairing with a stimulus that already evokes an emotional response. In conditioning terms, the affectively neutral stimulus is the conditioned stimulus (CS) and is paired with either a liked or disliked unconditioned stimulus (US), resulting in the CS evoking a response congruent with the US with which it was paired (see De Houwer, Thomas, & Baeyens, 2001, for a review). EC has been an elusive and controversial phenomenon with Stevenson, Boakes, and Wilson (2000), and Lovibond and Shanks (2002) recently noting that EC experiments using visual stimuli had come under considerable criticism. The controversy surrounding EC stems from failures to obtain the basic effect

Correspondence concerning this article should be addressed to Andy P. Field, Department of Psychology, School of Life Sciences, University of Sussex, Falmer, Brighton, East Sussex, BN1 9QH, e-mail: andyf@sussex.ac.uk

This research was funded by Unilever plc, Grant RBW3 0600 to Andy Field. The authors are grateful to Bob Boakes for his suggestions regarding Experiment 2, and to Leonora Wilkinson for invaluable discussions when revising the paper.

http://www.tandf.co.uk/journals/pp/02699931.html   DOI:10.1080/02699930441000292

(e.g., Field, 1997; Field & Davey, 1999; Field, Lascelles & Davey, 2003; Rozin, Wrzesniewski, & Byrnes, 1998); demonstrations that EC effects can be elicited when participants have never been exposed to CS-US presentations, which have illustrated that EC effects can emerge from nonassociative processes (Field & Davey, 1997, 1999); and criticisms that some early research could not rule out such nonassociative processes because of a failure to counterbalance CSs and USs (Shanks & Dickinson, 1990) or to use between-group controls in which participants are exposed to CSs and USs, but not in contingent pairings (Davey, 1994; Field & Davey, 1998, 1999).

Notwithstanding these problems, EC is intriguing theoretically because, despite being a paradigmatic example of classical conditioning, it appears prima facie to have several unusual characteristics; the two most important being that unlike conventional autonomic conditioning in humans, EC can occur without participants possessing awareness of the learning contingencies involved (Baeyens, Eelen, & Van den Bergh, 1990) and responses acquired through EC appear to be resistant to extinction (Baeyens, Crombez, Van den Bergh, & Eelen, 1988; Díaz, Ruiz, & Baeyens, this issue). Conditioning without contingency awareness is particularly important theoretically because, as Lovibond and Shanks (2002) point out, it rarely—if ever—occurs in autonomic conditioning. Lovibond and Shanks distinguish single process models, in which propositional learning causes contingency awareness which in turn causes the conditioned response, from dual-process models, in which propositional learning causes contingency awareness, but conditioned responding is caused by some nonpropositional system (so contingency awareness and learning need not correlate). If EC can occur without awareness then a dual process model is implied—EC would be a nonpropositional learning process. One further inference might, therefore, be that EC is a qualitatively distinct form of Pavlovian learning. Indeed, Baeyens, Eelen and Crombez (1995) and Baeyens and De Houwer (1995) suggest that EC is a form of learning in which CS-US associations are merely referential connections between stimuli: So, according to Baeyens et al. (1995), unlike Pavlovian learning it is not critical that the CS be accompanied by a genuine expectancy that the US will shortly follow.

However, the true value of work into EC using visual stimuli has been diminished by the criticisms alluded to earlier. Fortunately, some progress has been made in the visual domain; for example, Díaz et al. (this issue) incorporated between-group controls and replicated the finding that conditioned evaluative responses were resistant to extinction; Field (2003) has likewise shown evaluative conditioning to visual stimuli compared to such controls. To date though, few studies using visual stimuli have used the counterbalanced CS-US allocations suggested by Shanks and Dickinson (1990). Paired with the ubiquitous reports of failures to replicate EC effects in a variety of laboratories (Field & Davey, 1999; Field et al., 2003; Rozin et al., 1998), the cloud of doubt hanging over EC has still yet to fully disperse. The apparent fragility of the EC phenomenon has led some (De Houwer et al., 2000, 2001; Rozin et al., 1998) to allude to the possibility of boundary conditions that moderate conditioned responding, however, likely moderator variables have yet to be proposed or tested empirically. One such boundary condition could be attention.

In general terms, dividing attention seems to attenuate learning: Nissen and Bullemer (1987) demonstrated that under dual-task conditions participants could not learn a repeating sequence (as measured by the serial reaction time task, which they characterise as associative learning)—see also Shanks and Channon (2002). In addition, although divided attention did reduce conscious awareness of the sequence being learnt, Nissen and Bullemer concluded that it was not the lack of awareness that caused the lack of learning: amnesic patients could learn the sequence despite having no awareness of it (see also Reber & Squire, 1994, 1998).

Attention might also have a more specific role to play. The Rescorla-Wagner model (1972) formalises the idea that associations are formed between cues and surprising outcomes. This model famously incorporates a term representing a cue's individual associability, which represents an individual learning rate that the model acknowledges stems from differential attention. Mackintosh (1975), in a seminal paper, extended these ideas to suggest that the attention devoted to a given cue is a function of its importance in predicting an outcome: That is, animals will attend to relevant stimuli at the expense of not attending to irrelevant ones. Both models formalise learning in terms of a change in the association weights (associative strength) of a CS. Kruschke (2001) has followed up Mackintosh's ideas by proposing an attentional system involved in learning that has two goals: the first is to implement the assumption that any CS should receive some attention, and the second is to decide how attention should be distributed over multiple CSs. Kahneman's (1973) suggestion that attentional resources are finite is upheld in this model such that increased attention to one CS necessarily implies less attention to another. The system receives feedback and shifts attention in such a way as to reduce error, these shifts in attention lead to changes in the association weights (of the CSs), which themselves act to reduce the error in learning.

Interestingly, these attentional models provide explanations of failures to learn such as blocking (in which an organism fails to acquire a conditioned response to a stimulus, A, if it is presented in compound with another stimulus, B, that already predicts the US, Kamin, 1969) and latent inhibition (in which pre-exposure to a stimulus retards subsequent learning of a conditioned response to that stimulus during conditioning). Blocking, for example, results from learning not to attend to the stimulus A (Mackintosh, 1975) and has garnered empirical support (Krushke & Blair, 2000) and latent inhibition can be explained in terms of inattention (Kruschke, 2001). Lubow and Gerwitz (1995), in a review of latent inhibition, report that latent inhibition is strongest when a masking task is presented during pre-exposure; however, if this task is absent or is too difficult then latent inhibition will be small or nonexistent. Kruschke (2001) argues that these results can be explained in terms of attentional load: Only when the pre-exposed cue competes with the masking task for attention will subsequent latent inhibition occur. If the masking task is too difficult then it requires full attention and so none is available for the pre-exposed stimulus when it appears alongside the task.

The importance of both blocking and latent inhibition to failures to obtain EC is that they involve *failures to learn*. Learning fails because of a CS attracting insufficient attention. Based on this, one general explanation of the incon-sistencies in EC research could, therefore, be that in some experiments the CSs are sufficiently attention-grabbing for learning to occur, whereas in others learning fails because the CSs do not attract attention.

Given that divided attention reduces awareness of what is being learnt (see Nissen & Bullemer, 1987, above), attention may also go some way to explaining inconsistent findings with regard to contingency awareness and EC. There is evidence that contingency awareness *facilitates* conditioning, does not influence learning one way or another, and *impedes* learning (see Field, 2000 and 2001a for reviews). Contingency awareness has been defined (at least at the operational level) variously as the knowledge that a particular CS precedes a particular US (Baeyens et al., 1990; Field, 2000, for example), or that a particular CS precedes a US that evokes a particular emotional response (e.g., Baeyens et al., 1990). If, as Mackintosh (1975) and Rescorla-Wagner (1972) suggest, attention to a CS increases the strength of the associative connection between that CS and its US, then this may well have a knock on effect in terms of contingency awareness. Nevertheless, it is conceivable that contingency awareness can be dissociated from attention: Nissen and Bullemer "emphasize the importance of distin-guishing between attending to the task itself and being aware of information carried by the task" (p. 29).

The current study looks at these issues by manipulating general aspects of attention in an EC task using visual stimuli. In addition to this, it takes the novel step of using fully counterbalanced CS-US allocations to eliminate the artefact described by Field and Davey (1999) and uses comparison groups in which CSs and USs cannot be associated.

EXPERIMENT 1

In the first experiment an attempt was made to manipulate the attentional load during a visual EC task. This is comparable to the dual-task conditions described by Nissen and Bullemer and seeks to reduce the attention paid to the task itself. It is predicted that in dual-task conditions, EC will be attenuated. In addition, contingency awareness should be reduced in the dual-task condition, but based on other associative learning tasks (like sequence learning) it should be attention to the task, and not awareness of the contingencies that attenuates learning.

Method

Participants

A total of 96 paid volunteers were used as participants (32 per condition) and were tested individually. Their ages ranged from 19 to 55 years. The majority (76) were students from various disciplines at Sussex University and the remaining 20 were members of the general public. In the awareness-enhanced condition, 10 were male, 22 were female, 6 were members of the general public, and the mean age of the group was 22.41 ($SD = 5.10$). In the distraction condition, 10 were male, 22 were female, 8 were members of the general public and the mean age of the group was 28.00 ($SD = 11.29$). In the control condition 11 were male, 21 were female, 6 were members of the general public, and the mean age of the group was 23.50 ($SD = 3.51$).

Stimuli

A total of 50 colour photographs were taken from the International Affective Picture System CD-ROM (Lang, Bradley, & Cuthbert, 1997a), which contains a set of emotional stimuli with normative affective ratings collected over 10 years (Lang, Bradley, & Cuthbert, 1997b). The pictures chosen for this study had received similar ratings from both genders (and were, therefore, not gender-specific) and had elicited either neutral, very positive or very negative pleasure ratings. Four pictures were chosen as CSs based on them having completely neutral IAPS ratings (from Lang et al., 1997b). The USs consisted of two pictures that had very positive IAPS ratings and two that had very negative IAPS ratings. A list of CS and US pictures and their IAPS ratings are in the Appendix. The remaining 42 pictures contained a range of positive, negative and neutral pictures.

To avoid the artefact described by Field and Davey (1999), CSs were allocated to USs using a Latin-square counterbalancing order. There were four different CS-US allocations ensuring that each CS was paired with all four USs across participants.

Apparatus

The experiment was run on a Pentium PC using custom written computer software: *Ectests version 1.2* (Stevens et al., 1999). The experimental cubicle contained a table, a chair and the computer, monitor and mouse.

Procedure

Before the experiment, participants were randomly allocated to one of three groups (attention-enhanced, distraction, block/sub-block control) that differed in the instructions that they received (see stage 2 below).

All participants were initially given written instructions. Once the experimenter was satisfied that the instructions had been understood and that the participant was able to use the mouse to operate the on-screen rating scale, the participant was left alone in the room to complete the experiment. The experiment consisted of four stages, with instructions appearing on the screen before each stage to remind the participant of what to do.

Stage 1: Baseline assessment (preconditioning).   In this stage, the 50 IAPS photographs were randomly presented to participants. Each picture appeared in the centre of the computer screen, directly above a rating scale. The scale ranged from -100 (disliked) through 0 (neutral) to $+100$ (liked), in intervals of five. Using the mouse, a pointer on the scale could be dragged along the scale to the point that indicated the participant's feelings towards the picture. Below the scale, a screen button displayed the value indicated by the pointer. Participants moved the pointer until satisfied with their rating, after which they clicked on the on-screen button to proceed to the next picture. This encouraged participants to pay attention to the rating they had given a particular picture. It was emphasised to participants that they should rely on their spontaneous, instinctive reaction to the picture. The ratings given at this stage were the preconditioning ratings.

Stage 2: Acquisition.   Attention-enhanced and distraction groups received the same stimulus presentation schedule at this stage. The only difference between the groups was in the alleged aim of the experiment conveyed by the instructions. All participants were told to attend carefully to a series of pictures on the screen. However, the attention-enhanced group was told that the experiment examined memory and was asked to try to memorise the order of the pictures. The distraction group was led to believe the experiment was investigating multitasking and was correspondingly instructed to count backwards from 300, aloud, in intervals of three for the duration of the stage. (This task was intended to reduce attention to the CS-US contingencies.) The instructions stressed the importance of both attending to the screen and counting backwards. Both groups were asked to think about how the pictures made them feel.

During this stage, each participant saw four CS-US pairings: two CSs paired with positive USs (Neutral-Like, N-L) and two CSs paired with disliked USs (Neutral-Dislike, N-D). Each CS-US pairing was presented 10 times, and the presentation order was randomised with the restriction that no CS-US pairing could appear consecutively more than twice. Each stimulus appeared for 1 s, the interval between the CS and US (the trace interval) was set at 100 ms, and the interval between CS-US pairs (the intertrial interval, ITI) was 4 s. The trace interval was considerably shorter than the intervals used in early EC studies (e.g., Baeyens et al., 1988 and 1990).

The block/sub-block (BSB) control group were told to attend carefully to a series of pictures on the screen and to think about how the pictures made them feel. They were not told to memorise the order of pictures or asked to do the distracter task. The pictures were then presented in a BSB control procedure (Field, 1996, 1997) in which CSs and USs were selected and matched together using the same counterbalancing schedule as in the two experimental groups. However, during conditioning, the CSs and USs were not presented in a contiguous or contingent pattern. Instead, participants saw five pairings of a stimulus with itself (so participants saw each stimulus presented 10 times—as in the experimental conditions), using the same timing parameters as the experimental conditions. Thus, a stimulus appeared for 1 s, followed by a blank screen for 100 ms, followed by the same stimulus presented for 1 s, followed by a blank screen for 4 s, and so on until that stimulus had appeared 10 times. This set of self-presentations can be thought of as a block of pairings; because there were four different CS-US pairs in the experimental conditions, this control condition contained four CS blocks and four US blocks.

Half of the participants saw the four CS blocks presented in random order followed by the four US blocks, also in random order, and half saw the US blocks before the CS blocks. Keeping the CS blocks separate from the US blocks ensured that participants never saw a CS appearing contingently with a US. By randomising the presentation order of the blocks the possibility that participants could detect the US that corresponded to a CS was eliminated: Because, for example, a CS might appear as the first CS-block, whereas the corresponding US might appear as the third US-block presented. So, even if participants were aware that there were CS-US pairings, which is unlikely, it is improbable that they could determine exactly which CS was assigned to which US. If no conditioning effects are observed in this condition, then nonassociative accounts of the effects observed in the experimental condition can be ruled out.

Stage 3: Postacquisition assessment (postconditioning).   Participants were informed that they would be presented with another set of photographs, and that they must rate each one along a rating scale to indicate the degree to which they liked, disliked or felt neutral about it. The same 50 pictures as in stage one were shown in random order and re-rated. The ratings in this stage are the postconditioning ratings.

Stage 4: Measurement of contingency awareness.   Manipulations to attention will invariably enhance or hinder contingency awareness and these effects need to be examined, so three measures of contingency awareness were used in this stage in counterbalanced order across participants. The first two were the so-called strong and weak measures used in much of the EC literature (e.g., Baeyens et al., 1988, 1990; Baeyens, Eelen, Crombez, & Van den Bergh, 1992; Baeyens, Eelen, Van den Bergh, & Crombez, 1989; Hammerl & Grabitz,

1993) and the third was the recognition measure described by Field (2000). This stage of the experiment typically took participants 1–3 minutes to complete.

Strong measure: This measure of contingency awareness is so called because it measures precise knowledge of contingencies: Participants must know exactly which US was paired with which CS. In this procedure one randomly selected CS appeared on the left side of the computer screen and all four USs appeared on the right (in random positions). Participants were asked to click on the picture on the right that they believed always followed the picture on the left during stage 2 of the experiment. After selecting a picture, four buttons (Completely Sure, Rather Sure, Rather Unsure, and Completely Unsure) appeared at the bottom of the screen for participants to indicate their confidence in their decision. Following this selection, one of the remaining CSs appeared on the left of the screen, and the four USs appeared on the right (in a different random position). The participant repeated the selection process until a US had been selected for each of the four CSs.

Weak measure: This procedure measures knowledge of only the valence of the US paired with a CS, and as such is considered weak. In this measure, one randomly selected CS appeared in the centre of the screen above three on-screen buttons (Liked, Disliked, and Neutral). Participants used these buttons to indicate whether they believed the picture (CS) had been followed by a picture that they liked, disliked or felt neutral about during stage 2 of the experiment. Following this choice, participants indicated their confidence in the decision using one of four on-screen buttons (Completely Sure, Rather Sure, Rather Unsure, and Completely Unsure). This process was repeated for the three remaining CSs.

Recognition measure: This measure of awareness is described by Field (2000) and required participants to discriminate actual CS-US pairings from decoy pairings in which the US is replaced with a picture from stage 1 that had the same valence as the US that was actually used. These decoy USs appeared in the baseline phase, but not in the acquisition stage. Participants saw eight CS-US pairs in random order (four actual CS-US pairings and four decoy pairings). Underneath each CS-US pair there were three on-screen buttons labelled Remember, Know, and No. For each pair of pictures participants were asked whether the pair of pictures had always appeared together (sequentially) during stage 2 of the experiment. Participants could respond that they: (1) actually remembered seeing the pairing (remember); (2) had a feeling that they had seen the pairing (know); or (3) definitely did not see the pairing during stage 2 (no).

Criteria for contingency awareness: Participants were deemed to be aware of a given contingency if they met the following criteria. For the strong measure, participants had to correctly identified the US with which a CS was paired and be either completely or rather sure of their answer. For the weak measure, participants had to correctly identify the valence of the US with which a CS was paired and be either completely or rather sure of their answer. For the recognition measure, two conditions had to be met: participants had to correctly recognise the actual contingency (either by indicating that they remembered seeing it, or had a feeling that they had seen it) and also had to indicate that they had not seen the relevant decoy pairing.

For group analysis, a participant was classified as contingency aware for a given measure if they were aware of two or more of the four contingencies based on the relevant criteria for the measure. This criterion is based on the fact that for all three measures, by guessing alone, a participant should only be deemed aware of 0 or 1 of the four contingencies (to the nearest contingency). The final decision as to whether a participant was classified as aware was based on the majority decision of the three awareness measures: If two or more of the measures classified the participant as aware then that individual was deemed aware of the contingencies, if two or more of the measures classified a participant as unaware then that person was classified as unaware.

Results

All statistical tests used a cut-off point of $p = .05$ for significance and, where relevant, effect sizes are reported as Pearson's r.

Awareness measures

In the attention-enhanced condition all 32 participants were classified as contingency aware based on the criteria above. In the distraction condition 10 participants were deemed unaware; the remainder were contingency aware. For the analysis, the distracter condition was broken down into contingency aware and contingency unaware subgroups.

US ratings

The liked USs were rated positively in the attention-enhanced group ($M = 49.87$, $SE = 6.49$), the distraction group ($M = 45.00$, $SE = 10.76$), and the BSB control ($M = 55.20$, $SE = 6.09$). The disliked USs were rated very negatively in the attention enhanced group ($M = -82.73$, $SE = 4.75$), the distraction group ($M = -66.56$, $SE = 7.88$) and the BSB control ($M = -78.60$, $SE = 4.46$). Using a probability of .05, a three-way 4 (group: attention-enhanced, distraction (aware), distraction (unaware) or BSB control) $\times$ 2 (US type: liked or disliked) $\times$ 2 (picture: picture 1 or picture 2) ANOVA on the US ratings revealed a highly significant main effect of US type, $F(1, 66) = 479.69$, $r = .94$ but no other significant main effects or interactions. These results indicate that liked USs were rated significantly more positively than disliked USs across all three groups.

CS Ratings

One consideration with using a counterbalanced design is that it is assumed that CSs (neutral pictures) that are selected based on their IAPS ratings (Lang et al., 1997b) are actually perceived as neutral by the participants in the experiment. It also assumes that the US pictures are perceived as liked and disliked (which we have just demonstrated). However, not all participants found the CSs neutral to begin with (using Baeyens et al.'s 1988, 1989, 1990, 1992 criterion of ratings between ±20) which left two options: exclude their data (11 participants from the attention enhanced condition, 3 from the distracter aware condition, 5 from the distracter unaware condition, and 7 from the BSB control) or include CS neutrality (the initial ratings of the CSs) as a covariate within the analysis. To avoid data exclusion, CS neutrality was included as a covariate.

Within each level of the type of US two stimuli were used (pictures of rabbits and a seal for positive USs, and a mutilated head and hand for the disliked ones), and each of these stimuli has a unique CS neutrality variable that needs to be covaried out. To achieve this, it was necessary to incorporate a variable called picture, which compares the two pictures within each type of US. Therefore, the data were analysed with a three-way 4 (group: attention-enhanced, distraction (contingency aware), distraction (contingency unaware) or BSB control) × 2 (US type: liked or disliked) × 2 (picture: picture 1 or picture 2) ANOVA with repeated measures on the last two variables, CS neutrality was a varying covariate for each CS and the change in evaluative responses (postconditioning minus preconditioning) was the dependent variable.

There were no significant main effects of US type, $F(1, 91) < 1$, group, $F(3, 91) = 2.39$, stimulus, $F(1, 91) < 1$. All interactions involving the stimulus variable were non significant also, showing that the picture used as particular CS had no effect on change in rating.

The crucial group × US type interaction was significant, $F(3, 91) = 4.94$, indicating that the US type did affect changes in CS ratings, but these changes depended on the group to which participants belonged. Contrasts revealed a significant difference between N-L and N-D pairs in the attention enhanced group compared to the BSB control ($CI_{.95} = -23.83$ (lower), -3.43 (upper), $t = -3.26$, $r = .32$), but not between the distracter (aware) and the BSB control ($CI_{.95} = -9.67$ (lower), 12.74 (upper), $t < 1$, $r = .03$) or the distractor (unaware) and the BSB control ($CI_{.95} = -18.57$ (lower), 11.06 (upper), $t < 1$, $r = .06$).

Figure 1 shows the mean evaluative ratings of the CS at preconditioning and postconditioning dependent on the type of US with which they were paired and whether participants were part of the BSB control or were distracted and were aware or unaware of the contingencies. In the attention-enhanced condition the valence of the CSs paired with positive USs increased and the ratings of CSs paired with negative USs decreased. However, in all other conditions these effects were not present.

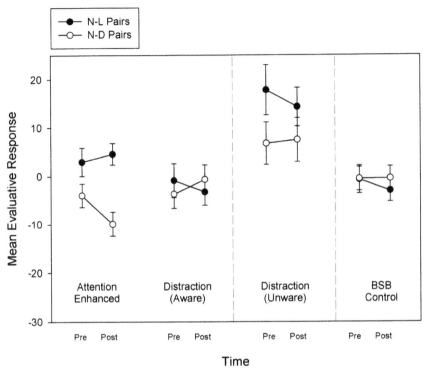

Figure 1. Graph showing the mean CS ratings (and *SE*) pre- and postconditioning for liked, disliked, and no USs according to whether participants were in the attention-enhanced (contingency aware), distracted (contingency unaware and aware), or in the BSB control.

Per-contingency analysis

As Field (2000, 2001a) has suggested, the analysis of awareness at a group level is problematic. Therefore, further analyses were conducted that included awareness at a per-contingency level (that is analysing the data by assigning each contingency a covariate that specifies the level of awareness of that particular contingency). For each CS, two awareness variables could be calculated: a dichotomous dummy variable (aware or unaware) or a continuous variable constructed from a combination of the correct response and the level of confidence in the response. For the strong and weak awareness measures, this continuous variable ranged from 0 (an incorrect response of which the participant was completely sure) to 7 (a correct response of which they were completely sure). The steps in between reflect varying degrees in confidence: 0 = incorrect and completely sure, 1 = incorrect and rather sure, 2 = incorrect and rather unsure, 3 = incorrect and completely unsure, 4 = correct and completely unsure, 5 = correct and rather unsure, 6 = correct and rather sure, 7 = correct and completely sure. For the recognition measure, the continuous variable ranged from 0 (any combination of responses in which participants said they had not seen the actual pairing), through 1 (if they recognised or knew they had seen the actual pairings, but also recognised the decoy pairing) and 2 (they recognised the actual pairing and only had a feeling they had also seen the decoy pairing, or they had a feeling they had seen the actual pairing and reported not seeing the decoy pairing) to 3 (they recognised the actual pairing and reported that they had not seen the decoy pairing).

As before, the change in evaluative responses (postconditioning minus pre-conditioning) were analysed. The analysis looked at the type of US used (liked or disliked) and, because within each of these levels two stimuli were used, another variable called picture was incorporated. The awareness measure could then be introduced as a covariate at each repeated level. Finally, a group variable was included (distraction task or no distraction task) and data from the BSB group were excluded (this group would confound with contingency awareness because of the large amount of contingency awareness across experimental groups and the universal absence of contingency awareness in the control group because they experience no contingencies). The analyses were, therefore, a 2 (US type: liked or disliked) × 2 (picture: picture 1 or picture 2) × distracter (distracter task or not) ANCOVA with four covariates representing the awareness of each of the four contingencies. Initial CS ratings were also included as covariates (CS Neutrality). In this analysis a main effect of US type reflects a conditioning effect, and an interaction between US type and distracter will indicate a different effect when a distracter task was not used. If awareness moderates the change in CS responses then this should show up as a significant covariate. The analysis was repeated using covariates based on the measures of awareness derived from the strong, weak, and recognition awareness measures. The effect of US type was significant in all analysis yielding effect sizes of $r = .38$ (weak dichotomous), .37 (weak continuous), .37 (strong dichotomous), .36 (strong continuous), .35 (recognition dichotomous), and .34 (recognition continuous). These effect sizes are not significantly different using Hedges' homogeneity of effect size test, $\chi^2 = 0.087, p = 1$ (see Field, 2001b for computational details). The US type effect significantly interacted with whether or not a distracter task was used in all cases, r (listed in the same order as above) = .38, .36, .41, .38, .41, and .40 (again these effect sizes are not significantly different, $\chi^2 = 0.17, p = 1$). The covariate effect of awareness was nonsignificant in all analyses and yielded effect sizes of r (listed in the same order as above) = .19, .17, .18, .15, .17, and .16. In no analysis did the type of picture or CS neutrality have an effect.

Discussion

This study has two important findings: (1) evaluative conditioning effects could be found compared to nonpaired control and these effects could not be prone to the artifact unearthed by Field and Davey (1999) and so reflect associative learning; and (2) distracting participants during conditioning eliminates conditioning effects.

On the first of these findings, Field and Davey (1999) discovered that when CSs and USs are selected based on an individual participant's subjective evaluation of them and are then paired based on perceptual similarity, evaluative-conditioning type effects are found even when participants see no conditioning trials. The conditioning-type effects were found to arise from an interaction between this stimulus selection procedure and participants tendency to engage in similarity-based category learning during the experiment. The current experiment eliminates this possibility by using the same CSs and USs for all participants and counterbalancing them across groups.

Given the controversy surrounding EC, these findings are very important because this study is one of the first to replicate the basic visual evaluative conditioning paradigm but with CSs and USs fully counterbalanced across participants[1] (although counterbalanced designs have been used in EC experiments using tastes). Shanks and Dickinson (1990) have suggested that a paradigm in which CSs and USs are counterbalanced across participants is a good control for nonassociative effects because all CSs enter into associations with all USs and so observed effects cannot possibly be attributed to stimulus properties. Field and Davey (1997, 1998, 1999) have taken a slightly stronger view. Essentially, they agree with Shanks and Dickinson but note that in autonomic paradigms some CSs are not paired with USs (so there is a discrimination between CSs that enter into associations and ones that do not). In EC studies this is typically not so because all CSs enter into associations with some form of US (be it liked, disliked, or neutral). Field and Davey (1998), therefore, argue that a nonpaired control (the BSB control) is a necessary additional control that allows comparison between CSs that enter into associations and those that do not. In terms of isolating cause and effect, this comparison of an association and no-association condition is necessary. As such, Experiment 1 has made important steps towards demonstrating EC using visual stimuli using a very strict methodology.

The most striking result is that a distraction task eliminated conditioning. There are two explanations: (1) the distraction task interfered with contingency awareness resulting in a failure to condition; or (2) the distraction task does not prevent contingency awareness, but prevents conditioned responding. The former is supported by evidence from the autonomic conditioning literature suggesting that repetitive CS-US pairings do not produce autonomic CRs when contingency awareness is prevented by using distracting masking tasks (Dawson, 1970; Dawson, Catania, Schell, & Grings, 1979; Dawson & Reardon, 1973). Dawson and Schell (1982) showed that in individuals who could not shift

---

[1] Some studies in the visual domain have used random CS-UC allocations (e.g., De Houwer et al., 2000), which reduces the possibility of artefacts, but fully counterbalancing eliminates any remote possibility that effects are stimulus-specific.

attention from a distraction task (in one ear) to a previously conditioned CS (presented in the opposite ear) no conditioning effects were observed. Although in this study CS-US relations were learnt without a distracter task, the results show that engaging in dual tasks interferes with conditioned responses by distracting attention from the conditioning task. However, this explanation is unlikely because the distraction task prevented awareness in only one third of the participants. Also, participants aware of the contingencies who were distracted showed no evidence of conditioning. This suggests that distracting participants interfered with conditioning without necessarily reducing contingency awareness.

A final possibility is that participants in the attention-enhanced condition were simply demand aware, whereas those in the distraction condition were not. For demand awareness to explain conditioned responding participants need to be aware of the contingencies and to have an expectation that the experimenter wants CS ratings to change in the direction of the US with which it was paired. Without contingency awareness, any expectation that CS ratings should change in the direction of the US cannot translate into behaviour because the participant does not know on which US to base the change. Therefore, to explain the current results would require an explanation of why the distraction task eliminated demand awareness in those participants who were contingency aware. Although it is not self-evident why demand awareness might have been present in the attention-enhanced group but not in the contingency aware distraction task group it, nevertheless, remains a possibility. One solution would be to reduce contingency awareness in both distracted and nondistracted participants: Because then even if demand awareness survives, it cannot translate into responses without contingency awareness.

Experiment 2

The exact role of contingency awareness and distraction were inseparable in Experiment 1 because: (1) nondistracted participants were always aware of contingencies, and relatively few distracted participants were unaware of the contingencies; (2) no baseline for the effects of distraction was available because BSB control participants did not engage in a distraction task; and (3) the spectre of demand awareness was not fully banished.

Experiment 1 looked at EC under dual-task conditions, but did not make specific attempts to reduce contingency awareness. Experiment 2 aimed to replicate the basic finding that dual-task performance inhibits EC, while dissociating these effects from those of contingency awareness. Specifically, attention was manipulated, as before, by using distracter tasks for half of the experimental and control participants. However, each person received normal presentations of CS-US contingencies and presentations in which the US was rapidly presented. By manipulating the speed at which the US was presented contingency awareness should be reduced *without* interfering with attention to the CS (and in models of associative learning it is the CSs that seem to vie for attentional resources). It is predicted that dual-task conditions will result in attenuated learning, whereas reduced contingency awareness will not.

Method

Participants

A total of 131 paid volunteers were used as participants (35 in the conditioning group with the distraction task and 32 in the other three groups) and were tested individually. Their ages ranged from 18 to 53 years. All participants were students from various disciplines at Sussex University. In the paired-distracter group, 10 were male and 25 female, with mean age of 21.91 (*SD* = 4.25). In the paired-no distracter group, 9 were male and 23 female, with mean age of 25.03 (*SD* = 8.25). In the BSB-distracter group, 8 were male and 24 female, with mean age of 21.38 (*SD* = 4.10). In the BSB-no distracter group, 13 were male and 19 female, with mean age of 22.63 (*SD* = 5.25).

Stimuli

The 50 colour pictures used in Experiment 1 were again used in this experiment.

Apparatus

The apparatus were the same as for Experiment 1 except that new software was written (ECAwarenessAttention version 1.0 by Field & Field, 2000).

Procedure

The procedure was, in essence, the same as that used in Experiment 1 except that within paired and BSB control groups half of the participants performed a distraction task during the acquisition stage. In addition, a within-participant manipulation of contingency awareness was achieved by using backward-masked fast-presented USs for half of the stimulus pairs (for convenience the pairings with masked USs will be referred to as subliminal pairs).

Stage 1: Baseline assessment (preconditioning).   This stage was identical to that described for Experiment 1.

Stage 2: Acquisition.   All participants viewed 10 semirandomised presentations of 4 CS-US pairs: 2 × N-L pairings, and 2 × N-D pairings. One N-L and one N-D pair had a backward-masked subliminal US, the remaining pairs had normal US presentations (with parameters identical to Experiment 1). As in

Experiment 1, the four different CSs were counterbalanced across the four USs across participants, but in addition the decision of which pairings had backward-masked USs was also counterbalanced across participants. All combinations of CSs and USs and masking arrangements were used resulting in 16 different counterbalancing conditions. For normal pairings, the presentation rates were identical to Experiment 1 (the US was presented for 1 s), however, in the subliminal pairings, the US and mask appeared over a 1 s interval with the US occupying 1 refresh rate of the monitor (approx. 17 ms) of the interval and the mask occupying the remaining 983 ms. It was important for the subliminal awareness check (see stage 4) that each US had a unique mask, therefore, four masks were constructed that consisted of a constant pattern of noise (random colour dots) that had either a green, blue, red, or yellow filter. As such, the masks had no recognisable features or similarity with the US that it masked.

Participants were split into one of four groups: (1) Paired-No Distraction in which participants viewed contingent CS-US presentations as described in the previous experiment; (2) Paired-Distraction, which was the same but partici-pants counted backwards from 300, aloud, in intervals of three for the duration of the stage; (3) BSB-No Distraction in which participants viewed CS and US block presentations as described in Experiment 1; and (4) BSB-Distraction, which was the same as the previous group but participants counted backwards as in the paired-distraction group.

Stage 3: Postacquisition assessment (postconditioning),   This stage was exactly as described for Experiment 1.

Stage 4: Measurement of contingency awareness.

Subliminal awareness: To assess awareness of the pairings in which the US was masked, participants were shown each mask used (the order of presentation was randomised) and asked to: "Think back to the second stage of the experiment when you were simply looking at images (but not rating them). Did you notice what image came IMMEDIATELY before the one above?" Parti-cipants could respond yes or no. If responding positively they were asked "What was the picture of?" and "How did the picture make you feel?" For each of these questions participants could type responses into a text box next to the question or click on a button labelled "Don't Know". A US was deemed to be undetected if participants answered no to the first question or incorrectly named the US picture or its valence.

Recognition awareness: In Experiment 1, the three awareness measures showed substantial correspondence (a meta-analysis of effect sizes from the different methods revealed considerable homogeneity); therefore, only one measure (the recognition measure) was used as a manipulation check in this experiment. This procedure was essentially the same as for Experiment 1 but with some subtle changes. Participants again saw eight CS-US pairs in random order (four actual CS-US pairings and the same CSs accompanied by four decoy USs). In the previous experiments, participants could conceivably discriminate real from decoy pairings on the basis of identifying US pictures they saw during stage 2 from those that they did not (remember the decoy USs were not from the conditioning stage). In this experiment, the decoy US was always the US of the same valence that was not paired with that CS. All other aspects of this stage were the same as in Experiment 1 and a participant was again deemed aware of a given contingency if: (1) they correctly recognised the actual contingency (either by indicating that they remembered seeing it, or had a feeling that they had seen it); (2) they correctly indicated that they did not see the relevant decoy pairing.

Results

All statistical tests used a cut-off point of $p = .05$ for significance and, where relevant, effect sizes are reported as Pearson's r.

Awareness measures

For the backward-masked pairings 130 of 131 participants were deemed unaware (i.e. unaware on both the subliminal awareness and recognition awareness measures) of the N-D pairing and 128 were unaware of the N-L pairing that they experienced. Therefore, in total 127 participants were unaware of the subliminal pairings. For the normal pairings we are interested only in the experimental group (because those in the control did not receive pairings and so could not be aware), of the 67 in the experimental group 51 were aware of the N-D pairing and 42 were aware of the N-L pairing.

US Ratings

The liked USs were rated positively in the paired-no distraction ($M = 64.66$, $SE = 5.78$), the paired-distraction ($M = 63.29$, $SE = 5.44$), BSB-no distraction ($M = 48.19$, $SE = 5.98$), and the BSB-distraction ($M = 58.08$, $SE = 5.69$). The disliked USs were rated very negatively in the paired-no distraction ($M = -78.13$, $SE = 5.18$), the paired-distraction ($M = -84.74$, $SE = 4.87$), BSB-no distraction ($M = -81.52$, $SE = 5.35$), and the BSB-distraction ($M = -83.47$, $SE = 5.10$). A three-way 2 (group: paired or BSB) $\times$ 2 (distract: distraction task or not) $\times$ 2 (US type: liked or disliked) ANOVA on the US ratings revealed a highly significant main effect of US type, $F(1, 123) = 1059.32$, $r = .95$ but no significant main effect of group, distract, or any interactions. As such, liked USs were rated significantly more positively than disliked USs and that this was true across all conditions.

CS Ratings

Figure 2 shows the mean evaluative ratings of the CS at preconditioning and postconditioning dependent on the type of US with which they were paired, whether these pairings had a normal or subliminally presented US, whether participants were part of the paired or BSB control groups and whether they were distracted or not. In the distracted conditions there were no substantial changes to any of the CS ratings in either the paired or BSB groups. However, in the nondistracted groups a differential shifts in CS ratings across the type of US were observed in the paired group but not the BSB control.

The change in CS ratings (postconditioning ratings minus preconditioning ratings) were analysed using a four-way 2 (group: paired or BSB control) × 2 (distraction: distraction task or not) × 2 (US type: liked or disliked) × 2(US speed: subliminal or normal) mixed ANOVA with repeated measures on the last two variables. The initial rating of the CS (CS neutrality) was entered as a varying covariate for each of the CSs, as was awareness of the contingency into which a particular CS entered (as measured by the recognition measure). As such, this analysis takes into account per-contingency awareness, and CS neutrality.

Rather than list all of the effects from this analysis, all main effects and interactions were nonsignificant unless otherwise stated. To demonstrate a basic conditioning effect CS ratings should change across time depending on the type of US with which it was paired (US type) and whether the CS and US were paired or not (group). Therefore, the dependent variable (the change in CS ratings) should be affected by the group × US type interaction and any higher order interactions involving this term. The group × US type interaction was significant, $F(1, 125) = 6.15$, $r = .22$. Distraction seemed to moderate this effect though as shown by a significant group × US type × distraction interaction, $F(1, 122) = 7.08$, $r = .23$. The final issue is whether US speed had any effect. The group × distracter × US type × US speed was nonsignificant, $F(1, 125) < 1$, $r = .06$. This indicates that the three-way interaction results described above were not influenced by the speed of US presentation. The CS neutrality and contingency awareness regression terms were nonsignificant throughout this analysis.

To break down the group × distracter × US type interaction, two-way 2 (group: paired or BSB) × 2 (US type: liked or disliked) mixed ANOVAs with repeated measures on the later variable were conducted separately for distracted and nondistracted groups and within these groups for normal and subliminal pairings. In all four analyses, the change in CS ratings was the outcome and CS neutrality and per-contingency awareness were entered as varying covariates for each CS. The crucial effect in each analysis is the group × US type interaction. For the distracted groups, this interaction was nonsignificant for normal pairs, $F(1, 63) < 1$, $r = .12$, and subliminal pairs, $F(1, 63) < 1$, $r = .02$. In the non-distracted groups, the group × US type interaction was significant for the normal pairings, $F(1, 60) = 4.06$, $r = .25$. Specifically, the effect of US type was

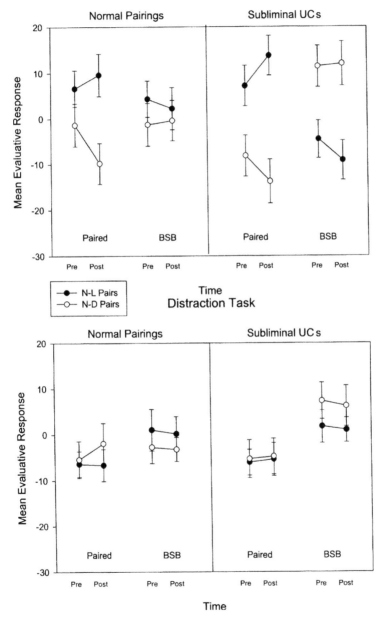

Figure 2. Graph showing the mean CS ratings (and *SE*) pre- and postconditioning for liked, disliked, and no USs according to whether stimuli were paired or unpaired (BSB), had backward masked subliminal USs, and participants were distracted or not during conditioning.

significant in the paired, $F(1, 60) = 7.23$, $r = .33$, but not the BSB group, $F(1, 60) < 1$, $r = .01$. Also in the nondistracted groups, the group × US type interaction was significant for the subliminal pairings, $F(1, 60) = 4.55$, $r = .27$. Specifically, the effect of US type was significant in the paired group, $F(1, 60) = 4.35$, $r = .26$, but not in the BSB control, $F(1, 60) = 1.09$, $r = .13$.

Figure 3 illustrates the dissociation between conditioning and awareness by plotting the size of the conditioning effect (changes in N-D and N-L pairings in experimental groups compared to the controls), and the percentage of participants aware of the contingencies for distracted and nondistracted participants, when USs were presented normally (unshaded bars and circles) and subliminally (shaded bars and triangles). A clear dissociation emerges: when No Distraction Task was used, conditioning occurred (as indexed by medium effect sizes) regardless of whether Subliminal/Normal pairs were used, and correspondingly, regardless of whether contingency awareness was extremely low or high. When Distraction was used, no conditioning occurred (the circle and triangle both indicate a small effect size), regardless of whether contingency awareness was extremely low or intermediate/high.

Discussion

Experiment 2 sought to dissociate the effects of awareness from the effects of distraction. The results demonstrated three very important points: (1) differential

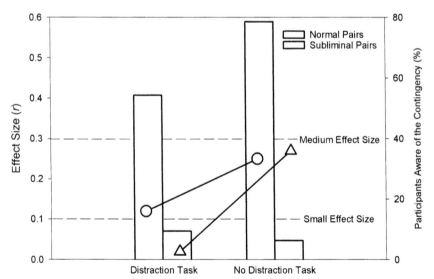

Figure 3. Graph showing the percentage of participants aware of contingencies (bars) and the size of the conditioning effect, r (lines), when distracted or not and when USs were presented normally (not shaded bars and circles) or subliminally (shaded bars and triangles).

conditioning could be observed compared to an unpaired control condition; (2) this conditioning was eliminated by a distraction task; and (3) the effect of distraction could not be explained by a reduction in contingency awareness.

One concern that could be raised with the data from Experiment 2 is that preconditioning ratings were sometimes quite different across conditions. In particular, one possible explanation of the observed effects when masked USs were used and there was no distraction task (top right panel of Figure 2) is that exposure to these stimuli during conditioning merely exaggerated the pre-conditioning ratings in a particular direction: When the preconditioning ratings were negative, exposure made them more negative and when preconditioning ratings were positive exposure make them more positive. This would be rather like the artifactual process found by Field and Davey (1999). There are several reasons why this explanation is unlikely. The most important point is that CSs were fully counterbalanced across USs. This is important because it makes it improbably that the effects were a product of a particular stimulus interacting with exposure effects (see Shanks & Dickinson, 1990). In addition, in Figure 2, all preconditioning ratings (16 in total) reflect averaged ratings of the same 4 CSs, and across conditions similar levels of preconditioning ratings can be seen to give rise to both positive and negative changes in ratings. Furthermore, the fact that CS neutrality did not feature as a significant variable in any analysis also suggests that these differences in baseline ratings were not responsible for the observed effects (remember that the effects observed controlled for CS neutrality). However, to further investigate this possibility statistically pre-conditioning ratings for trials involving "subliminal" USs and no distraction task were correlated with the change in evaluative ratings. If the explanation above is correct then high preconditioning ratings should create positive changes in evaluative ratings, and negative preconditioning ratings should create negative shifts in evaluative ratings. In short, a positive correlation should be observed. In fact, pre-conditioning ratings had a negative relationship with changes in evaluative ratings ($r = -.34$). If preconditioning ratings were contributing to the pattern of observed results (rather than the association into which a CS enters) then this would predict the exact opposite to the pattern of results shown in the top right panel of Figure 2 (if preconditioning ratings are above zero then ratings should fall, and if preconditioning ratings are below zero then they should rise). Nevertheless, these differences in baseline ratings across groups illustrate how difficult it is to find universally neutral stimuli.

Others might also suppose that demand awareness had a role to play in Experiment 2. However, for this to be true, it would be necessary to assume that the absence of contingency awareness did not imply the absence of demand awareness. The rationale for this second experiment was partly based on the idea that this cannot be the case. Although it is, of course, possible for participants to be aware that their ratings of CSs are expected to change, and that these changes depend upon the liked and disliked images that they have seen, without knowledge of which CS was paired with which US it is not so easy to imagine how this demand awareness would translate into behaviour. For demand awareness to explain these results, participants would have to know, at the very least, the valence of the US paired with a given CS. Given that when USs were rapidly presented the vast majority of participants could not identify them, this greatly reduces the credibility of a demand awareness explanation (at least for these pairings).

GENERAL DISCUSSION

The main finding in these experiments is that distraction has an effect on conditioning independent of contingency awareness. One obvious explanation of this finding is in terms of attentional resources being drawn away from the conditioning procedure. Kahneman (1973) has suggested that humans have limited attentional resources that are divided between tasks, as such, difficult tasks will consume the most attentional resources, and interference on difficult tasks will be less than on easy tasks (Zelniker, 1971). Pashler and colleagues have shown that when two tasks require different responses task performance will be limited because responses to both tasks are fighting for limited memory retrieval capacity (Carrier & Pashler, 1995; Fagot & Pashler, 1992; Pashler, 1990). Related to this evidence, studies on the psychological refractory period suggest that there is a fundamental limit on the performance on concurrent tasks, such that if the first task is occupying a central processing mechanism, then the second task will be put on hold (see Styles, 1997 for a review).

The role of attention in models of associative learning (e.g., Rescorla-Wagner, 1972, and Mackintosh, 1975) can be easily extended to fit the evaluative conditioning effects in Experiments 1 and 2: Participants may have found the distraction task (counting backwards) more cognitively demanding than watching the CS-US pairings. As a consequence, the limited attentional resources of these individuals may have been allocated to the counting task (the primary task) leaving few (if any) attentional resources for the processing of the emotional content of the CSs and USs. In Zelniker's (1971) terms, the greater distraction was observed on the easier task. In terms of Mackintosh's and Kruschke's formalisations of associative learning, this reduced attention would have an impact on the association weights of the CSs in these experiments.

However, the picture is probably more complex than this, because in both Experiments 1 and 2, contingency awareness remained relatively unaffected by distraction; therefore, attention clearly was being paid to the CS-US contingencies at some level. Therefore, it is not simply the case that participants ignored all of the CSs and USs because their attention was focused on the distraction task. One clue to what could be happening comes from recent findings from Katkin, Weins, and Öhman (2001) that ''gut-feelings'' to emotional stimuli may be based primarily on the perception of internal cues (such as heartbeats). Katkin et al. found that when an aversive US was used learning was best predicted by an ability to sense internal cues. Evaluative responses are based on such gut-feelings (at least in terms of how they are operationalised in evaluative conditioning experiments), and so may be moderated by individuals' abilities to sense internal responses to the experimental stimuli. As such, the distraction task in Experiments 1 and 2 may not have distracted participants from the stimuli per se (as indicated by the failure to reduce contingency awareness), but may have distracted them from processing the emotional content of these pictures by preventing them from paying attention to visceral cues. Of course, this explanation is tentative, but future work might look to explore the role of visceral cues in evaluative conditioning. Interestingly, one study using haptic stimuli did show conditioning effects relative to a BSB control when a very similar distracter task to the one employed in the current studies was used to inhibit contingency awareness (Hammerl & Grabitz, 2000). The difference between the current finding and theirs probably lies in the modality of the task. Hirst, Spelke, Reaves, Caharack, and Neisser (1980) have shown that dual processing is possible and in Hammerl and Grabitz participants the CS-US pairings, and the visceral cues they elicit, may simply have been more attention grabbing than in the current study (because they elicited a sensation on the skin). However, this does not explain why Hammerl and Grabitz found only EC when a distracter task was used.

A final consideration is what these results tell us at a process level and the implications for EC's status as a unique form of Pavlovian conditioning. In general terms, the results have some interesting implications for process models of associative learning such as those discussed by Lovibond and Shanks (2002). Lovibond and Shanks make the point that contingency awareness is interesting at a theoretical level because it may allow researchers to discount certain models of learning. In particular they make two quite strong predictions about a single process model: (1) this model predicts a close correspondence between aware-ness and the production of a conditioned response (CR); and (2) an adequate demonstration of conditioning without contingency awareness falsifies the sin-gle process model because contingency awareness is assumed to directly cause the CR. They go on to suggest that in a single process model a dissociation between conditioning and contingency awareness is unlikely to result from measurement error and so is the most theoretically interesting of the models. Although Lovibond and Shanks' logic is impeccable, they place the relationship between contingency awareness and conditioned responding in a vacuum. That is, they assume that other factors could not moderate the relationship between awareness and conditioned responding. The experiments presented in this paper shows that attention affected both contingency awareness (to some degree) and conditioned responding. This demonstrates how a single causal connection between awareness and learning could be moderated by some external factor. This perhaps suggests that a single process model is an overly simplistic view of associative processes, and that conditioning without awareness does not rule out such a process (because a single causal link may exist between conditioning and learning, but both are also influenced by other factors that are not part of a second process). Interestingly, the eventuality of external influences on learning and awareness opens up many possibilities for explaining the mass of conflicting evidence for the relationship between contingency awareness and conditioning, especially in evaluative conditioning (Field, 2001a).

Nevertheless, although the finding that conditioning effects did not seem to depend on contingency awareness lends further support to the idea that evaluative conditioning is both associative and can occur without contingency awareness, these results need to be treated cautiously. Although these experiments attempted to account for contingency awareness at a percontingency level, the data highlight the many problems faced by researchers trying to answer questions about awareness. For example, participants will never be aware or unaware of all contingencies, if only because of the degrees of error inherent in measuring awareness. As Shanks and St. John (1994) point out, measures need to be relevant to the conditioning effect, should assess awareness at the same time as conditioned responses, and should be comparably sensitive to measures of the conditioned response. The current experiments measured contingency awareness after evaluative responses were recorded, and even with a variety of measures it's unclear whether their sensitivity is comparable to that of the measures of conditioning. As such, no strong claims should be made about the role of contingency awareness.

REFERENCES

Baeyens, F., Crombez, G., Van den Bergh, O., & Eelen, P. (1988). Once in contact always in contact: Evaluative conditioning is resistant to extinction. *Advances in Behaviour Research and Therapy, 10*, 179–199.

Baeyens, F., & De Houwer, J. (1995). Evaluative conditioning is a qualitatively distinct form of classical conditioning: A reply to Davey (1994). *Behaviour Research and Therapy, 33*, 825–831.

Baeyens, F., Eelen, P., & Crombez, G. (1995). Pavlovian associations are forever: On classical conditioning and extinction. *Journal of Psychophysiology, 9*, 127–141.

Baeyens, F., Eelen, P., Crombez, G., & Van den Bergh, O. (1992). Human evaluative conditioning: Acquisition trials, presentation schedule, evaluative style and contingency awareness. *Behaviour Research and Therapy, 30*, 133–142.

Baeyens, F., Eelen, P., & Van den Bergh, O. (1990). Contingency awareness in evaluative conditioning: A case for unaware affective-evaluative learning. *Cognition and Emotion, 4*, 3–18.

Baeyens, F., Eelen, P., Van den Bergh, O., & Crombez, G. (1989). Acquired affective evaluative value: Conservative but not unchangeable. *Behaviour Research and Therapy, 27*, 279–287.

Carrier, L. M., & Pashler, H. (1995). Attentional limits in memory retrieval. *Journal of Experimental Psychology. Learning Memory and Cognition, 21*, 1339–1348.

Davey, G. C. L. (1994). Is evaluative conditioning a qualitatively distinct from of classical conditioning? *Behaviour Research and Therapy, 32*, 291–299.

Dawson, M. E. (1970). Cognition and conditioning: Effects of masking the CS-US contingency on human GSR classical conditioning. *Journal of Experimental Psychology*, *85*, 389–396.

Dawson, M. E., Catania, J. J., Schell, A. M., & Grings, W. W. (1979). Autonomic classicial conditioning as a function of awareness of stimulus contingencies. *Biological Psychology*, *9*, 23–40.

Dawson, M. E., & Reardon, D. P. (1973). Construct validity of recall and recognition post-conditioning measures of awareness. *Journal of Experimental Psychology*, *98*, 308–315.

Dawson, M. E., & Schell, A. M. (1982). Electrodermal responses to attended and nonattended significant stimuli during dichotic listening. *Journal of Experimental Psychology. Human Perception and Performance*, *8*, 315–324.

De Houwer, J., Baeyens, F., Vansteenwegen, D., & Eelen, P. (2000). Evaluative conditioning in the picture-picture paradigm with random assignment of conditioned stimuli to unconditioned stimuli. *Journal of Experimental Psychology. Animal Behavior Processes*, *26*, 237–242.

De Houwer, J., Thomas, S., & Baeyens, F. (2001). Associative learning of likes and dislikes: a review of 25 years of research on human evaluative conditioning. *Psychological Bulletin*, *126*, 853–869.

Díaz, E., Ruiz, G., & Baeyens, F. (2005). Resistance to extinction of human evaluative conditioning using a between-subjects design. *Cognition and Emotion*, *19*, 245–268.

Fagot, C., & Pashler, H. (1994). Repetition blindness: Perception of memory failure? *Journal of Experimental Psychology. Human Perception and Performance*, *21*, 275–292.

Field, A. P. (1996). *An appropriate control condition for evaluative conditioning.* (Cognitive Science Research Paper No. 431.) Brighton, UK: University of Sussex, School of Cognitive and Computing Science.

Field, A. P. (1997). *Re-evaluating evaluative conditioning.* Unpublished doctoral dissertation, University of Sussex, Brighton, UK.

Field, A. P. (2000). I like it, but I'm not sure why: Can evaluative conditioning occur without conscious awareness? *Consciousness and Cognition, 9*, 13–36.

Field, A. P. (2001a). When all is still concealed: Are we closer to understanding the mechanisms underlying evaluative conditioning? *Consciousness and Cognition, 10*, 559–566.

Field, A. P. (2001b). Meta-analysis of correlation coefficients: A Monte Carlo comparison of fixed- and random-effects methods. *Psychological Methods*, *6*, 161–180.

Field, A. P. (2003, March). *I don't like it because it eats Brussels sprouts: Evaluative conditioning in children.* Paper presented at the British Psychological Society Annual Conference, Bournemouth, UK. Unpublished manuscript.

Field, A. P., & Davey, G. C. L. (1997). Conceptual conditioning: Evidence for an artifactual account of evaluative learning. *Learning and Motivation, 28*, 446–464.

Field, A. P., & Davey, G. C. L. (1998). Evaluative conditioning: Arte-fact or -fiction? A reply to Baeyens, De Houwer, Vansteenwegen and Eelen (1998). *Learning and Motivation, 29*, 475–491.

Field, A. P., & Davey, G. C. L. (1999). Reevaluating evaluative conditioning: A nonassociative explanation of conditioning effects in the visual evaluative conditioning paradigm. *Journal of Experimental Psychology. Animal Behavior Processes*, *25*, 211–224.

Field, A. P., & Field, P. D. (2000). *ECAwarenessAttention version 1.0 for Windows*™ [Computer program]. Brighton, UK: Authors.

Field, A. P., Lascelles, K. R. R., & Davey, G. C. L. (2003). *Evaluative conditioning: Missing presumed dead.* Manuscript under review.

Fulcher, E. P., & Cocks, R. P. (1997). Dissociative storage systems in human evaluative conditioning. *Behaviour Research and Therapy, 35*, 1–10.

Hammerl, M., & Grabitz, H.-J. (1993). Human evaluative conditioning: Order of stimulus presentation. *Integrative Physiological and Behavioral Science, 28*, 191–194.

Hammerl, M., & Grabitz, H.-J. (2000). Affective-evaluative learning in humans: A form of associative learning or only an artifact? *Learning and Motivation, 31*, 345–363.

Hirst, W., Spelke, E. S., Reaves, C. C., Caharack, G., & Neisser, U. (1980). Dividing attention without alternation or automaticity. *Journal of Experimental Psychology. General, 109*, 98–117.

Kahneman, D. (1973). *Attention and effort.* Englewood Cliffs, NJ: Prentice Hall.

Kamin, L. J. (1969). Predictability, surprise, attention and conditioning. In B. A. Campbell & R. M. Church (Eds.), *Punishment and aversive behavior* (pp. 279–296). New York: Appleton-Century-Croft.

Katkin, E. S., Wiens, S., & Öhman, A. (2001). Nonconscious fear conditioning, visceral perception, and the development of gut feelings. *Psychological Science, 12,* 366–370.

Kruschke, J. K. (2001). Toward a unified model of attention in associative learning. *Journal of Mathematical Psychology, 45,* 812–863.

Kruschke, J. K., & Blair, N. J. (2000). Blocking and backward blocking involve learned inattention. *Psychonomic Bulletin and Review, 7,* 636–645.

Lang, P. J., Bradley, M. M., & Cuthbert, B. N. (1997a). *International Affective Picture System (IAPS)* [CD-ROM]. Gainesville, FL: NIMH Center for Emotion and Attention (CSEA).

Lang, P. J., Bradley, M. M. & Cuthbert, B. N. (1997b). *International affective picture system (IAPS): Technical manual and affective ratings.* Gainesville, FL: NIMH Center for Emotion and Attention (CSEA).

Lovibond, P. F., & Shanks, D. R. (2002). The role of awareness in Pavlovian conditioning: Empirical evidence and theoretical implications. *Journal of Experimental Psychology. Animal Behavior Processes, 28,* 3–26.

Lubow, R. E., & Gerwitz, J. C. (1995). Latent inhibition in humans: Data, theory and implications for schizophrenia. *Psychological Bulletin, 117,* 87–103.

Mackintosh, N. J. (1975). A theory of attention: Variations in the associability of stimuli with reinforcement. *Psychological Review, 82,* 276–298.

Nissen, M. J., & Bullemer, P. (1987). Attentional requirements of learning: Evidence from performance measures. *Cognitive Psychology, 19,* 1–32.

Pashler, H. (1990). Do response modality effects support multi-processor models of divided attention? *Journal of Experimental Psychology. Human Perception and Performance, 16,* 826–842.

Reber, P. J., & Squire, L. R. (1994). Parallel brain systems for learning with and without awareness. *Learning and Memory, 1,* 217–229.

Reber, P. J., & Squire, L. R. (1998). Encapsulation of implicit and explicit memory in sequence learning. *Journal of Cognitive Neuroscience, 10,* 248–263.

Rescorla, R. A. & Wagner, A. R. (1972). A theory of Pavlovian conditioning: Variations in the effectiveness of reinforcement and non-reinforcement. In A. H. Blake & W. F. Prokasy (Eds.), *Classical conditioning: II. Current research and theory* (pp. 64–99). New York: Appleton-Century-Croft.

Rozin, P., Wrzesniewski, A., & Byrnes, D. (1998). The elusiveness of evaluative conditioning. *Learning and Motivation, 29,* 397–415.

Shanks, D. R., & Dickinson, A. (1990). Contingency awareness in evaluative conditioning: A comment on Baeyens, Eelen and van den Bergh. *Cognition and Emotion, 4,* 19–30.

Shanks, D. R., & St. John, M. F. (1994). Characteristics of dissociable human learning systems. *Behavioral and Brain Sciences, 17,* 367–447.

Shanks, D. R., & Channon, S. (2002). Effects of a secondary task on ''implicit' sequence learning: Learning or performance? *Psychological Research, 66,* 99–109.

Stevens, A., Lascelles, K., Field, A. P., Matthias, R., Siddens-Corby, R., & Ives, R. (1999). *ECtests version 1.2 for Windows*™ [Computer program]. Brighton, UK: University of Sussex.

Stevenson, R. J., Boakes, R. A., & Wilson, J. P. (2000). Resistance to extinction of conditioned odor perceptions: Evaluative conditioning is not unique. *Journal of Experimental Psychology. Learning, Memory, and Cognition, 26,* 423–440.

Styles, E. A. (1997). *The psychology of attention.* Hove, UK: Psychology Press.

Zelniker, T. (1971). Perceptual attenuation of an irrelevant auditory verbal input as measured by an involuntary verbal response in a selective-attention task. *Journal of Experimental Psychology, 87,* 52–56.

APPENDIX

Stimulus type	Image	IAPS number	IAPS pleasure rating[a]
CS (Neutral)	Mug	7009	4.93
CS (Neutral)	Mushroom	5532	5.19
CS (Neutral)	Filing cabinet	7225	4.45
CS (Neutral)	Tissues	7950	4.95
US (Positive)	Seal pup	1440	8.19
US (Positive)	Puppies	1710	8.34
US (Negative)	Mutilated hand	9405	1.83
US (Negative)	Mutilated head	3010	1.79

[a] IAPS ratings range from 1 (unpleasant) to 9 (pleasant), with 5 representing neutral.

COGNITION AND EMOTION
2005, 19 (2), 245–268

Resistance to extinction of human evaluative conditioning using a between-subjects design

E. Díaz and G. Ruiz

University of Seville, Spain

F. Baeyens

University of Leuven, Belgium

Two experiments were conducted to examine whether the resistance to extinction obtained in evaluative conditioning (EC) studies implies that EC is a qualitatively distinct form of classical conditioning (Baeyens, Eelen, & Crombez, 1995a) or whether it is the result of an nonassociative artefact (Field & Davey, 1997, 1998, 1999). Both experiments included between-subjects control groups in addition to standard within-subjects control conditions. In Experiment 1, only verbal ratings were measured in order to evaluate the effect of postacquisition CS-only exposures on EC whereas in Experiment 2, verbal ratings and postextinction priming effects were measured. The results showed that the EC effects are demonstrable in a between-subjects design and that the extinction procedure did not have any influence on the acquired evaluative value of CSs regardless of whether the verbal ratings or the priming effects were used as dependent variables. The present results provide evidence that EC is resistant to extinction and suggest an interpretation of EC as a qualitatively distinct form of associative learning.

Evaluative conditioning is said to occur if the pairing of an affectively neutral stimulus (CS) with either a liked or disliked stimulus (US) results in a change of the evaluative tone of the CS in the same direction as the US with which it was paired (Levey & Martin, 1975). The basic procedure to establish this kind of learning consists of three sequential phases. In the first phase (baseline phase) the participants are asked to evaluate a set of stimuli on a scale ranging from −100 (very disliked) to +100 (very liked). On the basis of these subjective ratings, the stimuli most liked and most disliked are selected to be used as USs.

Correspondence should be addressed to E. Díaz, Department of Experimental Psychology, C/ Camilo Jose Cela, s/n, 41018 Seville, Spain; (e-mail: estredi@us.es.

This research was supported by a DGES (Spanish government) BSO2000-0323-C02-01 grant. The authors wish to thank Dirk Hermans, Deb Vansteenwegen, Paul Eelen, Tom Becker, Geert Crombez, Natividad Sanchez, and Gonzalo De la Casa for their help at various stages of the study or their helpful comments and thoughts.

http://www.tandf.co.uk/journals/pp/02699931.html   DOI:10.1080/02699930441000300

The stimuli most neutral are selected as CSs and each one is paired with one of the valenced stimuli. Additionally, a control condition is created by pairing two neutral stimuli. In the second phase (conditioning phase) all CS-US pairs are presented several times in a semi-randomised order. In the third phase (test phase) stimuli are rated a second time using the same rating scales as at the baseline phase. The standard findings from the test phase show that the hedonic value of CSs shifts towards the USs with which it was paired.

This kind of learning has been demonstrated in a wide variety of conditioning paradigms involving physically very different stimuli, like flavours (e.g., Baeyens, Crombez, De Houwer, & Eelen, 1996a; Baeyens, Crombez, Hendrickx, & Eelen, 1995b; Baeyens, Eelen, Van den Bergh, & Crombez, 1990b; Zellner, Rozin, Aron, & Kulish, 1983), visual stimuli (e.g., Baeyens, Eelen, Van den Bergh, & Crombez, 1992; De Houwer, Baeyens, Vansteenwegen, & Eelen, 2000; Díaz & De la Casa, 2002; Fulcher & Cocks, 1997; Hammerl & Grabitz, 1996; Shimp, Stuart, & Engle, 1991), haptic stimulation (e.g., Hammerl & Grabitz, 2000), olfactory stimuli (e.g., Baeyens, Wrzesniewski, De Houwer, & Eelen, 1996d) and social stimuli like human facial expressions of pleasure and displeasure (e.g., Baeyens, Kaes, Eelen, & Silverans, 1996b; Baeyens, Vansteenwegen, De Houwer, & Crombez, 1996c).

Although at a procedural level EC can be regarded as a form of Pavlovian conditioning, it is different from most other instances of human classical conditioning because it has been found that EC is highly resistant to extinction (e.g., Baeyens, Crombez, Van den Bergh, & Eelen, 1988; De Houwer et al., 2000) and it does not require CS-US contingency awareness (e.g., Baeyens, Eelen, & Van den Bergh, 1990a; De Houwer, Baeyens, & Eelen, 1994; Hammerl & Grabitz, 2000). These characteristics appear to define EC as a qualitatively distinct form of associative learning (Baeyens & De Houwer, 1995). Recently, De Houwer, Thomas, and Baeyens (2001) have pointed out that it is necessary to make a distinction between procedural and process levels, and that although EC is procedurally similar to other forms of Pavlovian conditioning, the underlying processes might be different. From this theoretical perspective Baeyens and colleagues have proposed that EC is also based on a CS-US association, but that the representation of this association is mediated by a referential system as opposed to an expectancy system which would mediate Pavlovian preparatory conditioning. According to this model, the referential system would operate automatically and it would only be sensitive to co-occurrences between events. Once a CS-US link has been established, the CS presentation would activate a US representation without necessarily generating an active expectancy that the US is actually going to occur. That is why EC is not influenced by procedures in which the events do not co-occur as in extinction (the referential system is only sensitive to CS-US co-occurrence) and why EC is not dependent on awareness of CS-US contingencies (the referential system can operate automatically).

However, other authors have proposed that these peculiar features could be attributed to procedural characteristics of the EC paradigm (e.g., Davey, 1994). Specifically, in the earlier EC experiments that showed resistance to extinction and conditioning without contingency awareness, the CSs and the USs were not paired on a random basis but on the basis of perceptual similarity of stimuli (e.g., Baeyens, et al., 1988; Baeyens, Eelen, Van den Bergh, & Crombez, 1989; Martin & Levey, 1987). According to Shanks and Dickinson (1990) this pairing procedure did not meet the requirement of a well-controlled within-subjects design (counterbalancing criterion or random assignment of the CSs to the USs) which raises important doubts about the nature of the effects obtained in these early experiments. Moreover, Field and Davey (1999) obtained conditioning-like changes of evaluation of the CSs when the CSs-USs pairs were constructed on the basis of perceptual similarity even in those control groups in which participants were never exposed to actual CS-US pairings.

The lack of between-subject control groups was proposed as another problematic procedural factor of the EC studies. Concerning this criticised aspect, it has been claimed that only an adequate between-group control (an unpaired group) would allow the possibility of demonstrating that EC effects are the result of associative learning. However, most EC studies used a within-subject control, so that, at least in principle the effects observed in these studies may be due to something other than associative learning (Davey, 1994; Field & Davey, 1997, 1998, 1999). Based on this argument, Davey (1994) pointed out that if the evaluative shifts obtained in the EC studies do not necessarily involve associative learning, it should come as no surprise that these evaluative shifts do not require contingency awareness (because the contingency would not be responsible of this learning) nor that they are resistant to extinction (as they are not based on a CS-US association).

In reply to these critiques, Baeyens, De Houwer, Vansteenwegen, and Eelen (1998) have pointed out that only a small minority of these early EC experiments used the perceptual similarity of CSs and USs as assignment procedure and that a within-subject design does represent an adequate procedure for demonstrating associative learning. Although we agree with these arguments, it should be noted that, apart from the criticised picture-picture experiments, only in the flavour-flavour EC studies has consistent evidence been obtained, showing that EC is resistant to extinction (e.g., Baeyens et al., 1996a; Baeyens et al., 1995b; Baeyens, Vanhouche, Crombez, & Eelen, 2004). However, this finding is less consistent when we consider other paradigms. Thus, studies using pictures of faces as CSs and electric shocks as USs obtained extinction when startle modulation was used as an index of evaluative learning but resistance to extinction when this learning was measured by an affective priming task or verbal ratings (Hermans, Crombez, Vansteenwegen, Baeyens, & Eelen, 2002b; Vansteewegen, Crombez, Baeyens, & Eelen, 1998). In addition, Field and Davey (1999) pointed out that the CSs and USs selection procedure on the basis of the participant's ratings and the lack of a between-subjects control do not rule out the possibility that the resistance to extinction obtained in these studies was the result of experimental biases.

The main purpose of the present study was to investigate whether the resistance to extinction obtained in EC studies represents a special characteristic of a qualitatively distinct form of associative learning (Baeyens, Eelen, & Crombez, 1995a) or whether it is the result of a nonassociative artefact of the EC paradigm (Field & Davey, 1997, 1998, 1999). To this end, we evaluated the effect of an extinction procedure on EC using between-subjects control groups in addition to the standard within-subjects control condition.

EXPERIMENT 1

In the typical extinction procedure when a stimulus previously conditioned is exposed without consequence (US), this results in a decreasing of the CR acquired during the conditioning. Although there is considerable agreement on interpreting this behaviour change in terms of a change in the associative structure relating the CS and US, the specific nature of such a change has been subject to considerable debate. Thus, some theories propose that the non-reinforced CS presentations result in a decreasing of the associative strength acquired by the CS through out the conditioning (Rescorla & Wagner, 1972; Wagner, 1979, 1981). On the other hand, other views consider that the absence of a consequence (US) that consistently follows the CS presentations produces a stimulus-no consequence association (Pearce & Hall, 1980). Finally, other theories that combine the role of the context and the CS-no US association, propose that through out the nonreinforced CS presentations, the context gains control over the expression of the CS-no US association, thus acquiring the properties of a retrieval cue (Bouton, 1993).

Despite the different accounts of extinction, it is clear that this phenomenon represents a basic learning process that permits organisms to adapt to environmental changes thus safeguarding them from responding persistently old relationships between stimuli that are no longer relevant. Therefore it would be relevant to determine whether the resistance to extinction of EC is the result of experimental biases (Field & Davey, 1999) or as Baeyens and De Houwer (1995) pointed out, or if it responds to the action of an associative learning system that involves a very low response cost so that the persistence of the response does not provide an adaptive disadvantage.

Experiment 1 was designed to examine whether exposure to Japanese letters, after having been paired with affective words, results in an extinction effect of EC to these Japanese letters. In order to prevent the experimental biases identified by Field and Davey (1999), the CSs and USs were not selected on the basis of participants' subjective ratings but were assigned on a random basis. Additionally, to control the stimulus exposure and pseudo-conditioning effects the block/sub-block control group (BSB) suggested by Field (1997) was used (see the Method section for a more detailed description).

Method

Participants

A total of 36 undergraduate Dutch-speaking students from the University of Leuven aged between 17 and 19 years participated as a partial fulfilment of course requirements. Each participant was tested individually. Test duration was about 45 minutes. Participants were randomly allocated to one of the three experimental groups (Extinction, Extinction Control, BSB Control).

Materials

Experimental events were presented on a SVGA colour monitor controlled by an IBM-compatible PC.

Three Japanese letters and three Dutch nouns were used as CSs and USs, respectively (see Table 1). Japanese letters were selected from the WP Japanese font available in the Microsoft Word 2000 program. Dutch words were selected from a previous study conducted by Hermans and De Houwer (1994) which provides affective (1 = very disliked; 7 = very liked) and familiarity (1 = not familiar at all; 7 = very familiar) ratings for 740 Dutch words. The nouns with the highest ($M = 6.92$, $SD = .27$) and the lowest ($M = 1.16$, $SD = .51$) mean evaluation were selected as Liked (L) and Disliked (D) US stimuli, respectively. A noun from categories 3–4 was taken to be used as Neutral (N) stimulus ($M = 3.53$, $SD = 0.82$). Additionally we selected three sets of 5 words each, rated as highly liked, disliked, or neutral from this study and 8 Japanese letters to be used as distracter stimuli in the rating phases. In addition, two Symbol letters were used as distracter stimuli in the Extinction phase (see Table 1). These letters were taken from symbol fonts available in the Microsoft Word 2000 program. The size of the letters was 255 mm.

All stimuli were presented centred on the computer screen in white uppercase letters on a black background. The size of the Japanese letters was 255 mm and the size of the letters which composed the words was 120 mm. The presentation of the stimuli was controlled by a Superlab for Windows 1.03 program.

Procedure

The experiment consisted of six sequential phases.

Baseline phase.   This phase was similar for the three groups. Participants were led to believe that the experiment concerned the study of semantic processing. This was said in order to minimise demand effects. Each participant was seated about 50 cm away from the computer screen and was handed a sheet

TABLE 1
Stimuli used as CSs (Japanese letters), distractors during the extinction phase (Symbol letters), and USs (liked, neutral, and disliked words)

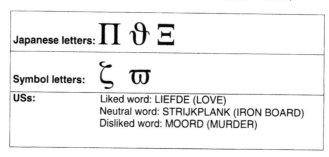

Japanese letters:	Π ϑ Ξ
Symbol letters:	ζ ω
USs:	Liked word: LIEFDE (LOVE) Neutral word: STRIJKPLANK (IRON BOARD) Disliked word: MOORD (MURDER)

containing 29 affective scales ranging from -10 to $+10$, in intervals of one by one (questionnaire 1). The 29 stimuli were randomly presented on the computer screen (3 CSs, 3 USs, and 23 distractor stimuli). Participants were instructed to rate each stimulus on questionnaire 1 selecting a score on the affective scales. It was indicated that a score of -10 meant that the stimulus was "very disliked", a score of $+10$ meant that the stimulus was "very liked" and a score of 0 meant that the stimulus was "completely neutral". Each stimulus remained on the screen untill participants pressed any key. Instructions stressed the importance of relying on the first immediate and spontaneous reactions toward the stimuli. The ratings given at this phase were the first evaluative responses (ER1).

Acquisition phase. This phase started immediately after the baseline phase. The instruction, which appeared on the computer screen, indicated that from that moment on the task would be simply to look carefully at all stimuli appearing on the screen. There were two possible presentation schedules which varied according to the condition the participants were assigned to:

(1) Paired condition. Both the Extinction group (Ext) and the Extinction control group (Excon) received this schedule. A random CS-US assignment was used for each participant. In this manner, three different stimulus pairs (N-L, N-N, N-D) were arranged for each participant. Each pair was presented 10 times intermixed with 4 CS-only trials (hence a partial reinforcement[1] schedule was used, such that $p(US/CS) = .7$ and $p(US/no\ CS) = 0$). Thus, a total of 42 presentation trials (14 trials for each stimulus pair times three pairs) were given in a randomised order. Each CS-US trial consisted of the following sequence of

---

[1] The selection of this contingency relation was motivated by the design of other studies at our lab, which had objectives that have no direct relation with the present investigation.

events: a warning tone followed by the presentation of the CS for a duration of 1 s, the offset of the CS coincided with the onset of the US, which was presented for 1 s. The intertrial interval was 6 s. In the CS-only trials, the US was not presented and the intertrial interval (in this case the time between the offset of one CS and the onset of the next warning tone) was set at 7 s. The Japanese letters were counterbalanced between-subjects in order to control for affective differences arising from the Japanese characters themselves.

(2) Unpaired condition. The BSB control group received this condition. CSs and USs were paired according to the same criteria as in the paired condition. However, the stimuli were not presented in a contiguous or contingent pattern. Instead, CSs and USs were separated and presented in two isolated blocks (CS block and US block). Within each of these blocks, each stimulus was paired with itself (7 times in CS blocks and 5 times in the US blocks) using the same parameters as in the CS-US trials of the paired condition. Thus, the warning tone was followed by the onset of a stimulus for 1 s, followed by the same stimulus presented by 1 s, followed by a black screen for 6 s, and so on, until that stimulus had been presented 14 times in the CS block and 10 times in the US block (thus participants saw each stimulus the same number of times as in the paired condition). Each set of such "self-paired presentations" is a sub-block. There were three CSs sub-blocks (each Japanese letter used as CS in the paired condition) and three USs sub-blocks (each word used as US in the paired condition). The three CS sub-blocks were randomly presented and also the three US sub-blocks were presented in random order. Half of the participants saw the CS block followed by the US block and the rest saw the US block before the CS block.

Postacquisition phase.   A new questionnaire (questionnaire 2) was given to the participants. New instructions were presented on the computer screen. Participants were informed that they would see a set of stimuli and that they were required to rate each one by the affective scales of the questionnaire 2. They were reminded to again rely on their first, immediate, spontaneous reaction at that exact moment. It was firmly stressed that we were only interested in their actual evaluation of the stimuli, and that they did not have to recall their previous ratings. The same 28 stimuli used in the baseline phase were presented in a random order. The ratings taken at this phase were the second evaluative responses (ER2).

Extinction phase.   This phase started immediately after the postacquisition phase. Participants were instructed to look carefully at the stimuli appearing on the screen. A different schedule was arranged according to the different groups.

(1) Ext group and BSB group. For these groups the CSs were now each presented in isolation 14 times. Each CS-only trial started with the warning tone. CS presentation duration was 1 s, the ITI (end of the CS of the previous trial to

onset of the warning tone of the following trial) was 7 s. CS-only trials were randomised

(2) Extcon group. In this group, in order to avoid generalisation effects from acquired affective values to stimuli that belong to the same class two new stimuli (symbol letters) were presented in isolation 14 times each one. The parameters of the letter presentation were identical to those used in the Ext group and BSB group in this phase.

Postextinction phase.   A new questionnaire (questionnaire 3) was given to the participants. The 28 stimuli were again presented in a random order. Participants were instructed to rate each stimulus on the questionnaire. It was firmly stressed that we were only interested in their actual evaluation of the stimuli, and that they did not have to recall their previous ratings. The ratings given at this phase were the third evaluative responses (ER3).

Contingency awareness assessment.   Participants were given a booklet with 3 pages. Each page contained one of the Japanese letters used as CS and four questions in relation to that stimulus. Participants were informed that the questions referred to the first observational phase of the experiment (acquisition phase). The first question asked participants to choose a score on a scale ranging from − 10 to +10 according to the valence of the stimulus that they may have remembered which occurred immediately after the stimulus that they were looking at, at the top of the page. The second question was whether the Japanese letter had been followed by a particular word. An affirmative answer let participants respond to the third question. This question asked participants to choose that word out of a list of 18 words (the same 18 words presented in the ratings phases). Finally, participants were invited to express the degree of confidence in their responses on a scale which ranged from 0 (completely unsure) to 100 (completely sure).

Results and discussion

Analysis of US ratings

The mean evaluative ratings of the USs are displayed in Table 2. The data were analysed using a Group (Ext, BSB, or Extcon) × US type (L, N, or D) × Moment of evaluative response measurement (ER1, ER2, or ER3) ANOVA. The analysis revealed a main effect of US type, $F(2, 54) = 853.73, p < .001$. As we expected, a priori contrasts confirmed that overall, the liked US received a higher rating than the neutral US, $F(1, 27) = 605.18, p < .001$ and than the disliked US, $F(1, 27) = 1208.38, p < .001$. Likewise, the disliked US was rated lower than the neutral US, $F(1, 27) = 493.27, p < .001$. No other effects were significant ($p > .05$ for all comparisons), which implies that the valence of the

TABLE 2

Mean evaluative ratings of (standard deviations) of the liked (L), neutral (N), and disliked (D) USs at each stage of the experiment (ER1, ER2, and ER3) in the three groups

Groups	L			N			D		
	ER1	ER2	ER3	ER1	ER2	ER3	ER1	ER2	ER3
Ext	9.1	9.3	8.7	−0.4	−0.6	−1	−9.3	−9.2	−9
	(1.44)	(1.56)	(2.05)	(1.50)	(1.95)	(2.98)	(1.05)	(1.47)	(1.63)
Extcon	9.2	9.4	9.3	−0.5	−0.6	−1.4	−8.4	−8.5	−8.8
	(0.91)	(0.84)	(0.94)	(2.06)	(1.77)	(2.31)	(2.31)	(2.06)	(1.75)
BSB	8.5	8.7	8.6	0	0.7	−0.1	−8.9	−8.4	−8.1
	(1.26)	(1.15)	(1.42)	(1.69)	(2.62)	(1.19)	(1.85)	(2.91)	(2.42)

Ext, extinction; Extcon, extinction control; BSB, block-sub-block lock.

USs remained stable throughout the different phases and that each USs type were similarly rated by the three groups.

Analysis of CS ratings

The mean evaluative ratings of the CSs at the baseline phase (ER1), the postacquisition phase (ER2), and the postextinction phase (ER3) for each pair type in each of the three groups (Ext group, Extcon group, and BSB group) are depicted in Figure 1. Data of six participants were removed from the analysis because they rated the CSs as affective stimuli (± 7) at the Baseline phase.

The data were analysed by means of a 3 (Group: Ext, BSB, or Extcon) × 3 (Pair type: N-L, N-N, or N-D) × 3 (Moment of evaluative response measurement: ER1, ER2, or ER3) analysis of variance (ANOVA) with repeated measures on the last two variables. Tests involving the Pair type variable (Mauchly $W = 0.506$), Moment of evaluative response variable (Mauchly $W = 0.585$) and Pair type × Moment of evaluative response interaction (Mauchly $W = 0.191$) violated the sphericity assumption, and so, Greenhouse-Geisser corrected F-values were used throughout. A main effect of the Pair type variable, $F(1.34, 36.14) = 10.68$, $p < .01$ was observed. A priori contrasts revealed that this effect implied an overall difference between N-L and N-N conditions, $F(1, 27) = 20.69$, $p < .01$; between N-D and N-N conditions, $F(1, 27) = 7.11$, $p < .01$; and between N-L and N-D conditions, $F(1, 27) = 8.73$, $p < .01$. No other main effects were obtained. We also observed a significant interaction between Group × Pair type variables, $F(4, 54) = 9.30$, $p < .01$, and a significant interaction between Pair type × Moment of evaluative response measurement, $F(2.11, 37) = 15.67$, $p < .001$. Finally, and of crucial importance the Groups × Pair type × Moment of evaluative response measurement interaction was also significant, $F(8, 108) = 4.61$, $p < .001$ which shows, as can be seen in Figure 1,

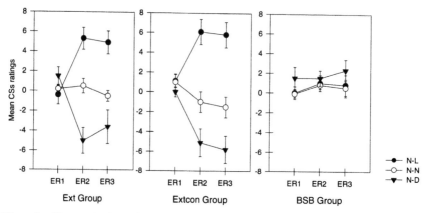

Figure 1. Mean evaluative ratings of the Conditioned Stimulus (CS) as a function of the Moment of evaluative measurement (ER1, ER2, and ER3) for each Pair type (N-L, N-N, and N-D) in the three Groups (Ext, extinction; Extcon, extinction control; BSB, block-sub-block). Error bars represent *SEMs*.

that the ratings of the different pair types at different moment of evaluative response measurement were different across the groups.

As expected, we observed no interaction between Pair type × Groups factors at baseline (ER1), $F(4, 54) = 1.62, p > .05$, showing that at this phase the ratings of the different pair types were the same across the groups.

At the second moment of measurement, ER2, a significant Pair type × Groups interaction was obtained, $F(54, 4) = 8.11, p < .001$, which implies that, after acquisition, the different groups rated the different pair types differently. A more detailed analysis revealed that this interaction was due to the fact that there was no effect of the factor Pair type in the BSB group ($p > .05$) but there was a significant effect in the Ext group, $F(2, 18) = 11.91, p < .001$, and a significant effect in the Extcon group, $F(2, 18) = 14.27, p < .001$. A priori contrasts showed that in the Ext group, there were significant differences between N-L and N-N pairs, $F(1, 27) = 10,12 \ p < .01$; between N-D and N-N pairs, $F(1, 27) = 22.46, p < .001$; and between N-L and N-D pairs, $F(1, 27) = 23.94, p < .001$. As we expected, the same pattern of results was observed in the Extcon group: a significant difference between N-L and N-N pairs, $F(1, 27) = 22.16, p < .001$; between N-D and N-N pairs, $F(1, 27) = 12.48, p < .001$; and also between N-L and N-D pairs, $F(1, 27) = 28.31, p < .001$.

A comparison between ERs at the baseline phase versus those after the acquisition phase revealed a significant difference for N stimuli from the N-L pair in the Ext group, $F(1, 27) = 18.98, p < .001$ and in the Extcon group, $F(1, 27) = 14.60, p < .001$ but no such difference was revealed in the BSB group ($p > .05$). The same comparison revealed a significant difference for the N-D pair in the Ext group, $F(1,27) = 27.46$, $p < .001$; and in the Extcon group, $F(1,27) = 16.90$, $p < .001$ but this comparison was not significant in the BSB group ($p > .05$). In the three groups, the ratings for the N-N pair after the acquisition phase were similar to those at the baseline phase ($p > .05$ for all comparisons). As we expected, these results show that evaluative conditioning took place during acquisition in the groups that received the paired condition: Ext and Extcon groups. However, this effect was not obtained in the BSB control group that received nonpaired presentations of CSs and USs. Additional comparisons between conditions confirmed that after the acquisition phase, the N-L pair was rated less positively by the BSB group than by the Ext and Extcon groups, $F(1,27) = 7.36$, $p < .05$ and $F(1,27) = 10.35$, $p < .01$ respectively, and the last two groups were similar in this comparison, $p > .05$. Similarly, the N-D pair was evaluated more negatively by the Ext and Extcon groups than by the BSB group, $F(1,27) = 13.59$, $p < .01$ and $F(1,27) = 14.02$, $p < .001$, respectively. Ratings of Ext and Extcon did not differ in this condition, $p > .05$. Comparisons between N-N pairs in the Ext, Extcon and BSB groups revealed similar ratings by all groups, ($p > .05$ for all comparisons).

As predicted from a resistance- to-extinction perspective, the pattern of results obtained after extinction phase was similar to those observed after the acquisition phase. At the third moment of measurement, ER3, a significant Pair type $\times$ Groups interaction was obtained, $F(4,54) = 8.02$, $p < .001$, which implies that, after extinction, the different groups rated the different pair types differently. In the Ext and Extcon groups, the ratings of the N-L stimuli were significantly higher than the ratings of the N-N stimuli, $F(1,27) = 12.81$, $p < .001$ and $F(1,27) = 23.41$, $p < .001$, respectively, and although the ratings of the N-D stimuli were lower than the ratings of the N-N stimuli, this comparison was only marginally significant in the Ext group, $F(1,27) = 4.07$, $p = .053$ and $F(1,27) = 7.84$, $p < .001$ respectively. The ratings of the N-L stimuli were significantly higher than the ratings of the N-D stimuli in the Ext group, $F(1,27) = 10.8$, $p < .01$. This comparison was also significant in the Extcon group, $F(1,27) = 20.11$, $p < .001$. In the BSB group there was no effect of the factor Pair type, $p > .05$. A comparison between ERs after acquisition (ER2) versus those after the extinction phase (ER3) revealed no significant differences for the different stimulus pairs in any of the three groups ($p > .05$ for all comparisons). Intergroup comparisons revealed there were no significant differences between Ext and Extcon groups at this phase ($p > .05$ for all comparisons). However, the ratings of the N-L pair were significantly higher in the Ext and Extcon groups than in the BSB group, $F(1,27) = 11.07$, $p < .001$ and $F(1,27) = 14.84$, $p < .001$, respectively. The ratings of the N-D pair were significantly lower in the Ext and Extcon groups than in the BSB groups, $F(1,27) = 8.10$, $p < .001$ and $F(1,27) = 15.26$, $p < .001$, respectively. The ratings of the N-N pair were similar in the three groups.

Awareness data

The answer to the first three questions revealed that all participants of the Ext and Extcon groups had noticed that each Japanese letter was frequently followed by a concrete word with a determinate valence. Moreover, all participants of these groups chose the correct word from the list of 18 words. The mean degree of confidence was 96.5% (ranging from 80 to 100). Therefore, all participants of these groups were classified as being aware of all three contingencies. As we expected, data from the BSB group in which the contingency relation was not established showed a different pattern of response. Given that, during the acquisition phase, each Japanese letter was paired with itself, in the first question they chose scores nearer to 0. Thus, the mean evaluation of these letters was 1.47 (ranging from -2 to $+3$). In addition, all participants of this group responded negatively to the second question. As all the participants were aware of all three contingencies further analysis concerning the relation between this variable and the evaluative response can not be made.

The results of Experiment 1 show that EC effects can be demonstrated in a between-subject design. The fact that CS-US pairs were constructed on a random basis and that the conditioning effects were only found in the paired groups (Ext and Extcon groups) whereas no conditioning-like effects occurred in the control group (BSB group) proposed by Field and Davey (1999) allows one to argue that the present results provide conclusive evidence for the associative nature of evaluative conditioning. Also, and of crucial importance, our data support the hypothesis that evaluative conditioning is resistant to extinction. In the Ext group we observed that 14 unreinforced presentations of the N stimuli did not have any influence on the previously acquired valence of the stimuli. Moreover, the ratings of the Ext group were similar to those of the Extcon group, which, after the conditioning did not receive any extinction trials. However, despite these results some questions can be raised concerning certain procedural factors that may favour this finding. Current extinction studies have demonstrated that a context change between extinction phase and test phase results in a recovery (renewal) of conditioned responding to extinguished CS (Bouton, 1994). It could be argued that the presentation of new instructions and the start of a new rating task after the extinction phase could constitute a change context. If so, the resistance to extinction observed in our experiment could be interpreted as a renewal effect. Moreover, Lipp, Oughton, and Lelievre (2003), have recently showed extinction of affective learning when the valence of CSs was measured during the extinction phase but showed resistance to extinction when, as in our experiment, the affective ratings were measured after the extinction phase. Although such an explanation is tenable, we consider that our findings do lead to such a conclusion. First, in relation to this issue, our procedure might be considered as an AAB design in which the acquisition and extinction contexts are identical (A context) and both differ on the test context (B context). In relation to this issue, most of the studies that have attempted to demonstrate a renewal effect with this kind of AAB procedure have failed to do so (e.g., Bouton & King, 1983; Bouton & Swartzentruber; 1989; Goddard, 1999; Nakajima, Tanaka, Urushihara, & Imada, 2000), or they have found a weak renewal effect (Thomas, Larsen, & Ayres, 2003). Moreover, from these studies it has been concluded that the similarity of the acquisition and extinction contexts helps thwart renewal. Due to this, it is difficult to assume that the high evaluative ratings obtained after the extinction phase in our experiment are due to a renewal effect. In addition, it is important to note that in order to obtain a renewal effect it is necessary for a clear differentiation to exist between the contexts of extinction and those of the test. Such a differentiation could be favoured, as in the Lipp et al. (2003) study as the experimenter entered the participant's room and removed electrodes used to present the unconditional stimulus during conditioning, before the postextinction rating phase. However, if we consider that in our study, stimuli were presented in a similar way in both phases (on the centre of computer screen, in white on a black background) it is much more difficult to think of the mere presentation of the instructions as a factor that produces such a clear context differentiation effect.

Also, it could be argued that, the partial reinforcement during acquisition could have retarded the extinction rate (Mackintosh, 1974). In fact, as it can be seen in Figure 1, there was a slight decrease of the evaluative ratings in the Ext group and although there was not a significant difference between ER2 and ER3, only a marginal difference between negative CSs and neutral CSs ($p = .052$) was obtained after extinction. Therefore, it could be possible to assume that the slight reduction of the ratings could have been greater if the number of extinction trials would have been greater. Nor can it be excluded that the evaluative response measurement after the extinction phase (ER3) was influenced by demand artefacts. In fact, the temporal interval between ER2 and ER3 was only 10 to 15 minutes so it is possible to assume that participants might be remembering their evaluations after the acquisition phase (ER2) and repeating them at the moment of ER3 measurement simply to appear consistent. The plausibility of these hypotheses was further investigated in Experiment 2.

EXPERIMENT 2

Experiment 1 revealed a clear effect of evaluative conditioning. However, data supporting that evaluative conditioning is resistant to extinction are vulnerable to alternative interpretations. A possible explanation for the resistance to extinction in Experiment 1 is that the partial reinforcement used during conditioning had retarded the rate of extinction. Specifically, exposure to nonreinforced Japanese letters trials during the acquisition phase similar to those encountered during the extinction phase may have decreased the salience of nonreinforcement during this last phase resulting in a slowed extinction rate. As it has been repeatedly reported, a greater number of extinction trials are necessary to disconfirm the expectation of reinforcement established for a partial schedule during acquisition (e.g., Alloy & Tabachnik, 1984; Mackintosh, 1974; Rescorla, 1999). In addition to this factor, demand characteristics could have promoted the stability of ERs across phases (Davey, 1994).

Experiment 2 was designed to examine whether one of these factors could determine the resistance to extinction observed in the Experiment 1. Specifically, we modified the original design by increasing the number of extinction trials in order to examine if this resistance to extinction was obtained because the partial reinforcement had retarded the rate of extinction. We decided not to remove the partial reinforcement in order to keep during the acquisition phase, some degree of masking of the experimental contingencies. Additionally, the effect of the extinction procedure was not only assessed by verbal ratings but also by means of an affective priming task, which provides an indirect measure of participants' stimulus evaluations, and is not affected by demand effects (e.g., Hermans, De Houwer, & Eelen, 1994 ; Hermans, Van den Broeck, & Eelen, 1998b). Finally, in order to simplify the design of this experiment and as the BSB group did not add any relevant information in relation to the objectives of this experiment, we decided to drop it.

In affective priming studies, two stimuli are presented in a sequential manner and participants are asked to respond as quickly as possible to the valence of the second stimulus. Results typically show that reaction times are shorter when both stimuli have the same valence—congruent trials—compared to when they have a different valence—incongruent trials (see Fazio, 2001, for a review). This phenomenon has been consistently demonstrated using different types of tasks, such as evaluative categorisation (e.g., Hermans, De Houwer, & Eelen, 1994), lexical decisions (e.g., Wentura, 1999), and pronunciation (e.g., Bargh, Chaiken, Raymond, & Hymes, 1996), and with a wide range of stimuli, such as nonsense words (e.g., De Houwer, Hermans, & Eelen, 1998); odours (e.g., Hermans, Baeyens, & Eelen, 1998a) and complex real-life colour pictures (e.g., Fazio, Jackson, Dunton, & Williams, 1995). Independently of the theoretical approach to affective priming—such as the spreading of activation account (e.g., Bower, 1991) or the Stroop-like reponse conflict account (e.g., Wentura, 1999—it is well established that this effect is based on an automatic process that it is unintentional, efficient, and that it can occur outside awareness (e.g., De Houwer, Hermans, Rothermund, & Wentura, 2002; Hermans, De Houwer, & Eelen, 2001). Therefore, the affective priming paradigm should be a good method to asses the effect of the extinction procedure on the acquired valence of CSs given its insensitivity to demand characteristics.

Method

Participants

A total of 24 Spanish-speaking students from the University of Seville participated. Their ages ranged from 18 to 20 years. All participants were tested separately and were volunteers.

Materials

Experimental events were presented on SVGA colour monitors controlled by IBM-compatible PCs. The conditioned stimuli were the same Japanese letters as Experiment 1. The unconditioned stimuli was the Spanish translation of the three words used in Experiment 1, which were previously rated as highly liked, disliked, and neutral in a pilot experiment conducted in our laboratory (Díaz, 2000). Primes for the affective priming procedure were 6 Japanese letters (the 2 Japanese letters that were used as CS-liked and CS-disliked, and 4 new Japanese letters). Targets for the affective priming procedure were a fixed set of six positive words (the word used as US-liked and 5 new words rated as liked in the pilot experiment) and six negative words (the word used as US-disliked and 5 new words rated as disliked in the pilot experiment).

Procedure

The procedure for Ext and Extcon groups was similar to Experiment 1 with the exception that during the extinction phase, each Japanese letter in the Ext group and each Symbol letter in the Extcon group were presented in isolation 24 times. After the postextinction phase, the two groups were given an affective priming phase. At this phase, the instructions explained that pairs of stimuli would be presented on the computer screen, the second of which would always be a word (the target), while the first would always be a nonword (the prime). Participants were instructed to attend to the word and to evaluate it as quickly as possible by pressing the ''P'' key (if the word had a positive meaning) or the ''N'' (if the word have a negative meaning) key on the computer keyboard. It was stressed that only the word was important and that the nonword should be ignored. Participants were, however, asked not to divert their eyes on the presentation of the nonword.

The affective priming task consisted of 72 experimental trials, preceded by 12 practice trials. Each trial started with a warning tone followed by the prime stimulus presented for 200 ms, followed, 100 ms after the offset of the prime (SOA 300 ms), by the target word. The target remained on the computer screen until the participants gave a response or 2000 ms had elapsed. The intertrial interval was 2 s. All combinations of the six primes and 12 targets were presented. The presentation order of these 72 trials was randomised. There were 12 trials in which the CS-liked was used as the prime, six followed by a positive target (congruent trials) and 6 followed by a negative target (incongruent trials). Also, the CS-disliked was used as prime in 12 trials, six followed by a positive target (incongruent trials) and six followed by a negative target (congruent trials). The rest of the 48 trials consisted of one of the 4 Japanese filler primes being followed by a positive target (24 trials) or a negative target (24 trials).

Finally, an awareness assessment similar to that used in Experiment 1 was conducted.

Results and discussion

Analysis of US ratings

The mean evaluative ratings of the USs are displayed in Table 3. The data were analysed using a Group (Ext, or Extcon) × US type (L, N, or D) × Moment of evaluative response measurement (ER1, ER2, or ER3) ANOVA. The analysis revealed a main effect of US type, $F(2, 40) = 829.70, p < .001$. A priori contrasts showed an overall difference between the liked US and the neutral US, $F(1, 20) = 542.79, p < .001$, between the liked US and the disliked US, $F(1, 20) = 2193.84$, and between the disliked US and the neutral US, $F(1, 20) = 257.03, p < .001$. As we expected, no other effects were significant ($p > .05$ for all comparisons).

Analysis of CSs ratings

Figure 2 shows graphs of the mean ERs for different groups at different moments of the experiment. Data of two participants were excluded from the analysis because they rated CSs as affective stimuli at the baseline phase. The data were analysed with a 2 (Group: Ext and Extcon) × 3 (Pair type: N-L, N-N, or N-D) × 3 (Moment of evaluative response measurement: ER1, ER2 or ER3) analysis of variance (ANOVA) with repeated measures on the last two variables.

TABLE 3
Mean ratings and (standard deviations) of the US type (L, N, and D) at the three stages of measurement (ER1, ER2, and ER3) for the groups

Groups	L			N			D		
	ER1	ER2	ER3	ER1	ER2	ER3	ER1	ER2	ER3
Ext	9.4	9.7	9.4	−1.2	−1.7	−1.4	−9.6	−9.7	−9.4
	(1.03)	(0.90)	(1.21)	(2.83)	(2.86)	(2.50)	(0.67)	(0.46)	(1.50)
Extcon	8.9	9.1	9.5	−0.2	−0.3	0	−8.9	−9.5	−9.5
	(1.92)	(1.32)	(0.93)	(0.90)	(0.67)	(0)	(1.92)	(1.21)	(0.93)

Ext, extinction; Extcon, extinction control.

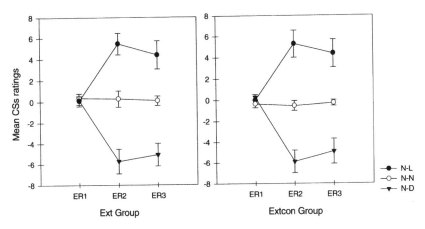

Figure 2.   Mean evaluative ratings of the Conditioned Stimulus (CS) as a function of the Moment of evaluative measurement (ER1, ER2, and ER3) for each Pair type (N-L, N-N, and N-D) in the two Groups (Ext, extinction; Extcon, extinction control). Error bars represent *SEM*s.

Tests involving the "Group" factor (Mauchly, $W = .329$), the "Pair type" $\times$ "Moment of evaluative response measurement" interaction (Mauchly, $M = .082$), violated the sphericity assumption, so Greenhouse-Geisser corrected F-values were used throughout. The analysis revealed a significant main effect of Pair type, $F(1.14, 22.72) = 36.94, p < .001$. A more detailed analysis with a priori planned contrasts showed an overall difference between (N-L) and (N-N) pairs, $F(1, 20) = 39.24, p < .001$; N-L and N-D pairs, $F(1, 20) = 39.67, p < .001$ and between N-N and N-D pairs, $F(1, 20) = 27.97, p < .001$. No other main effects were obtained.

We also observed an interaction between Pair type $\times$ Moment of evaluative response measurement, $F(1.27, 37.42) = 29.49, p < .001$. A priori contrasts revealed that this interaction was due to the fact that there was no effect of the Pair type at the baseline phase (ER1)($p > .05$), but a significant effect at the postacquisition phase (ER2), $F(2, 42) = 44.63, p < .001$, and a significant effect at the postextinction phase (ER3), $F(2, 42) = 28.95, p < .001$. After the acquisition phase (ER2) we obtained a differential pattern of response to the different stimulus pairs. Ratings for N-L were significantly more positive than ratings for N-N, $F(1, 20) = 40.17, p < .001$ and N-D, $F(1, 20) = 47.05, p < .001$. In addition, ratings for N-D were more negative than ratings for N-N, $F(1, 20) = 32.53, p < .001$. A comparison between ERs at the baseline with those after the acquisition phase revealed a significant difference for N stimuli from N-L pairs, $F(1, 20) = 38.32, p < .001$, and N-D pairs, $F(1, 20) = 46.40, p < .001$. The same comparison revealed no difference for N-N pairs ($p > .05$). After the extinction phase a similar pattern of results was obtained. There was a significant difference between N-L and N-N pairs, $F(1, 20) = 22.93, p < .001$, between N-L and N-D pairs, $F(1,20) = 29.65$, $p < .001$ and between N-N and N-D pairs, $F(1,20) = 25.47$, $p < .001$. A priori contrasts showed that there were no differences between ERs after extinction and those obtained after the acquisition phase, neither in the Ext group nor in the Extcon group ($p > .05$ for all comparisons).

Finally, comparisons concerning the "Group" factor were not significant, indicating that the pattern of responding in both groups were similar in each of the three rating phases ($p > .05$, for all comparisons). Thus, no extinction was observed.

Affective priming data

The data from trials on which an incorrect response was given or trials on which reaction times were faster than 250 ms or slower than 1500 ms were discarded to reduce the influence of outlier responses.

Figure 3 shows the mean reaction times of the groups as a function of the affective congruence and the target valence. We conducted a Groups (Ext vs. Extcon) × Target valence (Positive vs. Negative) × Affective congruence (congruent vs. incongruent) ANOVA with repeated measures on the two last variables. The main effect of Affective congruence was significant, $F(1,118) = 18.69$, $p < .001$. Reaction times for affectively congruent pairs ($M = 556.95$; $SE = 8.47$) were shorter than for affectively incongruent pairs ($M = 603.18$; $SE = 9.98$). Corroborating the data from evaluative ratings, the Groups × Affective congruence interaction was not significant ($p > .05$) indicating that the pattern of responding to pairs with different affective congruence was similar for both the Ext and Extcon groups (i.e., there was no extinction). All other main effects and interactions failed to reach significance ($p > .05$, for all comparisons).

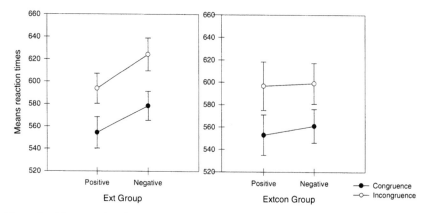

Figure 3. Mean reaction times of the groups (Ext, extinction; Extcon, extinction control) as a function of the Affective congruence (Congruent and Incongruent trials) and the Target valence (Positive and Negative). Error bars represent *SEM*s.

In summary, a different pattern of response to the Japanese letters used as CSs was observed after these stimuli were paired with the liked, neutral, and disliked affective US words. These acquired valences were not affected by an extinction procedure despite the number of extinction trials being twice as large as the number of conditioning trials. Moreover, different to Experiment 1, there was now no longer any sign of extinction on ER3. This finding allows one to question an interpretation in terms of a slower extinction rate because of the partial schedule used during the acquisition phase. In addition, this latter effect can also be disregarded as an effect of demand characteristic since, after extinction, the evaluative effect was still observed in the affective priming task, which is insensitive to demand effects.

Awareness data

Data from awareness questionnaire were similar to those of Experiment 1. All participants correctly recognised the specific US which had been paired with each of the Japanese letters used as CSs.

GENERAL DISCUSSION

The results of the present experiments show that EC effects can be demonstrated in a between-subjects design (Experiment 1), and that this conditioning is resistant to extinction (Experiment 1 and Experiment 2).

As we mentioned above, although evaluative conditioning effects have been widely demonstrated, Field and Davey (1997, 1999) argued that these effects at least in the picture-picture paradigm, might reflect an experimental bias induced by the CS and US assignment procedure and by the lack of a between-subjects control. Taking into account these critiques, CSs and USs were selected before the beginning of the experiments and CSs were randomly assigned to USs. Also, independent between-subject control groups were used in addition to the standard within-subject control condition. Having thus ruled out the potential artefact identified by Field and Davey (1999), and as no conditioning-like effects were observed in the control group, it is possible to suggest that the EC effects obtained in these experiments reflect learning of evaluative CS-US associations and therefore also that the resistance to extinction observed can not be criticised on the basis of these experimental biases. This is the first successful demonstration of this kind. Other studies exist that have demonstrated EC using a between-subject design, but these studies have used other paradigms and only one affective condition (negative or positive) was used to compare with the neutral condition (e.g., Hammerl & Grabitz, 2000; Stuart, Shimp, & Engle, 1987).

Of crucial importance, the present study points to the hypothesis that EC is resistant to extinction. In the standard preparatory Pavlovian conditioning pre-parations, a few CS-only trials are usually sufficient to cause a diminution or elimination of the previously acquired conditioning response (e.g., Biferno &

Dawson, 1977; Öhman, 1983). By contrast, our data show that the magnitude of the evaluative conditioning effect in the Ext group after 14- or 24-CS only presentations (Experiment 1 and Experiment 2, respectively) did not differ from the evaluative conditioning effect obtained in the conditioning group (Extcon group) indexed by both verbal ratings (Experiment 1 and Experiment 2) and postextinction affective priming effects (Experiment 2). Although we are aware that the partial schedule used during the acquisition phase could favour a retarded extinction rate, the fact that not the slightest reduction in the magnitude of EC effect was observed even when the number of extinction trials were almost twice as large as the number of acquisition trials, could hardly be explained exclusively by this factor (e.g., Alloy & Tabachnik, 1984; Mackintosh, 1974; Rescorla, 1999). Moreover, this effect also cannot be disregarded as an effect of demand characteristics. Even though the stability of the evaluative conditioning effect as indexed by the verbal ratings could have been determined in part by demands effect, the fact that the results obtained in the postextinction affective priming task, which is much less probably to be biased by demand effects, were in the same direction as the postextinction verbal ratings allow us to suggest that the resistance to extinction observed here is not entirely based on this bias (e.g., De Houwer et al., 2001; Hermans, Crombez, Vansteenwegen, Baeyens & Eelen, 2002a, 2002b). Although we are aware that it cannot be guaranteed that the reaction times obtained in the affective priming task were influenced purely by associative factors, because the BSB group was dropped from Experiment 2, we consider that it is difficult to consider that the differential effect observed between affectively congruent and incongruent trials is due exclusively to factors different from the affective value acquired by the Japanese letters during the acquisition phase.

Recent findings from research on causal judgements could provide an alternative account for our findings. From this research field it has been demonstrated that participants tend to integrate the information received through the acquisition and extinction phases if judgements are requested at the end of training, whereas trial-by-trial judgements are more sensitive to recency effects (e.g., Collins & Shanks, 2002; Matute, Vegas, & De Marez, 2002). As suggested by these findings, one might argue that the resistance to extinction observed in our experiments is the result of participants integrating the information of the two phases (acquisition and extinction) and rating the CSs on the basis of this integrated information at the postextinction phase. However, if this is true the pattern of results obtained in our study should have been different. First, the affective judgements obtained after the extinction phase (CS was followed by US in 28% of the trials in Experiment 1 and in 20% of the trials in Experiment 2) should be lower than those obtained after the acquisition phase (CS was followed by US in 70% of trials for both experiments). Second, the affective post-extinction judgement of the Extcon group which at the extinction phase was not presented with new information about the CSs (hence CS was followed by

US in 70% of trials) should be greater than those obtained after extinction in the Ext group.

Our results are in line with results from other studies that have shown that evaluative conditioning is resistant to extinction (e.g., Baeyens et al., 1995a, 1998, 1989; De Houwer et al., 2000). Although we are aware that this is a null finding that does not allow us to draw strong conclusions, taken together, the results of the present experiments seem to support the proposal that EC effects depend on the formation of a kind of CS-US association that is not sensitive to extinction. Although it has been suggested that this difference between EC and preparatory Pavlovian conditioning could be due to interparadigm differences— with regard to for example, number of CSs and USs, or the opacity of the design—(see De Houwer et al., 2001, for a review), the fact that the present experiments replicate this result in a procedure that uses only one CS-US pairing per condition and in which participants were aware of the contingencies seems to indicate that these differences with respect to extinction sensitivity can not be attributed or at least not exclusively to procedural elements. As such, these results apparently point to the kind of dissociation suggested by Baeyens et al. (1995a) between two associative learning systems that imply different levels of processing of the affective value and the predictive value of the stimuli. According to this view, EC, different from most Pavlovian paradigms, depends on the operation of a referential learning system which is only sensitive to co-ocurrences between neutral and valenced events and therefore it generates nonpredictive relations between events. As such, the resistance to extinction observed in our study would reflect that the associative structure underlying EC is not predictive but merely referential. From this account it would naturally follow that the acquired affective values were not affected by the changes in the predictive values of the CSs involved in the extinction procedure.

Finally, and from a more general point of view, the resistance to extinction of acquired affective valence has interesting implications for several areas of applied psychology. For example, clinical observations suggest that some affective emotional disorders might be partially based on acquired affective evaluations (e.g., some phobias, preferences, or compulsive behavioural disorders). Therefore, one would predict that interventions, such as exposure to the problematic stimuli, would not be able to alter or reduce the evaluative component of these disorders. Possibly a combination of exposure and other techniques, such as counterconditioning, might constitute a more effective therapy (e.g., Baeyens et al., 1989).

REFERENCES

Alloy, L. B., & Tabachnik, N. (1984). Assessment of covariation by humans and animals: The joint influence of prior expectations and current situational information. *Psychological Review, 91,* 112–149.

Baeyens, F., Crombez, G., De Houwer, J., & Eelen, P. (1996a). No evidence for modulation of evaluative flavor-flavor associations in humans. *Learning and Motivation, 27*, 200–241.

Baeyens, F., Crombez, G., Hendrickx, H., & Eelen, P. (1995b). Parameters of human evaluative flavor-flavor conditioning. *Learning and Motivation, 26*, 141–160.

Baeyens, F., Crombez, G., Van den Bergh, O., & Eelen, P. (1988). Once in contact always in contact: Evaluative conditioning is resistant to extinction. *Advances in Behaviour Research and Therapy, 10*, 179–199.

Baeyens, F., & De Houwer, J. (1995). Evaluative conditioning is a qualitatively distinct form of classical conditioning: a reply to Davey (1994). *Behaviour Research and Therapy, 33*, 825–831.

Baeyens, F., De Houwer, J., Vansteenwegen, D., & Eelen, P. (1998). Evaluative conditioning is a form of associative learning: On the artifactual nature of Field and Davey's (1997) artifactual account of evaluative learning. *Learning and Motivation, 29*, 461–474.

Baeyens, F., Eelen, P. & Crombez, G. (1995a). Pavlovian associations are forever: On classical conditioning and extinction. *Journal of Psychophysiology, 9*, 127–141.

Baeyens, F., Eelen, P., & Van den Bergh, O. (1990a). Contingency awareness in evaluative conditioning: A case for unaware affective-evaluative learning. *Cognition and Emotion, 4*, 3–18.

Baeyens, F., Eelen, P., Van den Bergh, O., & Crombez, G. (1989). Acquired affective-evaluative value: Conservative but not unchangeable. *Behaviour Research and Therapy, 27*, 279–287.

Baeyens, F., Eelen, P., Van den Bergh, O., & Crombez, G. (1990b). Flavour-flavour and colour-flavour conditioning in humans. *Learning and Motivation, 21*, 434–455.

Baeyens, F., Eelen, P., Van den Bergh, O., & Crombez, G. (1992). The content of learning in human evaluative conditioning: Acquired valence is sensitive to US-Revaluation. *Learning and Motivation, 23*, 200–224.

Baeyens, F., Kaes, B., Eelen, P., & Silverans, P. (1996b). Observational evaluative conditioning of embedded stimulus element. *European Journal of Social Psychology, 26*, 15–28.

Baeyens, F., Vanhouche, W., Crombez, G., & Eelen, P. (2004). *Human evaluative flavor-flavor conditioning is not sensitive to post-acquisition US-inflation.* Manuscript submitted for publication.

Baeyens, F., Vansteenwegen, D., De Houwer, J., & Crombez, G. (1996c). Observational conditioning of food valence in humans. *Appetite, 27*, 235–250.

Baeyens, F., Wrzesniewski, A., De Houwer, J., & Eelen, P. (1996d). Toilet rooms, body massages, and smells: Two field studies on human evaluative odor conditioning. *Current Psychology: Development Learning Personality Social, 15*, 77–96.

Bargh, J. A., Chaiken, S., Raymond, P., & Hymes, C. (1996). The automatic evaluation effect: Unconditional automatic activation with a pronunciation task. *Journal of Experimental Social Psychology, 32*, 104–128.

Biferno, M. A., & Dawson, M. E. (1977). The onset of contingency awareness and electrodermal classical conditioning: An analysis of temporal relationships during acquisition and extinction. *Psychophysiology, 14*, 164–171.

Bouton, M. E. (1993). Context, time, and memory retrieval in the interference paradigms of Pavlovian learning. *Psychological Bulletin, 114*, 80–99.

Bouton, M. E. (1994). Conditioning, remembering, and forgetting. *Journal of Experimental Psychology: Animal Behavior Processes, 20*, 219–231.

Bouton, M. E., & King, D. A. (1983). Contextual control of the extinction of conditioned fear: Test for the associative value of the context. *Journal of Experimental Psychology: Animal Behavior Processes, 9*, 248–265.

Bouton, M. E., & Swartzentruber, D. (1989). Slow reacquisition following extinction: Context, encoding, and retrieval mechanisms. *Journal of Experimental Psychology: Animal Behavior Processes, 15*, 43–53.

Bower, G. H. (1991). Mood congruity of social judgements. In J. P. Forgas (Ed.), *Emotion and social judgements* (pp. 31–54). Oxford, UK: Pergamon.

Collins, D. J., & Shanks, D. R. (2002). Momentary and integrative response strategies in causal judgment. *Memory and Cognition, 30,* 1138–1147.

Davey, G. C. L. (1994). Is evaluative conditioning a qualitatively distinct form of classical conditioning?. *Behaviour Research and Therapy, 3,* 291–299.

De Houwer, J., Baeyens, F. & Eelen, P. (1994). Verbal evaluative conditioning with undetected US presentations. *Behaviour Research and Therapy, 32,* 629–633.

De Houwer, J., Baeyens, F., Vansteenwegen, D., & Eelen, P. (2000). Evaluative conditioning in the picture-picture paradigm with random assignment of CSs to USs. *Journal of Experimental Psychology. Animal Behavior Processes, 26,* 237–242.

De Houwer, J., Hermans, D., & Eelen, P. (1998). Affective and identity priming with episodically associated stimuli. *Cognition and Emotion, 12,* 145–169.

De Houwer, J., Hermans, D., Rothermund, K., & Wentura, D. (2002). Affective priming of semantic categorisation responses. *Cognition and Emotion, 16,* 643–666.

De Houwer, J., Thomas, S., & Baeyens, F. (2001). Associative learning of likes and dislikes: A review of 25 years of research on human evaluative conditioning. *Psychological Bulletin, 127,* 853–869.

Díaz, E. (2000). *Efectos de extinción sobre el condicionamiento evaluativo con diseños entre-grupos.* [Extinction effects on the evaluative conditioning with between-subjects groups]. Unpublished doctoral dissertation, University of Seville, Seville.

Díaz, E., & De la Casa, L. G. (2002). Latent inhibition in human affective learning. *Emotion, 2,* 242–250.

Fazio, R. H. (2001). On the automatic activation of associated evaluations: An overview. *Cognition and Emotion, 15,* 115–142.

Fazio, R. H., Jackson, J. R., Dunton, B. C., & Williams, C. J. (1995). Variability of automatic activation as an unobtrusive measure of racial attitudes: A bona fide pipeline?. *Journal of Personality and Social Psychology, 69,* 1013–1027.

Field, A. P., & Davey, G. C. L. (1997). Conceptual conditioning: Evidence for an artifactual account of evaluative learning. *Learning and Motivation, 25,* 446–464.

Field, A. P., & Davey, G. C. L. (1998). Evaluative conditioning: Arti-fact or –fiction?- A reply to Baeyens, De Houwer, Vansteenwegen, and Eelen (1998). *Learning and Motivation, 29,* 475–491.

Field, A. P., & Davey, G. C. L. (1999). Reevaluating evaluative conditioning: A nonassociative explanation of conditioning effects in the visual evaluative conditioning paradigm. *Journal of Experimental Psychology: Animal Behavior Processes, 25,* 211–224.

Fulcher, E. P., & Cocks, R. P. (1997). Dissociative storage systems in human evaluative conditioning. *Behavioural Research and Therapy, 35,* 1–10.

Goddard, M. J. (1999). Renewal to the signal value of an unconditioned stimulus. *Learning and Motivation, 30,* 15–34.

Hammerl, M., & Grabitz, H.-J. (1996). Human evaluative conditioning without experiencing a valued event. *Learning and Motivation, 27,* 278–293.

Hammerl, M., & Grabitz, H.-J. (2000). Affective-evaluative learning in humans: A form of associative learning or only an artifact? *Learning and Motivation, 31,* 345–363.

Hermans, D., Baeyens, F., & Eelen, P. (1998a). Odours and affective processing context for word evaluation: A case of cross-modal affective priming. *Cognition and Emotion, 12,* 601–613.

Hermans, D., Crombez, G., Vansteenwegen, D., Baeyens, F., & Eelen, P. (2002a) Expectancy-learning and evaluative Learning in human classical conditioning: differential effects of extinction. In S. P. Shohov (Ed.), *Advances in Psychology Research* (Vol. 12, pp. 17–41). New York: Nova Science Publishers.

Hermans, D., & De Houwer, J. (1994). Affective and subjective familiarity ratings of 740 Dutch words. *Psychologica Belgica, 34,* 115–139.

Hermans, D., De Houwer, J., & Eelen, P. (1994). The affective priming effect: automatic activation of evaluative information in memory. *Cognition and Emotion, 8,* 515–533.

Hermans, D., De Houwer, J., & Eelen, P. (2001). A time course analysis of the affective priming effect. *Cognition and Emotion, 15,* 143–165.

Hermans, D., Van den Broeck, A., & Eelen, P. (1998b). Affective priming using a colour-naming task: A test of an affective-motivational account of affective priming effects. *Zeitschrift für Experimentelle Psychologie, 45,* 136–148.

Hermans, D., Vansteenwegen, D., Crombez, G., Baeyens, F., & Eelen, P. (2002b). Expectancy-learning and evaluative learning in human classical conditioning: Affective priming as an indirect and unobtrusive measure of conditioned stimulus valence. *Behaviour Research and Therapy, 40,* 217–234.

Levey, A. B., & Martin, I. (1975). Classical conditioning of human "evaluative" responses. *Behaviour Research and Therapy, 13,* 221–226.

Lipp, O. V., Oughton, N., & LeLievre, J. (2003). Evaluative learning in human Pavlovian conditioning: Extinct, but still there? *Learning and Motivation, 34,* 219–239.

Mackintosh, N. J. (1974). *The psychology of animal learning.* London: Academic Press.

Martin, I., & Levey, A. B. (1987). Learning what will happen next: Conditioning, evaluations & cognitive processes. In G. Davey (Ed.), *Cognitive processes and Pavlovian conditioning in humans* (pp. 57–81). Chichester, UK: Wiley.

Matute, H., Vegas, S., & De Marez, P. J. (2002). Flexible use of recent information in causal and predictive judgments. *Journal of Experimental Psychology. Learning, Memory, and Cognition, 28,* 714–725.

Nakajima, S., Tanaka, S., Urushihara, K., & Imada, H. (2000). Renewal of extinguished lever-press responses upon return to the training context. *Learning and Motivation, 31,* 416–431.

Öhman, A. (1983). The orienting response during Pavlovian conditioning. In D. Siddle (Ed.), *Orienting and habituation: Perspectives in human research* (pp. 315–363). New York: Wiley.

Rescorla, R. A. (1999). Within-subject partial reinforcement extinction effect in autoshaping. *Quarterly Journal of Experimental Psychology, 52B,* 75–87.

Rescorla, R. A., & Wagner, A. R. (1972). A theory of Pavlovian conditioning: Variations in the effectiveness of reinforcement and nonreinforcement. In A. Black & W. F. Prokasy (Eds.), *Classical conditioning II.* New York: Appleton-Century-Crofts.

Shanks, D. R., & Dickinson, A. (1990). Contingency Awareness in evaluative conditioning: A comment on Baeyens, Eelen, and Van den Bergh. *Cognition and Emotion, 4,* 19–30.

Shimp, T. A., Stuart, E. W., & Engle, R. W. (1991). A program of classical conditioning experiments testing variations in the conditioned stimulus and context. *Journal of Consumer Research, 18,* 1–12.

Stuart, E. W., Shimp, T. A., & Engle, R. W. (1987). Classical conditioning of consumer attitudes: Four experiments in an advertising context. *Journal of Consumer Research, 14,* 334–349.

Thomas, B. L., Larsen, N., & Ayres, J. J. B. (2003). Role of context similarity in ABA, ABC, and AAB renewal paradigms: Implications for theories of renewal and for treating humans phobias. *Learning and Motivation, 34,* 410–436.

Vansteenwegen, D., Crombez, G., Baeyens, F., & Eelen, P. (1998). Extinction in fear conditioning: Effects on startle modulation and evaluative self-reports. *Psychophysiology, 35,* 729–736.

Wagner, A. R. (1979). Habituation and memory. In A. Dickinson & R. A. Boakes (Eds.), *Mechanisms of learning and motivation.* Hillsdale, NJ: Erlbaum.

Wagner, R. A. (1981). SOP: A model of automatic memory processing in animal behavior. In N. Spear & G. Miller (Eds.), *Information processing in animals: Memory mechanisms.* Hillsdale, NJ: Erlbaum.

Wentura, D. (1999). Activation and inhibition of affective information: Evidence for negative priming in the evaluation task. *Cognition and Emotion, 13,* 65–91.

Zellner, D. A., Rozin, P., Aron, M., & Kulish, C. (1983). Conditioned enhancement of human's liking for flavor by pairing with sweetness. *Learning and Motivation, 14,* 338–350.

COGNITION AND EMOTION
2005, 19 (2), 269–282

No support for dual process accounts of human affective learning in simple Pavlovian conditioning

Ottmar V. Lipp and Helena M. Purkis

University of Queensland, Australia

Dual process accounts of affective learning state that the learning of likes and dislikes reflects a learning mechanism that is distinct from the one reflected in expectancy learning, the learning of signal relationships, and has different empirical characteristics. Affective learning, for example, is said not to be affected by: (a) extinction training; (b) occasion setting; (c) cue competition; and (d) awareness of the CS-US contingencies. These predictions were tested in a series of experiments that employed simple Pavlovian conditioning procedures. Neutral visual pictures of geometric shapes, or tactile conditional stimuli (CS) were paired with aversive electrotactile unconditional stimuli (US). Dependent measures were physiological (skin conductance, blink startle modulation) or verbal (US expectancy, on-line and off-line ratings of CS pleasantness). Different combinations of these dependent measures were employed across different experiments in an attempt to assess affective and expectancy learning simultaneously. Changes in CS pleasantness as indexed by ratings or blink startle modulation were readily observed. However, contrary to the predictions from dual-process accounts, results indicated that acquired CS unpleasantness is subject to extinction, occasion setting, cue competition, and not found in absence of CS-US contingency awareness.

The learning of likes and dislikes, affective learning,[1] is a pervasive phenomenon that occurs whenever we encounter novel stimuli or emotionally salient events. Given its ubiquity, it is surprising that the mechanisms that underlie

---

[1] Throughout the manuscript we use the term "affective learning" as a descriptive term to address the empirical phenomenon that the valence of a CS can change if it is paired with an emotionally salient US. The term "evaluative learning" was avoided as it is often used synonymously with a dual process account of affective learning.

Correspondence should be addressed to Dr Ottmar V. Lipp, School of Psychology, The University of Queensland, QLD, 4072, Australia; e-mail: O.Lipp@psy.uq.edu.au

Grants A10027218, A79600404, and 00/ARCS051 from the Australian Research Council supported this work. The present paper was conceptualised during two Special Interest Meetings on the Acquisition of Affect sponsored by the Fund for Scientific Research–Flanders (Belgium), LeLignely, Belgium, May 2001 and 2002.

http://www.tandf.co.uk/journals/pp/02699931.html   DOI:10.1080/02699930441000319

affective learning are a matter of debate, and have been so for at least the last 25 years (for reviews, see Baeyens, Eelen, & Crombez, 1995; De Houwer, Thomas, & Baeyens, 2001). Although there is some agreement that associative processes are involved in the acquisition and modulation of likes and dislikes (but see Davey, 1994, for a nonassociative account of affective learning), the nature of these processes is a matter of controversy. De Houwer et al. (2001) review three different theoretical approaches to accommodate affective learning. A conceptual-categorical account, which is non-associative, proposes that pairing of a neutral conditional stimulus (CS) and a valenced unconditional stimulus (US) enhances the emphasis on CS elements that match the valence of the US resulting in a change in CS evaluation. The holistic account holds that as a result of CS-US pairings characteristics of the US, such as valence are transferred to the CS. In this account, affective learning is seen as a fundamental component of Pavlovian conditioning and does not require the postulation of a distinct learning system. Third, the referential account, which is based on the work of Baeyens and colleagues (see for example, Baeyens et al., 1995), stipulates that affective learning is mediated by a learning mechanism that is qualitatively distinct from the one that mediates expectancy learning (i.e., the Pavlovian learning of signal relationships). This dual-process account holds that affective learning is affected by the contiguity between CS and US, and not by the contingency. Thus, it is said that affective learning is not subject to contingency manipulations or to cue competition. Moreover, as affective learning supposedly reflects a rather primitive form of learning it is said not to be affected by occasion setting or to require awareness of the CS-US contingencies. Finally, and important for some applied contexts, affective learning has been proposed not to extinguish across repeated presentations of the CSs after acquisition. On the other hand, the necessity for a dual-process account has been questioned (Field & Davey, 1997; Purkis & Lipp, 2001; Shanks & Dickinson, 1990). Proponents of a single-process account entertain that expectancy and affective learning are manifestations of a single learning mechanism and that they may differ quantitatively (i.e., in the number of trials required for a particular effect), but not qualitatively in their response to experimental manipulations.

The question of whether the acquisition of likes and dislikes is mediated by a specific learning mechanism or by one that follows the established rules of associative learning (Pearce & Bouton, 2001) is of interest beyond the discussion of theories of learning. The design of behaviourally based interventions dedicated to the reduction of dislikes in their most extreme form, apprehensions, fears, and phobias, is one of the applications of theories of associative learning. If it were correct that acquired dislikes are not subject to extinction, then exposure-based therapies would be limited in their ability to change the affective component of learned psychopathologies like anxiety disorders. Thus, an understanding of the basic mechanisms that mediate affective learning is essential for the design of effective therapies. However, the design of procedures for behaviour modification is not the only context that will benefit from a delineation of the mechanisms that mediate affective leaning. Recent research in applied social psychology has considered affective learning as one mechanism critically involved in the acquisition of prejudice (Olson & Fazio, 2001) and a better understanding of affective learning may aid the prevention or even correction of prejudice.

The claim that affective and expectancy learning reflect two distinct learning mechanisms is supported by findings obtained mainly in two paradigms, the picture-picture and the flavour-flavour paradigms (for a review see De Houwer et al., 2001, but see also Rozin, Wrzesniewski, & Byrnes, 1998). In the picture-picture paradigm, participants are trained with paired presentations of pictures depicting, for instance, human faces that differ in valence as established in a prior rating session. During training, neutral pictures (CSs) are followed by pictures that are either positive, negative, or neutral (USs). The emotionally salient pictures serve to change the valence of the neutral pictures that precede them, whereas the neutral USs provide a control baseline against which valence changes can be assessed while controlling for mere exposure effects. Usually, several picture pairs are presented per valence category, with pictures appearing briefly (e.g., for 2 second) at a rather rapid rate (e.g., 10 per minute). The acquisition training may be followed by an extinction session in which the CS pictures are presented alone without the USs. Changes in CS valence that were acquired during training are assessed in a postexperimental rating session in which participants rate the stimulus materials for a second time. Estimates of contingency knowledge are also based on postexperimental assessments. The flavour-flavour paradigm follows the same basic design as the picture-picture paradigm, but flavours are used as CSs and USs instead of pictures.

The picture-picture and flavour-flavour paradigms have been criticised for a number of reasons. Many of the earlier criticisms that related to shortcomings in experimental control (see Field & Davey, 1997; Shanks & Dickinson, 1990) have been addressed in subsequent studies that replicated the basic findings in more tightly controlled experiments. More recently, however, the paradigms have been criticised on conceptual grounds in that they do not permit the concurrent assessment of affective and expectancy learning and assess valence changes or contingency awareness after, rather than during learning. Shanks and St. John (1994) provided a review of the potential shortcomings of posttraining assessment in the context of measuring contingency awareness, which are relevant to the discussion of posttraining assessment of CS valence. In brief, Shanks and St. John advocate that changes in contingency awareness be assessed during acquisition training rather than after the completion of the experiment to minimise the potential of interference. Thus, it may be that participants who were contingency aware during acquisition do not reveal this on a postexperimental questionnaire due to effects of other experimental stages, such as extinction or simple forgetting. Similarly, valence ratings collected after completion of extinction training may, for instance, reflect renewal rather than the effects of extinction training (Bouton, 1994).

Research conducted in our laboratory over the last 10 years has attempted to address these issues in a simple Pavlovian conditioning paradigm as employed in studies of human autonomic conditioning (Öhman, Hamm, & Hugdahl, 2000). This paradigm employs only a small number of CSs, usually pictures of simple geometric shapes, and a single, electrotactile US. In the prototypical differential conditioning procedure, presentations of one CS, the CS+, are followed by the US whereas a second CS, the CS−, is presented alone. As the interstimulus interval between CS and US onset is usually long (e.g., 8 s) dependent measures, such as physiological responses (electrodermal or cardio-vascular responses and blink startle modulation) or ratings of valence or US expectancy can be collected during training without contamination by the unconditional response, which otherwise might interfere with measures of conditional responding. In addition, the measures taken in the picture-picture paradigms, pre-postratings or affective priming can be obtained (see Hermans, Vansteenwegen, Crombez, Baeyens, & Eelen, 2002). The simple conditioning procedure described here has the advantage of permitting the assessment of affective and expectancy learning at the time of training. Moreover, it is closely related to the procedures used in conditioning studies in rodents which permit investigations of the neural bases of the acquisition of affect. Recent functional magnetic resonance imaging (fMRI) studies of simple conditioning in humans (e.g., Büchel, Dolan, Armony, & Friston, 1999) have confirmed the conditioned fear circuitry identified in rodents (LeDoux, 2000).

Using this simple Pavlovian conditioning procedure, our laboratory has provided evidence that is inconsistent with a dual-process approach to affective learning. Moreover, we have provided some suggestions for alternative inter-pretations of the findings in support of dual-process accounts of affective learning. However, before presenting the results of studies that tested predictions from dual-process accounts relating to extinction, occasion setting, cue com-petition, and the role of contingency awareness, it has to be acknowledged that the simple conditioning procedure has also attracted some criticism that requires consideration.

Potential problems of the simple conditioning paradigm

The stimulus contingencies used in the simple conditioning paradigm are rather transparent. Thus, it has been argued that the procedure due to its simplicity favours a problem-solving approach to learning which may bias the outcomes in favour of expectancy learning and may prevent the observation of affective learning. This criticism is well founded in that the contingencies used in the simple procedure are indeed easy to learn, although not all participants succeed.

However, one may argue that the stimulus elements involved in the simple procedure are a better representation of real-life events, at least as concerns the acquisition of fears and phobias, than is, the quick presentation of a large number of relatively unobtrusive stimuli as employed in the picture-picture paradigm. The parallels found between the results from animal fear learning and from human simple conditioning seem to attest to its external validity in the realm of psychopathology.

A second criticism is concerned with the validity of one of the dependent measures used in the simple conditioning paradigm to index acquired stimulus valence, blink startle modulation (Vansteenwegen, Crombez, Baeyens, & Eelen, 1998). The fact that acquired fear elicited by a CS can potentiate startle reflexes has been well documented in animal research to the extent that the neural circuits mediating the effect have been identified (LeDoux, 2000). In humans, a similar relationship between stimulus valence and startle elicited during stimulus presentations, the affect-startle effect, has been shown repeatedly in a picture viewing paradigm (Lang, Bradley, & Cuthbert, 1990). In this paradigm, startle reflexes elicited during unpleasant pictures are larger than startles during neutral pictures whereas startles elicited during pleasant pictures are reduced. This observation has prompted the use of startle modulation as an index of acquired valence that can be obtained online during Pavlovian training in human conditioning procedures. Hamm and Vaitl (1996), for instance, found larger startles during CS+ than during CS− in anticipation of an aversive electrotactile US, but not in anticipation of a nonaversive tactile stimulus that served as the imperative stimulus of a reaction time task. Vansteenwegen et al. (1998) replicated this finding and also showed that the enhanced startle modulation during CS+ was lost during extinction training. However, verbal ratings of the CSs taken after extinction training continued to show a difference in valence between CS+ and CS−.

The validity of startle as an index of acquired CS valence has been questioned for two reasons. First, Cuthbert, Bradley, and Lang (1996) have shown that the affect-startle effect holds only for pictures that are highly arousing, but not for pictures that are rated as low in arousal. This prompted Vansteenwegen et al. to suggest that the loss of differential startle modulation seen during extinction may reflect a loss of stimulus arousal rather than of valence, a suggestion supported by the observation that differential electrodermal responses, an index of arousal, were lost across extinction as well. This suggestion seems, however, inconsistent with reports by Bradley, Lang, and Cuthbert (1993) who found that habituation across repeated presentations of pictures that differed in valence reduced arousal as indexed by electrodermal responses, but not the affect-startle effect. Thus, differential startle facilitation was observed even though the arousal of the pictures had been reduced.

A second set of findings that questions whether blink startle modulation during a Pavlovian conditioning procedure reflects CS valence comes from studies that found facilitated startle in anticipation of a nonaversive US (Lipp, 2002; Lipp, Siddle, & Dall, 2003b) and from studies that found facilitated startle in anticipation of a pleasant picture US (Lipp, Cox, & Siddle, 2001a; Sabatinelli, Bradley, & Lang, 2001). These studies clearly indicate that blink startle modulation in anticipation of a Pavlovian US may not reflect a change in CS valence, but changes in CS arousal or attentional processes. In absence of further research that clarifies the roles of attentional and emotional processes during aversive, nonaversive, and appetitive human Pavlovian conditioning, blink startle modulation results have to be interpreted with care and in the context of other measures.

However, as stated above, studies that failed to confirm predictions from dual-process accounts of affective learning in simple conditioning procedures did not rely solely on evidence from startle modulation. Their contribution is considerable even if one was to disregard the evidence from blink startle modulation entirely.

Even if care in the interpretation of startle modulation findings during simple conditioning is required, it seems unreasonable to dismiss these studies as irrelevant because most did not solely rely on evidence from blink startle modulation. They also provided evidence inconsistent with the predictions of dual-process accounts of affective learning using the very index on which they were founded, verbal ratings of stimulus valence. Moreover, such an all out dismissal ignores that there is indisputable evidence that blink startle modulation is sensitive to stimulus valence in human (Lang et al., 1990) and nonhuman animals (LeDoux, 2000). Thus, we will include startle modulation results in our subsequent discussion, but refer to the potential problem they may pose.

Evidence for extinction of affective learning

If we have to question the validity of evidence from studies that found extinction of affective learning using blink startle modulation as a concurrent measure of changes in CS valence (Lipp, Baker-Tweney, & Siddle, 1997; Vansteenwegen et al., 1998), is there other evidence to suggest that extinction of acquired valence indeed occurs? Moreover, does this evidence suggest an alternative explanation for the observation that affective learning, as assessed in postexperimental questionnaires, appears resistant to extinction? Lipp, Oughton, and LeLievre (2003a) reported two experiments that can answer both questions. Reports of resistance to extinction are derived from studies that employed verbal ratings of CS valence collected in testing sessions before and after Pavlovian training (e.g., Baeyens, Crombez, Van den Bergh, & Eelen, 1988). Rather than relying on pre/ post measures, it would be preferable to assess stimulus valence during Pavlovian acquisition and extinction to avoid the influence of multiple sources of interference that plague posttraining ratings (for a review see, Shanks & St. John, 1994), and more specifically, to avoid the effects of renewal (Bouton,

1994). Renewal refers to the well-documented fact that previously extinguished conditional responses can recur if, after extinction, the CS is presented in a context that differs from the context of extinction. In order to avoid these potential confounds, Lipp et al. (2003a) asked participants to use a dial and pointer continuously throughout acquisition and extinction training in order to indicate the valence of CS+ and CS −. In addition, they collected ratings of CS valence before and after training in a manner similar to that of previous studies. Replicating previous results of resistance to extinction, Lipp et al. found that in the posttest, the CS+ was rated as more unpleasant than the CS − even after 16 presentations of each CS without the US. The on-line ratings of CS valence collected throughout conditioning training, however, tell a different story. Both experiments confirmed that rated unpleasantness of the CS+ that was acquired during acquisition was lost during extinction. The CS+ was rated as neutrally at the end of extinction as it was rated at the beginning of acquisition. This finding is in stark contrast to the pattern of results suggested by the pre/post ratings whereby the CS+ was rated as more unpleasant after training.

In their second experiment, Lipp et al. (2003a) also collected dial and pointer ratings during the pre- and posttest sessions. A comparison between the ratings taken during the last presentations of CS+ and CS − during extinction and during the posttest indicated the re-emergence of differential ratings in the posttest that had been absent during extinction. This finding strongly suggests that previous reports of resistance to extinction derived from posttests may not provide a true reflection of CS valence at the end of extinction training. Rather, they may reflect the effects of renewal. Alternatively, the discrepancy between on-line and postratings may reflect that the participants employed different strategies to derive CS valence during extinction and in the posttest. Collins and Shanks (2002) have shown in a study of causal learning that causality judgements taken at different stages during training reflected the momentary predictive status of the CSs whereas ratings taken during a posttest reflected an average predictiveness taken across the entire training session. It will be up to future studies to decide whether the mode of assessment has similar effects on the manner in which valence judgements are generated.

Evidence for occasion setting in affective learning

Occasion setting refers to the observation that the effectiveness of a target CS to elicit a conditional response may depend on the presence of an occasion setter that signals whether the CS will be followed by the US (Holland, 1992). In feature positive occasion setting, conditional responses are displayed in presence of the occasion setter, but not in its absence whereas in feature negative occasion setting the presence of the occasion setter results in the absence of conditional responses. According to dual-process theory, affective learning will occur whenever the CS is paired with an affectively salient US. Thus, affective learning should not be affected by occasion setting.

Baeyens, Crombez, Hermans, and Eelen (1996) and Baeyens, Hendrickx, Crombez, and Hermans (1998) failed to find evidence for occasion setting in a flavour-flavour paradigm, a result consistent with the predictions of dual-process theory. Hardwick and Lipp (2000), on the other hand, found evidence for occasion setting in a sequential feature positive discrimination procedure. Participants were presented with a picture of a circle (or a tactile stimulus) as the target CS. This CS was followed by an aversive electrotactile stimulus if preceded by a tactile (or visual) occasion setter, but not if presented alone. Blink startle during the target stimulus, elicited by an acoustic probe stimulus, was larger after the presentation of the occasion setter than in its absence. Thus, there seems to be evidence for occasion setting from a simple conditioning procedure, although one may argue that this conclusion is tentative, as Hardwick and Lipp relied on blink startle modulation as the sole measure of affective learning.

Evidence for cue competition in affective learning

In cue competition procedures, such as in blocking, several CSs are presented in a compound followed by the US. Associative learning to a particular cue in these situations is critically dependent on the extent to which the US is already predicted by the other cues presented simultaneously. If the US is well predicted already, the novel CS will not come to elicit a conditional response. If affective learning occurs whenever the CS is paired with an affectively salient US then it should not be subject to cue competition.

To date, there are no published studies that investigated cue competition in the picture-picture or flavour-flavour paradigms. Lipp, Neumann, and Mason (2001b) investigated cue competition in affective and expectancy learning in a simple conditioning procedure in a series of three experiments. Participants were presented with a training sequence that consisted of two acquisition phases and a test phase presented without interruptions. In the first acquisition phase, two CSs were trained in a differential conditioning procedure (A-US, B-). In the subsequent compound conditioning phase, two CSs were added, one in a AC compound on AC-US trials and one in a BD compound on BD-US trials (A-US, B-, AC-US, BD-US). Conditioning to novel CS C should be blocked as it is presented with an excitatory CS, A, whereas conditioning to novel CS D should be facilitated as it is presented with an inhibitory CS, B, and followed by the US. Cue competition was assessed during a subsequent test phase in which CSs C and D were presented alone. Geometric shapes served as CSs and the US was an aversive electrotactile stimulus. Dependent measures in Experiment 1 were skin conductance and on-line ratings of US expectancy. In experiments 2 and 3, pre/postratings of CS valence and blink startle measurement were added, respectively. All experiments provided clear evidence for cue competition in expectancy learning as indicated by larger electrodermal responses and increased US expectancy during stimulus D than during C in the test stage. Moreover, stimulus D was rated as more unpleasant than was stimulus C in the post test, although both stimuli had been paired with the US equally often. These results are not consistent with the prediction that affective learning is not subject to cue competition.

Evidence that affective learning is affected by contingency awareness

Whether human learning can occur in absence of knowledge of the stimulus contingencies has been the matter of a very long standing debate not only in the context of affective learning (Lovibond & Shanks, 2002; Shanks & St. John, 1994). Reports that the acquisition of CS (un-) pleasantness can occur in absence of explicit contingency knowledge have been provided in a number of procedures from a number of different laboratories (e.g., Baeyens, Eelen, & Van den Bergh, 1990). However, these reports share in common the weakness that they rely on measures of contingency awareness that are collected after the completion of learning, and not during learning. As summarised by Shanks and St. John (1994) this procedure is problematic in that a lack of reported awareness at the time of test may not necessarily imply that there was no awareness during training. Thus, it would be preferable to assess awareness of the CS-US relationship during training rather than afterwards.

Purkis and Lipp (2001) employed such an assessment of awareness in a modified simple conditioning procedure using an on-line measure of US expectancy as a trial by trial index of contingency awareness. Asking participants to report their expectancy of the US is likely to direct their attention to the CS-US contingency and in doing so, facilitate learning. In order to prevent facilitated acquisition, Purkis and Lipp inserted the CS-US contingency in a more complex stimulus sequence that was presented to participants in the guise of a visual memory task. Participants were presented repeatedly with two randomised sequences of four different colour pictures that were preceded by a slide depicting a permutation of the numbers 1 to 4 and followed by a tone. Participants were instructed to memorise the pictures and, upon presentation of the tone, to list them in the sequence as shown on the numbers slide. Correct performance of this quite challenging task could earn a small monetary reward for the participants. Moreover, participants were told that an electrotactile stimulus would be presented from time to time, and that they were to indicate whether they expected this stimulus using a dial and pointer device. The electrotactile stimulus was presented at the offset of one of the pictures in one sequence, but not in the other. In addition to the dial and pointer ratings of US expectancy, pre- and postratings of CS valence, postexperimental assessment of

CS-US contingency knowledge, electrodermal responses, and blink startle modulation served as dependent measures.

Sixteen of the 36 participants who provided complete data sets were classified as non-verbalisers based on the data derived from the on-line expectancy dial. These participants failed to indicate increased US expectancy during the CS+ on two consecutive trials throughout the total of 32 picture sequences. The postexperimental assessment of contingency knowledge confirmed this classification. The data were subjected to two sets of analyses, one comparing the responses of verbalisers with those of nonverbalisers, and the second comparing the responses of verbalisers before and after they had reached the criterion of verbalisation. The latter was based on the on-line expectancy dial data. The between subject analysis found evidence for expectancy and affective learning as indicated by electrodermal responses, blink modulation, and verbal ratings of CS valence in verbalisers, but not in nonverbalisers. The within-subject analysis found evidence for differential electrodermal responses and blink modulation in verbalisers after they had reached the criterion of contingency awareness, but not before. These results, obtained in a tightly controlled procedure that avoided the shortcomings of previous studies, clearly indicate that contingency knowledge is a prerequisite for expectancy and affective learning.

SUMMARY AND CONCLUSIONS

The present review of studies of affective learning in simple conditioning procedures failed to provide any support for the proposal that affective and expectancy learning reflect qualitatively distinct learning mechanisms. Rather, the studies indicate clearly that affective learning, like expectancy learning, is subject to extinction, occasion setting, and cue competition, and is not found in absence of contingency awareness. This conclusion holds even if blink startle modulation results are disregarded and only results from verbal ratings are considered. Moreover, it should be noted that there are further studies that failed to support predictions from dual process accounts (e.g., Lipp, Neumann, & Siddle, 1998). What are the implications of these results for dual process accounts of affective learning?

One way of dealing with these findings is to point to the obvious procedural differences between simple conditioning and, for instance, the picture-picture paradigm and to dismiss the results reviewed above as not relevant. After all, the procedures differ in the number of different stimuli used, the nature of the stimulus materials, and the conditioning paradigm. This approach, however, seems too simplistic if the intention is to develop a general theory of human affective learning that has scope across procedures. Thus, a more detailed analysis of the implications of the present findings seems required. A second approach is to reconsider the dichotomous nature of single and dual-process accounts as described here and to ask whether changes in CS valence may be mediated by different systems. LeDoux's (1995) analysis of the neurobiology of rodent fear learning seems to suggest such an approach (Baeyens et al., 1995).

LeDoux (1995) reviewed evidence that the lateral nucleus of the amygdala is the point of convergence for inputs from a number of cortical structures that mediate fear learning in different experimental paradigms. Simple single cue conditioning in a delay design, for instance, can be mediated by the sensory thalamus in absence of any cortical involvement. Discrimination learning on the other hand, requires input from neocortical regions whereas context-dependent learning or learning in trace conditioning paradigms in mediated via the hippocampus. In a similar fashion, one could argue that affective learning in some paradigms, especially those that require more complex discriminations, will be mediated by higher cortical structures and also share the characteristics of a more complex learning process. On the other hand, affective learning in a more simple learning procedure may be mediated on the subcortical level, perhaps on the level of the sensory thalamus (see Baeyens et al., 1995). This approach has some merit, but seems to fall short for one reason. The differential delay conditioning procedure used in the simple conditioning studies in our laboratory are more basic than the ones employed, for instance, in the picture-picture paradigm that employs multiple CSs and USs in a trace conditioning procedure. Thus, if anything it would be reasonable to assume that a more basic learning mechanism should become apparent in the simple conditioning paradigms used in the studies reviewed above.

The affective learning results obtained in simple human conditioning procedures as reviewed above seem at odds with those described in the literature. These discrepancies in findings can be seen as an advantage rather than a disadvantage in that they permit an analysis of the boundary conditions that determine which pattern of results will emerge given a particular conditioning procedure and a particular experimental manipulation. Such research can also address some of the problems that have emerged from previous research and which seem to limit the conclusions that can be drawn from some of the studies currently available in the literature.

The finding of extinction of affective learning using on-line measures of CS valence and the two alternative explanations for the apparent lack of extinction in previous studies that employed only postextinction tests questions the internal validity of those studies. These findings require further investigation of the claims that affective learning does not extinguish. This can be done by integrating the on-line measure or repeated assessments of CS valence in a picture-picture or flavour-flavour procedure. For applied contexts, the finding that affective learning is subject to extinction is reassuring. It seems to confirm the validity of extinction-based interventions such as exposure. On the other hand, the suggestions that dislikes that have been reduced during extinction may be subject to renewal is a reason for concern in that it suggests the necessity of pre-empting context effects when designing behavioural interventions. Renewal has been discussed as a source for relapse as observed after therapeutic interventions, behaviour-based or otherwise (Bouton, 2000). If, on the other hand, the findings of different response strategies during causal learning reported by Colins and Shanks (2002) extend to affective learning, the manner in which long-term therapeutic effects are assessed may require reconsideration. The fact that most follow-up assessments of therapeutic effects rely on verbal report data not unlike those collected in postexperimental test sessions suggests that these follow-ups may underestimate the actual effectiveness of therapeutic interventions.

The findings of occasion setting, cue competition, and necessity for contingency awareness for affective learning in the simple conditioning procedure are also of interest for the delineation of boundary conditions. Although one may want to dismiss the finding of occasion setting in affective learning as it is based on evidence from blink startle modulation only, this does not seem wise as it is only a question of time until experiments that employ other measures, such as on-line ratings, are conducted. Moreover, this argument is not relevant for the reports of cue competition and of the effects of contingency knowledge in affective learning. Both findings require an extension to other affective learning paradigms. The assessment of contingency awareness in affective learning needs to include on-line measures of US expectancy as postexperimental assessments are not sufficient to assess contingency knowledge at the time of training. The masking task used by Purkis and Lipp (2001) may provide some suggestions as to the design of such studies if there is concern about the effects of on-line measures on learning. A detailed analysis of the role of contingency awareness in affective learning can also inform research in other areas in which claims about learning in absence of contingency awareness have emerged recently. These areas include learning with fear-relevant stimuli (Öhman & Soares, 1998), rule learning in decision-making tasks (Tranel, Bechara, & Damasio, 2000), or the acquisition of simple motor responses (Clark, Manns, & Squire, 2002). In the absence of better controlled studies the conclusion drawn by Lovibond and Shanks (2002) in a recent review that there is no convincing evidence for human associative learning in absence of contingency knowledge still stands.

In summary, the present review of studies that employed a simple conditioning design did not provide any support for the contention that human affective learning is mediated by a distinct learning mechanism. At a minimum, this implies that affective learning within the simple conditioning design does not fall within the scope of the recently proposed dual-process accounts of affective learning. Such a conclusion would severely limit their importance excluding, for instance, Pavlovian fear learning. At a maximum, the present findings question the validity of dual-process accounts. The findings from the simple conditioning studies are inconsistent with all predictions from dual-process accounts that were tested. Moreover, they provided alternative interpretations for some of the key findings in support of dual-process theories, like for instance that claim that affective learning is resistant to extinction. On the other hand, the evidence presented in support of dual-process theory cannot be discounted. Thus, a more detailed analysis of affective learning across experimental paradigms seems required before a final conclusion can be drawn. The evidence presented above seems to suggest, however, that the necessity for a dual-process account of affective learning should be carefully considered.

REFERENCES

Baeyens, F., Crombez, G., Hermans, D., & Eelen, P. (1996). No evidence for color-modulation of evaluative flavor-flavor associations in humans. *Learning and Motivation*, *27*, 200–241.

Baeyens, F., Crombez, G., Van den Bergh, O., & Eelen, P. (1988). Once in contact always in contact: Evaluative conditioning is resistant to extinction. *Advances in Behaviour Research and Therapy*, *10*, 179–199.

Baeyens, F., Eelen, P., & Crombez, G. (1995). Pavlovian associations are forever: On classical conditioning and extinction. *Journal of Psychophysiology*, *9*, 127–141.

Baeyens, F., Eelen, P., & Van den Bergh, O. (1990). Contingency awareness in evaluative conditioning: A case for unaware affective-evaluative learning. *Cognition and Emotion*, *4*, 3–18.

Baeyens, F., Hendrickx, H., Crombez, G., & Hermans, D. (1998). Neither extended sequential nor simultaneous feature positive training result in modulation of evaluative flavor-flavor conditioning in humans. *Appetite*, *31*, 185–204.

Bouton, M. E. (1994). Context, ambiguity, and classical conditioning. *Current Directions in Psychological Science*, *3*, 49–53.

Bouton, M. E. (2000). A learning theory perspective on lapse, relapse, and the maintenance of behavior change. *Health Psychology*, *19*, 57–63.

Bradley, M. M., Lang, P. J., & Cuthbert, B. N. (1993). Emotion, novelty and the startle reflex: Habituation in humans. *Behavioral Neuroscience*, *107*, 970–980.

Büchel, C., Dolan, R. J., Armony, J. L., & Friston, K. J. (1999). Amygdala-Hippocampal involvement in human aversive trace conditioning revealed through event-related functional magnetic resonance imaging. *Journal of Neuroscience*, *19*, 10869–10876.

Clark, R. E., Manns, J. R., & Squire, L. R. (2002). Classical conditioning, awareness, and brain systems. *Trends in Cognitive Sciences*, *6*, 524–531.

Collins, D. J., & Shanks, D. R. (2002). Momentary and integrative response strategies in causal judgment. *Memory and Cognition*, *30*, 1138–1147.

Cuthbert, B. N., Bradley, M. M., & Lang, P. J. (1996). Probing picture perception: Activation and emotion. *Psychophysiology*, *33*, 103–112.

Davey, G. C. L. (1994). Defining the important questions to ask about evaluative conditioning: A reply to Martin and Levey (1994). *Behaviour Research and Therapy*, *32*, 307–310.

De Houwer, J., Thomas, S., & Baeyens, F. (2001). Associative learning of likes and dislikes: A review of 25 years of research on human evaluative conditioning. *Psychological Bulletin*, *127*, 852–869.

Field, A. P., & Davey, G. C. L. (1997). Conceptual conditioning: Evidence for an artifactual account of evaluative learning. *Learning and Motivation*, *28*, 446–464.

Hamm, A. O., & Vaitl, D. (1996). Affective learning: awareness and aversion. *Psychophysiology*, *33*, 698–710.

Hardwick, S., & Lipp, O. V. (2000). Modulation of affective learning: An occasion for evaluative conditioning. *Learning and Motivation*, *31*, 251–271.

Hermans, D., Vansteenwegen, D., Crombez, G., Baeyens, F., & Eelen, P. (2002). Expectancy-learning and evaluative learning in human classical conditioning: affective priming as an indirect and unobtrusive measure of conditioned stimulus valence. *Behaviour Research and Therapy*, *40*, 217–234.

Holland, P. C. (1992). Occasion setting in Pavlovian conditioning. In D. L. Medin (Ed.), *The psychology of learning and motivation* (pp. 69–125). New York: Academic Press.

Lang, P. J., Bradley, M. M., & Cuthbert, B. N. (1990). Emotion, attention and the startle reflex. *Psychological Review, 97*, 377–395.

LeDoux, J. E. (1995). In search of an emotional system in the brain: Leaping from fear to emotion and consciousness. In M. S. Gazzaniga (Ed.), *The cognitive neurosciences* (pp. 1049–1061). Cambridge, MA: MIT Press.

LeDoux, J. E. (2000). Emotion circuits in the brain. *Annual Review of Neuroscience, 23*, 155–184.

Lipp, O. V. (2002). Anticipation of a non-aversive reaction time task facilitates the blink startle reflex. *Biological Psychology, 59*, 147–162.

Lipp, O. V., Baker-Tweney, S. R., & Siddle, D. A. T. (1997). The extinction of conditioned fear potentiated startle in humans [Abstract]. *Psychophysiology, 34*, S58.

Lipp, O. V., Cox, D., & Siddle, D. A. T. (2001a). Blink startle modulation during anticipation of pleasant and unpleasant stimuli. *Journal of Psychophysiology, 15*, 155–162.

Lipp, O. V., Neumann, D. L., & Mason, V. (2001b). Stimulus competition in affective and relational learning. *Learning and Motivation, 32*, 306–331.

Lipp, O. V., Neumann, D. L., & Siddle, D. A. T. (1998). Evaluative learning is sensitive to manipulations of the CS-US contingency [Abstract]. *Australian Journal of Psychology, 50*, S56–S57.

Lipp, O. V., Oughton, N., & LeLievre, J. (2003a). Evaluative learning in human Pavlovian conditioning: Extinct, but still there? *Learning and Motivation, 34*, 219–239.

Lipp, O. V., Siddle, D. A. T., & Dall, P. J. (2003b). The effects of unconditional stimulus valence and conditioning paradigm on verbal, skeleto-motor, and autonomic indices of human Pavlovian conditioning. *Learning and Motivation, 34*, 32–51.

Lovibond, P. F., & Shanks, D. R. (2002). The role of awareness in Pavlovian conditioning: Empirical evidence and theoretical implications. *Journal of Experimental Psychology. Animal Behavior Processes, 28*, 3–26.

Öhman, A., Hamm, A. O., & Hugdahl, K. (2000). Cognition and the autonomic nervous system: Orienting, anticipation, and conditioning. In J. T. Cacioppo, L. G. Tassinary, G. G. Berntson (Eds.), *Handbook of psychophysiology* (pp. 533–575). New York: Cambridge University Press.

Öhman, A., & Soares, J.J.F. (1998). Emotional conditioning to masked stimuli: Expectancies for aversive outcomes following nonrecognized fear-relevant stimuli. *Journal of Experimental Psychology: General, 127*, 69–82.

Olson, M.A., & Fazio, R.H. (2001). Implicit attitude formation through classical conditioning. *Psychological Science, 12*, 413–417.

Pearce, J. M., & Bouton, M. E. (2001). Theories of associative learning in animals. *Annual Review of Psychology, 52*, 111–139.

Purkis, H. M., & Lipp, O. V. (2001). Does affective learning exist in the absence of contingency awareness? *Learning and Motivation, 32*, 84–99.

Rozin, P., Wrzesniewski, A., & Byrnes, D. (1998). The elusiveness of evaluative conditioning. *Learning and Motivation, 29*, 397–415.

Sabatinelli, D., Bradley, M. M., & Lang, P. J. (2001). Affective startle modulation in anticipation and perception. *Psychophysiology, 38*, 719–722.

Shanks, D. R., & Dickinson, A. (1990). Contingency awareness in evaluative conditioning: A comment on Baeyens, Eelen, and van den Bergh. *Cognition and Emotion, 4*, 19–30.

Shanks, D. R., & St. John, M. F. (1994). Characteristics of dissociable human learning systems. *Behavior and Brain Sciences, 17*, 367–447.

Tranel, D., Bechara, A., & Damasio, A. R. (2000). Decision making and the somatic marker hypothesis. In M. S. Gazzaniga (Ed.), *The new cognitive neurosciences* (pp. 1047–1061). Cambridge, MA: MIT Press.

Vansteenwegen, D., Crombez, G., Baeyens, F., & Eelen, P. (1998). Extinction in fear conditioning: Effects on startle modulation and evaluative self reports. *Psychophysiology, 35*, 729–736.

COGNITION AND EMOTION
2005, 19 (2), 283–306

Beyond evaluative conditioning?
Searching for associative transfer of nonevaluative
stimulus properties

Tom Meersmans

University of Leuven, Belgium

Jan De Houwer

Ghent University, Belgium

Frank Baeyens

University of Leuven, Belgium

Tom Randell

University of Southampton, UK

Paul Eelen

University of Leuven, Belgium

Evaluative conditioning refers to the changes in liking of an evaluatively neutral stimulus (the conditional stimulus or CS) as a result of merely pairing it with another, already liked or disliked stimulus (the unconditional stimulus or US). We examined whether other, non-evaluative stimulus properties of a US can also be associatively transferred to a CS. In a series of experiments, we tried to transfer perceptions of the gender of children and the gender of first names. We found evidence for the associative transfer of these properties but only when participants were aware of the contingencies.

What people like or dislike is in most cases based on individual experience rather than on the genetic makeup of that individual (Rozin & Millman, 1987). One of the mechanisms responsible for the development of likes and dislikes is

Correspondence should be addressed to Jan De Houwer, Department of Psychology, Ghent University, Henri Dunantlaan 2, B-9000 Ghent, Belgium; e-mail: Jan.DeHouwer@UGent.be

This research was supported by University of Leuven grant OT/99/11 to Paul Eelen and ESRC-ROPA grant R022250197 to Jan De Houwer and Steven Glautier. We thank Hilde Hendrickx, Michael Olson, Deb Vansteenwegen, and Eva Walther, for providing us with information about their unpublished studies concerning non-evaluative stimulus transfer.

http://www.tandf.co.uk/journals/pp/02699931.html   DOI:10.1080/02699930441000328

associative learning and was named evaluative conditioning (EC) by Martin and Levey (1978). EC refers to the changes in liking of a stimulus as a result of merely pairing it with another liked or disliked stimulus. For example, repeatedly pairing an affectively neutral picture (i.e., neither liked nor disliked) with a liked/disliked picture, will make that originally neutral picture more positive/ negative.

At a procedural level, EC can be regarded as a form of Pavlovian conditioning. In traditional Pavlovian conditioning or preparatory conditioning (PC), a biologically neutral stimulus (conditional stimulus or CS) is repeatedly paired with a biologically significant stimulus (unconditional stimulus or US), after which the originally neutral stimulus elicits preparatory behaviour (e.g., Pavlov, 1927). In EC, an affectively neutral stimulus (CS) is repeatedly paired with an affectively relevant (positive or negative) stimulus (US), after which the perceived valence of the originally neutral stimulus changes (e.g., Martin & Levey, 1978).

At the functional level, however, there appear to be differences between PC and EC (for an overview, see De Houwer, Thomas, & Baeyens, 2001). In contrast to PC, EC seems to be resistant to extinction: Repeated presentations of the CS by itself after conditioning do not make the CS neutral again (e.g., De Houwer, Baeyens, Vansteenwegen, & Eelen, 2000). Some evidence also suggests that EC is less sensitive to contingency awareness (e.g., Olson & Fazio, 2001), CS-US contingency (Baeyens, Hermans, & Eelen, 1993) and modulation (e.g., Baeyens, Hendrickx, Crombez, & Hermans, 1998a).

The apparent functional differences between EC and PC suggest that they depend on different processes. Baeyens and colleagues (Baeyens, Eelen, Crombez, & Van den Bergh, 1992; Baeyens, Eelen, & Crombez, 1995; Baeyens & De Houwer, 1995) argued that PC is a form of expectancy learning, while EC is a form of merely referential learning. The expectancy learning system is thought to be responsible for the detection of reliable predictors of (biologically) significant events with the purpose of preparing the organism as well as possible for the US. The CS leads to an expectation that the US will actually occur. This triggers a conditional response that is relatively costly for the organism. Because of this cost, the system responds only to reliable, nonredundant predictors. The referential learning system is less complex, using only information about the co-occurrences of stimuli. In this system, the CS also activates the US representation but not in such a way that the US is expected to occur here and now. The activation of the US representation changes only the perception of the CS: The activated US-valence is "misattributed" to the CS. As such, the cost of this system is relatively low, explaining why reliability and redundancy play a lesser roll than in expectancy learning. Importantly, if EC is caused by misattributing the US-valence to the CS, then maybe other properties of the US can also be misattributed to the CS.

There are also other reasons to assume that nonevaluative stimulus properties can transfer between associated stimuli. Davey (1994) proposed that EC effects are due to factors that influence the categorisation of stimuli. The essence of this account is that pairing a CS and a US makes salient the properties that the two stimuli have in common. For instance, pairing an evaluatively neutral CS (e.g., a picture of a man with brown eyes, long-shaped face, full lips, and long hair) and a liked US (e.g., a picture of a man with blue eyes, round shaped face, full lips, and long hair) could make salient the liked features of the CS (e.g., full lips, long hair). As a result, after the CS-US pairings, the CS will no longer be categorised as neutral but as positive. Field and Davey (1997) pointed out that such an account leads to the prediction that not only evaluative but also other properties can be transferred by pairing two stimuli. For instance, if one pairs the picture of a baby whose gender is difficult to determine with certainty (e.g., because he/she possesses both male- and female-like features) with the picture of a baby who is clearly perceived as male, this could increase the salience of the male-like features of the first baby and thus increase the likelihood that the baby is categorised as male (but see Baeyens, De Houwer, Vansteenwegen, & Eelen, 1998b, for a critical evaluation of the categorisation model and the evidence that Field and Davey, 1997, obtained for this model). Note that according to the categorisation model of Davey (1994), associative transfer of stimulus properties should be especially likely to occur if the paired stimuli share certain features and thus are similar to a certain extent.

Based on both the model of Baeyens and colleagues (Baeyens et al., 1992, 1995; Baeyens & De Houwer, 1995) and the model of Davey (1994; Field & Davey, 1997) one can thus predict that nonevaluative stimulus properties can transfer from one stimulus to another by pairing these stimuli. The central question of this paper is whether associative transfer of nonevaluative stimulus properties can indeed be found. We deemed it important to examine this question not only because it could inform us about the validity of a prediction of models of EC, but also because associative transfer of nonevaluative stimulus properties could be an important mechanism that determines the meaning and perception of various kinds of stimuli. If we are able to find a procedure that results in reliable associative transfer of nonevaluative stimulus properties, this would allow us to examine the functional characteristics of this potentially important learning mechanism. Experiments by Stevenson and colleagues suggest that it is indeed possible to associatively transfer non-evaluative properties. In a series of studies, they repeatedly paired a flavour (CS) with a sweet or sour taste (US). Afterwards, participants experienced the smell of the flavour as being sweeter or sourer, respectively. This shift appeared to be resistant to extinction (Stevenson, Boakes, & Wilson, 2000), independent of contingency awareness (Stevenson, Boakes, & Prescott, 1998), and independent of changes in liking of the CS. These results could be seen as evidence for associative transfer of nonevaluative stimulus properties: by repeatedly pairing a CS-flavour with a US-taste, the "sweetness/sourness" of the US transfers to the CS. But Stevenson et al. (2000) suggest that flavour-taste transfer might be something unique: Flavours and tastes are sensory very close to one another and might be stored holistically. This nonevaluative transfer might therefore be unique for olfactory-gustatory stimuli.

Other studies that show associative transfer of non-evaluative stimulus properties are sparse. Some evidence comes from the marketing literature. In one experiment, Kim, Allen, and Kardes (1996) paired a picture of a pizza box of a nonexisting brand (CS) with a picture of a fast racing car (US). This crucial pair was presented 10 times intermixed with 30 fillers. When asked how long it would take to deliver pizzas from this brand, participants assessed the pizza brand to deliver faster than in a control-condition in which all the pictures were presented at random (and the crucial CS was never paired with the US). This could be seen as transfer of the "speed" of the US (car) onto the CS (pizza brand). But one third of the participants were able to describe the research as some sort of associative learning study and might thus have been aware of the contingency. No subsequent analysis of the impact of contingency awareness on transfer was reported. In a second experiment, Kim et al. also succeeded in transferring the "softness" of a picture of kittens (US) onto a picture of a box of tissues (CS). In this experiment, no information about contingency awareness was given. Both experiments suggest associative transfer of nonevaluative stimulus properties, but it is unclear whether this effect depended on participants becoming aware of the contingencies. The issue of contingency awareness is, nonetheless, an important one. First, if associative transfer of nonevaluative stimulus properties indeed depends on contingency awareness, it would suggest that such transfer effects have different functional characteristics than EC that does not seem to depend on contingency awareness. Second, when participants are aware of the contingencies, they could intentionally use this knowledge to comply to what they think the experimenter wants them to do. That is, awareness of the contingencies renders it possible that transfer is due to demand effects rather than to a genuine change in the perception of the CSs. There is evidence that demand effects can indeed play a role in studies on EC (see Field, in press, for an overview).

To conclude, more research is needed before one can claim that associative transfer of nonevaluative stimulus properties is a general phenomenon. Most importantly, more evidence for associative transfer of nonevaluative stimulus properties with nongustatory stimuli is needed. The main aim of our research was to look for such evidence. In Experiments 1–6, we used a picture-picture paradigm to examine whether the gender of persons can be transferred associatively. In two subsequent studies, we examined the transfer of gender of first names onto Japanese characters. In order to obtain information about the possible role of contingency awareness and demand effects, we also assessed the degree to which participants were aware of the CS-US contingencies (all experiments except Experiment 2), used indirect measures of learning that are assumed to be less sensitive to demand effects (Experiments 2–5, 7, & 8), and/or assessed the extent to which participants consciously and deliberatively based their ratings on knowledge about the CS-US pairs (Experiments 7 and 8).

EXPERIMENTS 1–6

Stimulus valence, the property transferred in EC, is a basic and easily activated stimulus property (Zajonc, 1980) that might be very hard to rival in importance. In our experiments, we chose gender as the property that we wanted to transfer because intuitively we believed that gender is an important property of a person that might thus be more easy to transfer than other, less biologically important features. In Experiments 1–6, we tried to influence the gender-assessment of gender-ambiguous infants by repeatedly pairing them with pictures of clearly male or female infants. The procedure used in these experiments was conceptually similar to that of the picture-picture EC studies of Baeyens and colleagues (e.g., Baeyens et al., 1992). In most of these picture-picture studies, three types of CS-US pairs were presented: neutral-liked, neutral-disliked and neutral-neutral pairs. After repeated presentations of these pairs, the valence of the previously neutral CS-picture had shifted in the direction of the valence of the US with which it had been paired. We used a similar procedure but focused on the transfer of gender rather than on the transfer of valence. In four of the six experiments, we also used indirect gender measures in addition to a gender scale measure. It has been argued that such indirect measures are less susceptible to demand effects and thus provide a useful addition to traditional rating measures of learning (e.g., De Houwer, Hermans, & Eelen, 1998; Hermans, Vansteenwegen, Crombez, Baeyens, & Eelen, 2002a). Given that all experiments were highly similar, we will present them in one section. A summary of the most important procedural differences can be found in Table 1.

Method

Participants. A total of 31 (4 men and 27 women), 37 (7 men and 30 women), 26 (13 men and 13 women), and 44 (7 men, 37 women) first year psychology and economy students participated in exchange for course credits in Experiments 1, 4, 5, and 6, respectively. In Experiment 2, 32 (1 man and 31 women) second year psychology students participated in exchange for course credits. In Experiment 3, 40 students (6 men and 34 women) from various faculties at the University of Southampton were paid £6.00 for taking part.

Stimuli and measures. A colour photograph (face and chest) was taken from 58 different babies between 2 and 18 months old. They were digitised with a resolution of 300 × 333 pixels and were 9.50 cm high and 11 cm wide on the

TABLE 1
Most important procedural differences between Experiments 1–6

Experiment	Preview	Premeasure	CS selection	US selection	Dependent variables	Awareness test	Participants
1	no	no	Preselected	Preselected	Gender scale	yes	1st year economies
2	no	yes	Individually	Individually	Gender scale priming measure	no	2nd year psychology
3	no	yes	Individually	Individually	Gender scale priming measure	yes	Paid students
4	yes	yes	Individually	Individually	Gender scale name measure	yes	1st year psychology
5	yes	yes	Individually	Preselected	Gender scale name measure	yes	1st year economy
6	yes	yes	Preselected	Preselected	Gender scale	yes	1st year psychology

Note: Preview refers to whether participants saw each picture before the preacquisition scale measure. Premeasure refers to whether there was a preacquisition gender scale measure. CS and US selection refers to whether CSs or USs were selected for each individual separately on the basis of the preacquisition ratings or were selected on the basis of a pilot study.

screen. This set of pictures was used in all experiments except in Experiment 1 where we presented only CSs and USs that were selected on the basis of a small pilot study ($N = 20$). In the pilot study, participants assessed the gender of the 58 pictured children on a scale from very certainly a girl ($= 0$) to very certainly a boy ($= 100$). Twelve pictures received a mean rating between 45 and 55 (and SD < 25) on this scale. These 12 pictures were used as "gender-neutral" stimuli (CSs and US-neutrals). The 3 highest and 3 lowest scoring pictures scored above 90 and below 10 (and SDs < 15) respectively and were used as US-males and US-females, respectively.

In all experiments, the conditioning and rating phases were controlled by custom made Java-programs. Reaction-time tasks were implemented using the computer software Affect (Hermans, Clarysse, Baeyens, & Spruyt, 2002b). Experiment 3 was run in English, all others in Dutch.

We always used a scale from 0 (*very certainly a girl*) to 100 (*very certainly a boy*) to assess perceived gender. Because this scale measure is very transparent and thus vulnerable to demand effects, we also developed two more indirect gender measures. In Experiments 2 and 3, we used a gender priming procedure (similar to an affective priming procedure, e.g. Fazio, Sanbonmatsu, Powell, & Kardes, 1986) in which on each trial a target-picture was presented that showed either a male or female face. The task was to determine the gender of the target picture as quickly as possible by pressing a left or right key. A prime-picture was presented 300 ms before each target for a duration of 200 ms The target remained on the screen until the participant responded or 3000 ms elapsed. In a pilot study, we used pictures of adult men and women as primes and targets, and observed that when the gender of the prime and target picture were the same (congruent trials), participants were faster to classify the gender of the target picture than when the gender of prime and target differed (incongruent trials). This suggests that the priming procedure can be used to measure the gender-perception of the primes: If we find that, after a certain prime-picture, participants are faster to classify male targets than female targets whereas for another prime-picture the opposite effect is obtained, we can conclude that the first prime is seen as more male than the second prime (see De Houwer et al., 1998, and Hermans et al., 2002a, for studies in which priming tasks were also used as an indirect measure of associative learning). In Experiments 2 and 3, the nine CSs were used as primes and combined with four target pictures of adult men and four target pictures of adult women. Each prime-target pair was presented twice, resulting in 144 trials. Note that this priming task, and all other reaction time tasks described in this paper, started with practice trials with other, but similar stimuli. The stimuli used during practice were four pictures of babies that were rated as gender-ambiguous in a pilot study. The four practice pictures were not presented at any other time during the experiment.

The second indirect gender measure was a "name task" in which participants saw the picture of an infant (a CS) together with three male and three female first names. Participants in Experiments 4 and 5 were instructed to guess what the first name of the presented infant was. We predicted that infant pictures that were previously paired with a male US would be assigned a male name more often than infant pictures that were paired with a female US.

Procedure. The cover story for these experiments was that men look differently at children than women, and that we were testing if this would affect heartrate when looking at infant pictures. During acquisition, participants were instructed to just look at the pictures while a heartrate device (in reality a heartbeat measure device in which one can slide a finger) would do the rest.

In Experiments 1–5, nine pairs were generated for acquisition. Each CS was randomly assigned to a US with the restriction that there would be three neutral-male, three neutral-female, and three neutral-neutral pairs. In Experiments 2, 3, and 4, CSs and USs were selected on the basis of an individual preacquisition measure: Before acquisition, each participant was asked to rate all 58 pictures on the gender scale. On the basis of these ratings, we selected for each participant separately the most male, female, and neutral pictures. In Experiment 1, however, the CSs and USs were selected on the basis of the pilot study (described in the Measures section above) and participants did not rate pictures before acquisition. In Experiment 5, CSs were selected individually but USs were selected on the basis of the pilot study. In Experiment 6, finally, both CSs and USs were selected on the basis of the pilot study, but now only six CS-US pairs were constructed and presented (three neutral-male and three neutral-female). In all experiments, each CS-US pair was presented nine times during acquisition (1 s CS, 0 s ISI, 1 s US, 6 s ITI).

After acquisition, the postmeasures were administered. The gender scale measure was used in all six experiments. In Experiments 2 and 3, the gender-priming procedure was added. It was replaced by the naming measure in Experiments 4 and 5. All experiments except Experiment 2 ended with a contingency awareness test in which we checked to what extent participants recognised which CS had been paired with which US. On the left third of the screen, a CS picture was presented. On the right side, six US pictures were presented: two US-male, two US-female and two US-neutral pictures. One of the pictures on the right side was the US with which that CS had been paired during acquisition. Participants were asked to guess, for each CS, which US had been paired with that CS. At the bottom of the screen, they also indicated how sure they were of their choice, by checking one of the four check boxes that were labelled as ''very uncertain'', ''uncertain'', ''certain'', and ''very certain''. Note that in Experiment 6, all three US-male and three US-female USs were presented on the right side of the screen during all trials of the awareness test.

There were also other small differences between the experiments. The most important other differences include: the order of the measures, whether the neutral pictures were chosen because their ratings were close to the individual mean or close to the midpoint of the scale, and whether participants could scan through all pictures before rating them for the first time. Due to space limitations, we will not discuss these differences in detail (but see Table 1).

Results

Gender ratings. The mean gender rating of the CS-male (gender-neutral picture that was paired with a male one) and CS-female stimuli (gender-neutral picture that was paired with a female one) are presented in Table 2. The data were analysed using CS category (CS-male or CS-female) and moment (pre- or postacquisition) ANOVAs except in Experiment 1 where only CS category was used as a variable because there were no preacquisition ratings. In the six experiments, we obtained evidence for gender transfer only once, namely in Experiment 2 where participants after but not before acquisition rated the CS-males as more male than CS-females, $F(1, 31) = 8.24$, $p = .007$, $d = 0.52$. In the other experiments, we did not find a transfer-effect on the scale measure (all Fs < 1, ds between -0.03 and 0.19, see Table 2).

Indirect measures. In Experiments 2 and 3, the gender priming task was used as an demand-insensitive indirect measure of transfer. The mean reaction time on the congruent and incongruent trails of the priming phase are presented in Table 3. Congruent trials are trials on which the CS-category of the prime and

TABLE 2
Mean gender ratings as a function of rating moment and CS category and size of the transfer effect (Cohen's *d*) in Experiments 1–6

| Experiment | CS category | Pre-acquisition | | Post-acquisition | | d |
		M	SE	M	SE	
Experiment 1	CS-male	–		57.92	1.94	0.10
	Cs-female	–		56.58	2.62	
Experiment 2	CS-male	57.88	1.19	60.38	1.88	0.52
	CS-female	57.42	1.02	54.07	1.73	
Experiment 3	CS-male	50.04	0.63	51.46	1.91	0.14
	CS-female	51.01	0.68	50.08	2.14	
Experiment 4	CS-male	57.39	0.62	58.82	2.19	0.12
	CS-female	58.21	1.07	57.01	3.43	
Experiment 5	CS-male	50.46	0.57	51.88	2.13	−0.03
	CS-female	51.24	0.62	52.95	2.28	
Experiment 6	CS-male	57.73	2.42	56.92	2.12	0.19
	CS-female	58.29	1.98	54.03	1.66	

TABLE 3
Mean reaction times during the gender priming task as a function of
congruence and size of the transfer effect (Cohen's *d*) in Experiments 2 and 3

	Congruence				
	Congruent		Incongruent		
Experiment	M	SE	M	SE	d
Experiment 2	489	9	489	9	0.01
Experiment 3	525	12	525	11	0.04

gender of the target matched (i.e., male-male or female-female). On incongruent trials, the CS-category of the prime and the gender of the target differed (i.e., male-female or female-male). As was the case for each reaction time task described in this paper, reaction times on trials with an incorrect response were discarded and a cut-off procedure was used to remove outliers. For both congruent and incongruent trials, reaction times that fell above or below 2.5 standard deviations from a person's mean reaction time on those trials were discarded. ANOVAs with congruence as within-subjects variable failed to reveal a main effect of congruence ($Fs < 1$, ds of 0.01 and 0.04 in Experiments 2 and 3, respectively).

In Experiments 4 and 5, we used the gender name task as an indirect measure of transfer. The percentages of male names given to CS-male and CS-female pictures during the naming phase are presented in Table 4. ANOVAs with CS-category as the only within-subjects variable did not reveal a main effect of CS-category ($F(1, 36) = 2.42$, $p = .13$, $d = 0.26$, and $F < 1$, $d = 0.06$, in Experiments 4 and 5, respectively).

TABLE 4
Mean percentage of male names chosen during the name task as a
function of CS category and size of the transfer effect (Cohen's *d*) in
Experiments 4 and 5

	CS type				
	CS-male		CS-female		
Experiment	M	SE	M	SE	d
Experiment 4	60.37	5.82	52.32	6.08	0.26
Experiment 5	57.74	5.98	55.02	6.04	0.06

Awareness data. Category awareness was determined by counting the number of CSs for which the participant selected a US from the correct category (i.e., either the US with which the CS was paired or a different US from the same category). During the awareness test, participants selected a US from the correct category (US-male or US-female) for on average 43%, 37%, 53%, 44%, and 60% of all pairs in Experiments 1, 3, 4, 5, and 6, respectively. Note that no awareness test was administered in Experiment 2.

In order to investigate whether category awareness was related to the magnitude of the transfer effect, we calculated a transfer effect score in the following manner. First, we subtracted the preacquisition rating of each CS-male from the corresponding postacquisition rating. Next, we subtracted the postacquisition rating of each CS-female from the corresponding preacquisition rating. Finally, we took the sum of these two differences. A positive score thus reflects a transfer effect in the expected direction (i.e., a CS-male is perceived as more male after than before acquisition and/or a CS-female is perceived as more female after than before acquisition). The transfer effect score was calculated in a similar way in all experiments except Experiment 1. Because there was no preacquisition rating phase in that experiment, we first assigned a value of 50 (i.e., the midpoint of the scale) to all preacquisition ratings and then calculated the transfer effect score in the same way as in the other experiments. The correlation between the category awareness score and the transfer effect score was not significant in Experiment 1, $r = -.11$, Experiment 3, $r = -.02$, Experiment 4, $r = .27, p = .10$, and Experiment 5, $r = .26, p = .21$. In Experiment 6, however, the category awareness score was correlated significantly with the transfer effect score, $r = .38, p = .008$. To examine this relation further, we divided participants into those who did ($N = 12$) and did not ($N = 32$) perform above chance on the awareness test.[1] One sample t-tests revealed a significant positive transfer effect score for the category aware participants, $t(11) = 2.43, p = .03, d = 0.70$, but not for the other participants, $t(31) < 1, d = 0.01$.

We also examined whether the category awareness score was related to the transfer effect as indexed by the indirect gender measures. The gender priming transfer score was calculated by subtracting the reaction time on congruent trials from the reaction time on incongruent trials. The transfer score in the gender

---

[1] We assumed that each choice during the awareness test was independent of the other choices and that the number of correctly identified pairs was thus binomially distributed when participants guess. Given these assumptions, in Experiment 6, a participant was classified as category aware if at least five of the six selected USs were from the correct category. The probability of achieving this category awareness score by chance is smaller than .05. In the other experiments, the criterium for classifying a participant as category aware was a category awareness score of at least 6 out of 9 (Experiments 1–5) or at least 4 out of 4 (Experiments 7 and 8). Due to space limitations, we only report separate analyses for category aware and unaware participants if prior analyses show that category awareness was related to the transfer effect.

naming task corresponded to the number of male names given to CS-males minus the number of male names given to CS-females. The correlation between the category awareness score and the gender priming score was not significant in Experiment 3, $r = -.17$. There was a marginally significant positive correlation between category awareness and the gender naming task in Experiment 4, $r = .27$, $p = .10$, and Experiment 5, $r = .35$, $p = .08$.

Overall analysis. In order to increase the power of our statistical tests, we aggregated the gender rating data of all six experiments.[2] A one sample t-test on the transfer effect score of all 209 participants showed that the transfer effect was small but significant, $t(208) = 2.28$, $p = .02$, $d = 0.16$.

We also performed an analysis on all data except the data of Experiment 2 in which no awareness measure was present. This allowed us to examine the relation between category awareness and transfer. In this set of data, the transfer effect was no longer significant, $t(176) = 1.59$, $p = .11$, $d = .12$. The correlation between the category awareness score and the transfer effect score was, however, significant, $r = .15$, $p = .04$. For the 43 participants who were significantly category aware (see footnote 1), we found a significant positive transfer effect, $t(42) = 2.14$, $p = .04$, $d = 0.33$. For the remaining 134 participants, who were not significantly category aware, we found no trace of a transfer effect, $t < 1$, $d = 0.04$, even though this test had sufficient power (.82) to detect a small effect ($d = 0.25$).

Discussion

We found a significant transfer of gender effect in Experiment 2 and in the data of the category aware participants of Experiment 6. When we combined the gender rating data of all six experiments, the transfer effect was also significant. In the experiments where an awareness test was present (i.e., all experiments except Experiment 2), the transfer effect was positively correlated with category awareness and present only in the participants who were category aware. We can thus conclude that associative transfer of gender can be found. The data also showed that such transfer depends on conscious knowledge of the CS-US contingencies. One interpretation of this finding is that associative transfer of gender is functionally different from EC, which is often found to be independent

---

[2] We are aware of the fact that aggregating data of different experiments is not entirely appropriate when the design and procedure of the experiments is not identical. However, the different gender transfer experiments were similar to a large degree. Also, when the transfer scores of all 209 participants were analysed using an ANOVA with experiment (1–6) as between-subjects variable, the main effect of experiment was not significant, $F < 1$. Another option would have been to perform a meta-analysis on the data of the six experiments. However, such a meta-analysis would have too little power to reveal possible moderating variables and could yield an inflated estimate of significance of the overall transfer effect (e.g., Field, 2003).

of contingency awareness (see De Houwer et al., 2001, and Field, in press, for reviews). Another interpretation is that the observed transfer effects were due to demand compliance. When: (a) participants are aware of the fact that certain CSs are consistently paired with a male US-picture and other CSs with a female US-picture; and (b) are afterwards asked to rate how male or female the CS-pictures look, they might infer that the experimenter wants them to rate the CSs according to the gender of the US with which it was paired. According to this demand interpretation, the observed transfer effects were not due to an actual change in the gender-perception of the CSs but were merely due to the fact that participants intentionally wanted to conform with what they thought was expected of them (see Field, in press, and Page, 1969, for an in depth discussion of the problem of demand effects in EC research). The fact that no transfer effects were found on demand-insensitive indirect measures of valence is also consistent with this interpretation. Also note that Experiment 2, in which a significant transfer was found, was the only experiment in which second year psychology students took part. These students had participated in many previous experiments and might thus have been more apt to discover the purpose of the experiment.

EXPERIMENT 7

The demand-interpretation of the results of Experiments 1–6 implies that participants intentionally used their conscious knowledge of the CS-US con-tingencies as a basis for their gender ratings. Because we did not assess the strategies of the participants directly, we cannot be sure about whether the observed transfer effects were actually due to demand. We therefore decided to conduct a new experiment in which we did interview the participants about the strategies they used when giving their gender ratings. Because the size of the transfer effects in Experiments 1–6 tended to be small, we also used a new gender transfer procedure in which Japanese characters functioned as CSs and first names typical of men and women served as USs. This procedure was based on the studies of Diaz, Ruiz, and Baeyens (this issue) who found strong EC effects when Japanese symbols were paired with positive and negative words. A procedure that is able to show EC might enhance the possibility of finding nonevaluative stimulus transfer. Moreover, Japanese characters are also good neutral stimuli: They are (relatively) easy to discriminate and ambiguous concerning gender. Finally, in Experiment 7 we used a gender priming task rather than a gender name task as an indirect measure of gender transfer. In Experiments 4 and 5, the gender name effects tended to correlate with category awareness. This raises the pos-sibility that the gender name task might be somewhat susceptible to demand effects. Given that participants have ample time to deliberate about their responses in the gender name task, it is indeed possible that they take into account conscious knowledge of the CS-US contingencies.

Method

Participants.   A total of 26 (6 men and 20 women) first year psychology students participated in exchange for course credits.

Stimuli and measures.   Four clearly differentiable Japanese characters were used as CSs for acquisition, and two more were used as fillers for the gender priming. Four (two male and two female) first names were used as USs. Another eight first names (four male and four female) were used as targets for the gender priming measure.

As dependent variables, we used a gender scale and an associative gender name priming procedure to check for gender transfer. For the scale measure, participants were told that the Japanese characters (the CSs) referred to a Japanese first name and they were asked to guess on a scale from 0 (*female*) to 20 (*male*) what the gender of that Japanese name was. The priming measure was based on an existing gender name priming procedure. In previous gender priming experiments, participants responded faster when the gender of a target name, that had to be categorised as male or female, was the same as the gender of the preceding prime name (e.g., Draine & Greenwald, 1998). We replicated this gender priming effect in a pilot study. Therefore, if we find that after a certain prime, participants are faster to classify the target as a male than as a female name, and if for another prime name an opposite or smaller effect is obtained, we have evidence that the first prime is seen as more male than the second prime. In our experiments, the four CSs and two fillers were used as primes and combined with eight target first names, resulting in 48 trials per block. We used Affect software to implement the experiment (Hermans et al., 2002b).

Procedure.   The experiment was presented as a study on differences in psychophysiological reactions when seeing familiar and unfamiliar words and symbols. During acquisition, participants were instructed to just look at words and symbols while a heartrate device (see Experiments 1–6) would do the rest.

The experiment started with an acquisition phase in which each of the Japanese characters (CSs) was paired either with a male (US-male) or with a female name (US-female). Which CS was paired with which US was counter-balanced. Each of the four pairs was presented 10 times (1 s CS, 0 ISI, 1 s US, 2 s ITI).

In the gender priming procedure, the four CSs were used as primes together with the four male and four female target names. Participants were instructed to ignore the prime and to quickly categorise the target name as male or female by pressing one of two buttons on the keyboard. Each prime-target combination was presented three times, divided over three blocks that were separated by a short break. The primes were presented for 200 ms. The target appeared 50 ms after the offset of the prime (i.e., SOA = 250 ms). During the scale measure, participants were asked to indicate the gender of the CSs. The order of these two gender measures (priming measure first or scale measure first) was counterbalanced.

The experiment ended with a contingency awareness measure in which participants were asked to indicate for each character with what name it had been paired. We also assessed whether participants had consciously and intentionally used their knowledge of the CS-US pairs as a basis for their ratings of the CSs, as would be the case if they followed a demand strategy. We first asked whether the participant had noticed that each Japanese character had always been paired with one particular name. If they answered yes to this question, they were asked whether they had consciously used their knowledge about the gender of the name with which a character was paired to determine the male/female rating of the character. Participants who answered "yes" to the latter question were regarded as demand aware.

Results

Gender ratings. The mean gender ratings of the CS-male (neutral symbol that was paired with a male name) and CS-female (neutral symbol that was paired with a female name) stimuli are presented in Table 5. We found gender transfer on the gender scale: After acquisition, a CS-male was perceived as more male than a CS-female, $F(1, 25) = 38.76$, $p < .0001$, $d = 1.25$.

Gender priming data. The mean reaction times for the congruent and incongruent trials from the priming procedure are presented in Table 6. An ANOVA with congruence as a within-subjects variable revealed a main effect of congruence, $F(1, 25) = 4.60$, $p = .04$, $d = 0.43$.

TABLE 5

Mean gender ratings as a function of CS category and size of the transfer effect (Cohen's *d*) in Experiments 7 and 8

| | CS-type | | | | |
| | CS-male | | CS-female | | |
Experiment	M	SE	M	SE	d
Experiment 7	15.18	0.92	4.87	0.88	1.25
Experiment 8	12.63	0.81	8.34	0.71	0.64

TABLE 6
Mean reaction time during the gender priming task as a function of
congruence and size of the transfer effect (Cohen's *d*) in Experiments 7 and 8

	Congruence				
	Congruent		Incongruent		
Experiment	M	SE	M	SE	d
Experiment 7	519	12	527	13	0.43
Experiment 8	514	9	516	9	0.12

Awareness data.   During the awareness test, participants selected a US from the correct category for on average 88% of all pairs. There was a strong positive correlation between the category awareness score and the transfer effect score, $r = .69, p < .001$. Subsequent one sample t-tests revealed that the transfer effect was significant for those participants who selected a US from the correct category for all four pairs $(N = 20), t(19) = 9.07, p < .001, d = 2.03$, but not for the other participants $(N = 6), t < 1, d = -0.07$. The awareness questions also showed that 62% of participants claimed that in their assessment of the CS-gender, they consciously took into account the gender of the US with which it had been paired during acquisition. When we divided participants on the basis of their claim that they consciously used the CS-US pairings to make the ratings (demand aware vs. demand unaware), we found a marginally significant interaction effect, $F(1, 24) = 4.01, p = .06$. One-sample t-tests showed that the transfer effect was positive in the data of participants who were demand aware $(N = 16), t(15) = 6.69, p < .001, d = 1.67$, but also in the data of the other participants $(N = 9), t(9) = 2.37, p = .04, d = 0.75$. When we selected those participants who were both category aware and demand aware $(N = 14)$, the transfer effect was large, $t(13) = 8.22, p < .001, d = 2.20$. The transfer effect was more than three times as small but still significant in the other participants $(N = 12), t(11) = 2.38, p = .04, d = 0.65$.

We also investigated the relation between contingency awareness and the gender priming effect. The correlation between both was significant, $r = .42, p = .02$. Further analyses revealed that for the category aware participants, a significant priming effect was found, $F(1, 19) = 6.61, p = .02, d = 0.59$, but not for the other participants, $F(1, 5) < 1, d = -0.11$. To investigate the relation between demand awareness and the gender priming effect, we conducted an ANOVA with demand awareness (demand aware or unaware) and congruence (congruent or incongruent priming trials) as variables. The interaction between both variables was not significant, $F < 1$. Nevertheless, additional analyses revealed that the effect of congruence tended to be significant only in the data of the demand aware participants.

Discussion

We again found a significant transfer effect that depended on contingency awareness. This result emerged both in the scale measure and in the gender priming task. The transfer effect in the gender ratings also depended on whether participants said that they used their knowledge of the CS-US contingencies as a basis for their gender ratings. Although this suggests that the transfer effect in the gender rating data was due to demand compliance, there are two observation that raise doubts about this interpretation. First, a significant transfer effect was found in participants who claimed that they did not intentionally use conscious knowledge of the CS-US contingencies to make their gender ratings. One could, however, argue that our demand awareness questions were not sensitive enough. It is thus possible that the effect in the demand unaware group might have been due to a small number of demand aware participants that were not detected as being demand aware. Second, a significant transfer effect was found in the gender priming data. Given the automatic nature of the processes that underlie priming effects, it seems unlikely that this effect could have been due to demand compliance. On the other hand, the gender effect in the priming data was positively related to contingency awareness and found only for contingency aware participants. We will discuss this puzzling pattern of data in the general discussion. Before making more definite conclusions, we ran an additional experiment in order to investigate whether we could replicate the present effects.

EXPERIMENT 8

Method

Participants.   A total of 21 (7 men and 21 women) first year psychology students participated in exchange for course credits.

Stimuli, measures, and procedure.   The stimuli and measures were the same as in Experiment 8 except that eight other first names (four male and four female) were added as targets for the gender priming measure. These eight new first names replaced the original ones in the last two blocks of the priming procedure.

The procedure was identical to that of Experiment 7, with two exceptions. First, the gender priming task always came before the gender scale measure (this order was counterbalanced in Experiment 7). Second, while the first two priming blocks were the same as in Experiment 7, the next priming block was replaced by two blocks that used a second set of eight new target names. This adjustment was made to counter a possible floor effect due to repeated presentations of the targets.

Results

Gender rating data. The mean gender ratings of the CS-male (neutral symbol that was paired with a male name) and CS-female (neutral symbol that was paired with a female name) stimuli are presented in Table 5. We again found a transfer effect on the gender scale, $F(1, 27) = 10.94$, $p = .003$, $d = 0.64$.

Gender priming data. The mean reaction times for the congruent and incongruent trials from the priming task can be found in Table 6. An ANOVA with congruence as a within-subject variable failed to show an effect of congruence, $F(1, 27) = 1.12$, $d = 0.12$.

Awareness data. During the awareness test, participants selected a US from the correct category for on average 73% of all pairs. The category awareness score correlated with the transfer effect score, $r = .38$, $p = .05$, showing that the transfer effect increased in magnitude as category awareness increased. As in Experiment 7, the transfer effect was significant only for those participants who scored above chance on the awareness test ($N = 15$), $t(14) = 3.11$, $p = .008$, $d = 0.80$, but not for the other participants ($N = 13$), $t(12) = 1.60$, $p = .14$, $d = 0.44$. Only 39% of participants claimed that in their assessment of the CS-gender they took into account the gender of the US with which it had been paired during acquisition. If we divided participants based on this claim (demand aware vs. demand unaware), we found a significant transfer effect for the demand aware participants ($N = 11$), $t(10) = 6.12$, $p < .001$, $d = 1.94$, but not for the demand unaware participants ($N = 17$), $t < 1$, $d = 0.09$. An ANOVA with demand awareness and type of CS (CS-male or CS-female) showed that the interaction between both variables was significant, $F(1, 26) = 28.38$, $p < .0001$. A very strong transfer effect was found in those participants who were both category aware and demand aware ($N = 7$), $t(6) = 8.52$, $p < .001$, $d = 3.22$, but the effect was virtually absent in the data of the other participants ($N = 21$), $t(20) = 1.31$, $d = 0.28$.

Unlike to what was the case in Experiment 7, there was no correlation between category awareness and the transfer effect in the priming measure, $r = -.11$, $p = .58$. An ANOVA with demand awareness and congruence as variables did not reveal an interaction, $F(1, 26) = 1.27$.

Discussion

Once again we found a significant gender transfer effect in the data of the category aware participants but not in the data of the other participants. In contrast to the data of Experiment 7, no transfer effect was found in the gender priming task and in the gender rating data of the demand unaware participants. These findings suggest that the observed transfer effect was in a large part due to demand compliance.

One possible reason why we did not find a transfer effect in the priming task of Experiment 8 was that the priming task always came before the scale measure whereas in Experiment 7, the order of two measures was counterbalanced. This might be important because during the scale measure, participants were informed that the Japanese characters were actually first names of men or women. As a result of these instructions, participants might have consciously inferred that they learned the Dutch translation of the Japanese characters. Previous research has shown that such conscious inferences are sufficient to induce priming effects (e.g., De Houwer et al., 1998). It might thus be that the priming effect that was observed in Experiment 7 depended on the fact that participants made these conscious inferences during the scale measure. This argument is also in line with the observation that, in Experiment 7, the transfer effect in the priming data was correlated with category awareness. In Experiment 8, participants were not told that the Japanese characters were names of men or women until after the priming task (because the scale measure always came last). This could be the reason for why no priming effect was found in Experiment 8.

To investigate this issue further, we re-analysed the priming data of Experiment 7 to investigate whether the priming effect depended on the order of the tasks. Although the Order × Congruence ANOVA failed to show an interaction between both variables, $F < 1$, closer inspection of the data revealed that the priming effect (incongruent minus congruent) was smaller in magnitude when the priming task came first, $M = 6$ ms, than when the scale measure came first, $M = 14$ ms. Moreover, when only taking into account those participants who were classified as demand unaware and who completed the priming task before the scale measure ($N = 5$), a mean priming effect of only 3 ms was found. Although statistically not significant (probably because of low power), these data are consistent with the idea that transfer effects in the priming task might have depended on conscious inferences. More research is of course needed before definite conclusion can be drawn regarding this issue.

GENERAL DISCUSSION

The main aim of the present research was to find evidence for associative transfer of nonevaluative stimulus properties of visual stimuli. We indeed consistently found evidence for a transfer of gender, but only in participants who were aware of the CS-US contingencies. This raises two questions. First, how should we interpret the transfer effect in the category aware participants? Second, why did we fail to observe a significant effect in category unaware participants?

Regarding the first question, we see three possible interpretations. First, it is possible that an associative transfer of gender can occur only after participants have become aware of the crucial contingencies. This interpretation would imply that associative transfer of gender is functionally different from associative transfer of valence (i.e., EC) because the latter does not seem to depend on contingency awareness (e.g., De Houwer et al., 2001; Field, in press). Note that according to this interpretation, the observed gender transfer effects are genuine in the sense that they reflect an actual change in how participants perceive the gender of the CSs.

Second, the fact that the gender transfer effects depended on contingency awareness can be regarded as evidence for the fact that the transfer effects were not genuine but due to demand compliance. That is, participants could have intentionally used their conscious knowledge of the CS-US contingencies as a basis for rating the gender of the CSs *because they believed that this was what the experimenter wanted them to do*. In line with this interpretation: (a) we failed to find transfer effects in the demand-insensitive indirect measures of Experiments 2, 3, 4, 5, and 8; (b) we found that a substantial percentage of the participants in Experiments 7 and 8 claimed that they based their gender ratings on conscious knowledge of the CS-US contingencies; (c) the transfer effect in the rating data of Experiments 7 and 8 depended on demand awareness; and (d) no transfer effect was found in the demand unaware participants of Experiment 8. On the other hand, a significant transfer effect was found in the rating data of the demand unaware participants of Experiment 7 and in the demand-insensitive gender priming task of Experiment 7. The latter result is particularly problematic because it is difficult to see how participants could strategically control the outcome of the priming measure in order to comply with perceived demand characteristics.

There is also a third interpretation of the finding that gender transfer effects depended on contingency awareness. De Houwer, Baeyens, and Field (this issue) pointed out that EC effects can be based both on justified and unjustified preferences. Justified preferences are those for which participants can give valid reasons. For instance, participants might dislike a certain CS because they learnt that the CS is a reliable signal for an upcoming aversive US (e.g., an electric shock). Such a justified dislike is based on an intentional use of conscious knowledge about the CS-US contingency. But unlike to what is the case with demand compliance, conscious knowledge is not used to comply to the perceived wishes of the experimenter. Rather, it is used to form a genuine personal opinion about the nature of the CS. The gender transfer effects that we observed in the present experiments might have arisen in a similar manner. When asked to rate the gender of the CSs, participants might have believed that the CS-US pairings provided valid information about the gender of the CSs. For instance, in Experiments 7 and 8, they might have believed that the US-names provided a translation of the Japanese characters. As a result, conscious knowledge of the CS-US contingencies could have provided a basis to form a personal opinion about the gender of the CSs. This interpretation of the data is compatible with the fact that transfer effects depended on contingency awareness and on whether participants claimed that they used their knowledge of the CS-US contingencies as a basis for their ratings. Moreover, unlike the demand compliance account, an account in terms of justified beliefs is also compatible with the observation that a significant gender priming effect was found in Experiment 7 and that this priming effect correlated with contingency awareness. As De Houwer et al. (this issue) pointed out, the conscious inferences that underlie justifiable preferences and beliefs can also lead to effects on indirect measures, such as priming. Moreover, additional analyses of the priming data of Experiment 7 (see Discussion of Experiment 8) suggested that gender priming effects were more pronounced for participants who completed the gender scale measures before the gender priming measure. This could have been due to the fact that participants were only informed about the nature of the CSs (i.e., that they were Japanese first names) during the instructions for the gender scale measure. Such information allows the participants to form justifiable beliefs about the gender of the CSs, which in turn could have been responsible for priming effects. It should be clear, however, that an account of our findings in terms of justifiable beliefs is highly speculative and that more research is needed to differentiate this account form a demand compliance account.

The second question that was raised by our findings is why we failed to find transfer effects in the absence of contingency awareness. As we pointed out above, EC typically does not depend on contingency awareness. Likewise, in the studies of Stevenson and colleagues (e.g., Stevenson et al., 1998, 2000), associative transfer of the sweetness and sourness of drinks was found in the absence of contingency awareness. This forces us to consider whether there might have been procedural elements in our studies that prevented us from observing associative transfer of nonevaluative stimulus properties in the absence of contingency awareness (i.e., unconscious transfer).

One possible reason might have been that we selected a stimulus feature (i.e., gender) that is difficult to transfer in an unconscious manner. Although we see no compelling a priori reasons for why this would be the case, maybe other features are more easy to transfer in such a manner. One should note, however, that there are many unpublished studies that have failed to provide evidence for (unconscious) associative transfer of a variety of features: the age of persons (Meersmans, 2004), emotional expressions (Vansteenwegen, 1994), size, brightness of pictures, semantic category of words (De Houwer, Meersmans, Baeyens, & Eelen, 2002), ambitiousness of persons (Walther, 2002), and location of sounds (Olson & Fazio, 2002). It is therefore not clear to us what other features might be more suitable to transfer in an associative manner. The fact that Kim et al. (1996) did find transfer of perceived speed and softness should be interpreted with caution because they did not take into account contingency awareness. Finally, although the results of Stevenson and colleagues (e.g., Stevenson et al., 1998, 2000) demonstrate that the sweetness and sourness of tastes can be transferred in an unconscious manner, it is possible that these effects are limited to tastes and odours. For instance, Stevenson et al. argued that such stimuli are processed in a more holistic manner than visual stimuli. That is, the CS and US are experienced as one event and stored within a single memory representation. When the CS is presented during the test phase, this activates the memory representation of those prior experiences and thus biases the perception of the CS in the direction of the US.

One could also argue that other elements of our procedure were responsible for the fact that we did not find evidence for an unconscious transfer of gender. For instance, we used complex stimuli that were presented only briefly and on a small number of trials. It is indeed possible that this seriously reduced the size of the unconscious conditioning effects. Although it is difficult to refute this argument in a definite manner, one can point out that the stimuli and procedures that we used were highly similar to those used in other studies that did provide evidence for (unconscious) EC. But it might well be that a procedure that produces unconscious EC is not necessarily suited for producing unconscious nonevaluative transfer effects.

The categorisation account of Davey (1994) implies that associative transfer of stimulus properties will occur to the extent that the CS and US share certain perceptual properties. Although we did not manipulate this variable explicitly, it should be noted that the CSs and USs that were used in Experiments 1–6 were to a large degree perceptually similar (i.e., both CSs and USs were pictures of babies). Also, unconscious associative transfer of valence has been found when comparable stimuli were used (e.g., Baeyens et al., 1992). We therefore think it is unlikely that our failure to find reliable unconscious transfer of gender was due to a lack of similarity between the CSs and USs. Nevertheless, a new study in which the degree of similarity between CSs and USs is manipulated could be useful to test the impact of this potential boundary condition more carefully.

It is possible that there are still other reasons why we failed to find transfer effects in the absence of contingency awareness. We also acknowledge that perhaps we would have found evidence for unconscious gender transfer effects if we would have increased the power of our tests even further. We therefore do not exclude the possibility that unconscious transfer effects with visual stimuli can be found under certain conditions. Our data do clearly show, however, that associative transfer of nonevaluative properties can depend heavily on contingency awareness. It is therefore necessary that contingency awareness is assessed in all future studies on associative transfer of nonevaluative stimulus properties. Moreover, our analysis of the reasons for why associative transfer depends on contingency awareness leads to the conclusion that one should also assess the justification that participants give for their ratings. This could allow one to determine whether the observed transfer effects are due to demand compliance or based on justified beliefs. Additional information about the validity of these two accounts might by provided by studies that look at the effect of contingency awareness and instructions about the nature of the CSs on indirect measures of transfer.

REFERENCES

Baeyens, F., & De Houwer, J. (1995). Evaluative conditioning is a qualitatively distinct form of classical conditioning: A reply to Davey (1994). *Behaviour Research and Therapy*, *33*, 825–831.

Baeyens, F., De Houwer, J., Vansteenwegen, D., & Eelen, P. (1998b). Evaluative conditioning is a form of associative learning: On the artifactual nature of Field and Davey's (1997) artifactual account of evaluative learning. *Learning and Motivation*, *29*, 461–474.

Baeyens, F., Eelen, P., & Crombez, G. (1995). Pavlovian associations are forever: On classical conditioning and extinction. *Journal of Psychophysiology*, *9*, 127–141.

Baeyens, F., Eelen, P., Crombez, G., & Van den Bergh, O. (1992). Human evaluative conditioning: Acquisition trials, presentation schedule, evaluative style and contingency awareness. *Behaviour Research and Therapy*, *30*, 133–142.

Baeyens, F., Hendrickx, H., Crombez, G., & Hermans, D. (1998a). Neither extended sequential nor simultaneous feature positive training result in modulation of evaluative flavor-flavor conditioning in humans. *Appetite*, *31*, 185–204.

Baeyens, F., Hermans, D., & Eelen, P. (1993). The role of CS-US contingency in human evaluative conditioning. *Behaviour Research and Therapy*, *31*, 731–737.

Davey, G. C. L. (1994). Is evaluative conditioning a qualitatively distinct form of classical conditioning. *Behaviour Research and Therapy*, *32*, 291–299.

De Houwer, J., Baeyens, F., Vansteenwegen, D., & Eelen, P. (2000). Evaluative conditioning in the picture-picture paradigm with random assignment of conditioned stimuli to unconditioned stimuli. *Journal of Experimental Psychology. Animal Behaviour Processes*, *26*, 237–242.

De Houwer, J., Hermans, D., & Eelen, P. (1998). Affective and identity priming with episodically associated stimuli. *Cognition and Emotion*, *12*, 145–169.

De Houwer, J., Meersmans, T., Baeyens, F., & Eelen, P. (2002, April). Associative transfer of non-evaluative stimulus properties. In A. P. Field & J. De Houwer (Chair), *Evaluative conditioning*. Symposium conducted at the Experimental Psychology Conference, Leuven, Belgium.

De Houwer, J., Thomas, S., & Baeyens, F. (2001). Association learning of likes and dislikes: A review of 25 years of research on human evaluative conditioning. *Psychological Bulletin*, *127*, 853–869.

Draine, S.C., & Greenwald, A.G. (1998). Replicable unconscious semantic priming. *Journal of Experimental Psychology: General*, *127*, 286–303.

Fazio, R.H., Sanbonmatsu, D.M., Powell, M.C., & Kardes, F.R. (1986). On the automatic activation of attitudes. *Journal of Personality and Social Psychology*, *50*, 229–238.

Field, A. P. (2003). Can meta-analysis be trusted? *The Psychologist*, *16*, 642–645.

Field, A. P. (in press). Learning to like (or dislike): Associative learning of preferences. In A. J. Wills (Ed.), *New directions in human associative learning*. Mahwah, NJ: Erlbaum.

Field, A. P., & Davey, G. C. L. (1997). Conceptual conditioning: evidence for an artifactual account of evaluative learning. *Learning and Motivation*, *28*, 446–464.

Hermans, D., Clarysse, J., Baeyens, F., & Spruyt, A. (2002b). *Affect (Version 1.0 and 3.0)* [Computer software; retrieved from http://www.psy.kuleuven.ac.be/leerpsy/affect]. University of Leuven, Belgium.

Hermans, D., Vansteenwegen, D., Crombez, G., Baeyens, F., & Eelen, P. (2002a). Expectancy learning and evaluative learning in human classical conditioning: Affective priming as an indirect and unobtrusive measure of conditioned stimulus valence. *Behaviour Research and Therapy*, *40*, 217–234.

Kim, J., Allen, C.T., & Kardes, F.R. (1996). An investigation of the mediational mechanisms underlying attitudinal conditioning. *Journal of Marketing Research, 33*, 318–328.

Meersmans, T. (2004). *Associative transfer of non-evaluative stimulus properties.* Unpublished Doctoral Dissertation, University of Leuven, Belgium.

Martin, I., & Levey, A.B. (1978). Evaluative conditioning. *Advances in Behaviour Research and Therapy, 1*, 57–102.

Olson, M.A., & Fazio, R.H. (2001). Implicit attitude formation through classical conditioning. *Psychological Science, 12*, 413–417.

Olson, M.A., & Fazio, R.H. (2002, February). *Implicit covariation learning: evaluative versus non-evaluative associations.* Poster session presented at the annual meeting of the Society for Personality and Social Psychology, Savannah.

Page, M. M. (1969). Social psychology of a classical conditioning of attitudes experiment. *Journal of Personality and Social Psychology, 11*, 177–186.

Pavlov, I. (1927). *Conditioned reflexes.* New York: Oxford University Press.

Rozin, P., & Millman, L. (1987). Family environment, not heredity, accounts for family resemblances in food preferences and attitudes: A twin study. *Appetite, 8*, 125–134.

Stevenson, R.J., Boakes, R.A., & Prescott, J. (1998). Changes in odor sweetness resulting from implicit learning of a simultaneous odor sweetness association: An example of learned synesthesia. *Learning and Motivation, 29*, 113–132.

Stevenson, R.J., Boakes, R.A., & Wilson, J.P. (2000). Resistance to extinction of conditioned odor perceptions: Evaluative conditioning is not unique. *Journal of Experimental Psychology: Learning, Memory, and Cognition, 26*, 423–440.

Vansteenwegen, D. (1994). *In welke mate wordt de perceptie van een prikkel beïnvloed door zijn referentiele relaties met andere prikkels?* [To what extent can the perception of a stimulus be influenced by its referential relation with other stimuli]. Unpublished master's thesis, University of Leuven, Belgium.

Walther, E. (2002). Guilty by mere association: Evaluative conditioning and the spreading attitude effect. *Journal of Personality and Social Psychology, 82*, 919–934.

Zajonc, R.B. (1980). Feeling and thinking: Preferences need no inferences. *American Psychologist, 35*, 151–175.

SUBJECT INDEX

Advertising
  mood, 190–191
  unconditioned stimulus revaluation,
    181
Affective emotional disorders, 265
Affective-evaluative learning
  phenomenon, 197
Affective learning
  contingency awareness, 277–278, 280
  cue competition, 276–277, 280
  extinction, 274–275, 279
  occasion setting, 275–276, 280
  theories, 270
  underlying mechanism, 269–270
  use of term, 269
Affective perseverance, 184
Affective priming
  compared to evaluative conditioning,
    182
  extinction, 258
  indirect measure of evaluative
    conditioning, 192, 198
  preferences, 170
  unconscious processes, 213
Amygdala, 279
Associative learning
  evaluative conditioning as qualitatively
    distinct form, 246
  extinction, 248
  process models, 239–240
  use of term, 162
Associative processes, 270
Associative transfer of nonevaluative
    stimuli, 285–286, 294–295, 299, 300,
    301–302, 303–304
Attention
  contingency awareness, 220
  evaluative conditioning, 165–166, 238
  learning attenuation, 219
  resource limitation, 219, 238

Attitude conditioning, 177–182, 197
Automatic effective processing, 167
Automatic processes, 167
Aversions, 189–190
Awareness, learning and, 164, 214; see
    also Contingency awareness

Balance theory, 184–186
Balanced sentiment triad, 185–186
Bell-food paradigm, 176
Between-subject controls, 163, 218, 247,
    256
Blink startle modulation, 273–274
Blocking, 219
Bogus pipeline, 199–200, 212
Boundary conditions, 166–167, 219
Brand extension, 191

Categorisation model, 285, 304
Category awareness, 293
Classical conditioning, 168, 175–176
Clinical psychology, 189, 265
Commercials, 191
Compulsions, 265
Conceptual–categorical account, 213, 270
Conditioned attitudes, 177–182, 197
Conditioning
  conceptual analysis, 168
  distraction, 229–230, 238
Connectionism, 213
Conscious inferences, 301, 303
Conscious propositional knowledge,
    169–170
Consciousness
  evaluative conditioning, 169–170, 213
  learning, 198–199
Consumer research, 190–191
Contingency, 177–178
Contingency awareness
  affective learning, 277–278, 280

assessment, 252
associative transfer of nonevaluative
   stimuli, 286, 303, 304–305
attention, 220
defined, 220
evaluative conditioning, 164–165, 177,
   198–199, 218, 246, 284
gender priming, 298
measurement, 207, 223–225, 240
theoretical level, 239
Counterbalancing, 220, 229, 247
Counterconditioning, 178, 184, 189, 265
Cue competition, 276–277, 280

Demand awareness, 230, 297, 298, 299
Demand effects, 295
stability of evaluative responses, 258,
   264
Depression, 189
Discounting, 213
Distraction, 198, 229–230, 238
Dual process model, 218, 270, 278,
   280–281

Effect, 168–169
Evaluative conditioning
   advantages, 192–193
   applied settings, 189–191
   artefact, 162–163
   associative nature, 256
   attention, 165–166, 238
   automatic processes, 167
   baseline phase, 198
   bogus pipeline, 212
   boundary conditions, 166–167, 219
   conceptual–categorical account, 213
   connectionism, 213
   consciousness, 169–170, 213
   contingency awareness, 164–165, 177,
      198–199, 218, 246, 284
   controversies, 162–166, 217–218
   description, 176, 284
   different processes, 167–171
   dual process model, 218
   effect, 168–169
   evaluative phenomena, 192
   experimental bias, 248, 263

extinction, 165, 178, 218, 246, 247–248,
   256, 263–265, 284
failure, 163, 192, 213, 218
functional properties, 163–166
genuine phenomenon, 162–163
holistic account, 180, 213
intuition, 167
justified preferences, 171, 302–303
learning phase, 198
manifestations, 182–189
misattribution, 284
nonassociative processes, 218
Pavlovian conditioning, 218, 239, 246,
   265, 284
perceptually similar stimuli, 162–163,
   247
procedure, 168
referential account, 213, 284
sequential phases, 198
single process model, 218
stability, 182
stimulus categorisation, 285
stimulus evaluation, 167
test phase, 198
theoretical models, 213
transfer of affect, 176
unconscious, 177, 213
use of term, 162
visceral cues, 239
visual stimuli, 217, 218
Evaluative generalisation, 182
Expectancy learning, 284
Experimental bias, 248, 263
Exposure-based therapies, 265, 270
Extinction
   affective learning, 274–275, 279
   affective priming, 258
   associative learning, 248
   evaluative conditioning, 165, 178, 218,
      246, 247–248, 256, 263–265, 284
   experimental biases, 248, 263
   partial reinforcement, 257–258
   renewal effect, 256–257, 274–275,
      279–280

Fear, 272, 279
Flavour–flavour paradigm, 246, 271–272

Flavour–taste transfer, 285–286
Functional magnetic resonance imaging, 272

Gender priming, 289, 296, 298
Gut-feelings, 238–239

Haptic stimulation, 246
Hippocampus, 279
Holistic representation, 180, 213, 270

Implicit Association Test (IAT), 170, 198
Implicit learning, 167
Impression formation, 213
Independent control groups, 206
Ingroup favouritism, 188–189
Intuition, 167

Justified preferences, 170–171, 302–303

"Kill-the-messenger effect", 183

Latent inhibition, 219–220
Learning
    attention, 219
    awareness, 164, 214
    consciousness, 198–199
    failure, 219–220
    preferences, 161
Luncheon technique, 197

Magnetic resonance imaging, 272
Marketing, 286
Mere ownership effect, 186
Mood-congruency hypothesis, 190
Mood induction, 190–191

Name letter effect, 186

Occasion setting, 275–276, 280
Olfactory stimuli, 246

Partial reinforcement, 257–258
Pavlovian conditioning, 218, 239, 246, 265, 270, 272, 284
Perception, 213
Persuasion, 182–183

Phobias
    counterconditioning, 265
    evaluative conditioning, 189–190
    exposure therapy, 265
Picture–picture paradigm, 176, 271–272, 287
Postconditioning revaluation, 213
Predictions, 176
Preferences
    crucial role, 161
    implicit measures, 170
    justified/unjustified, 170–171, 302–303
    learning, 161
Prejudice, 180, 271
Procedure, 168
Psychological reactance, 199, 200, 204, 206, 212, 213

Reactance, 199, 200, 204, 206, 212, 213
Referential account, 213, 270, 284
Renewal effect, 256–257, 274–275, 279–280
Rescorla-Wagner model, 219

Salience, 285
Self-anchoring, 187
Self-evaluation, 186–189
Self-projection, 187
Sensory preconditioning, 178–180, 213
Sentiment relation, 184–186
Signal learning, 176
Simple conditioning paradigm, potential problems, 272–274
Single process model, 218, 239–240
Social stimuli, 246
Spreading attitude effect, 179–180, 191
Startle reflexes, 273–274
Stigmatisation, 183
Stimulus
    categorisation, 285
    evaluation, 167
    subliminal, 177, 198
    valence, 287
Subliminal stimuli, 177, 198

Thalamus, 279

Therapy
  counterconditioning, 189, 265
  effectiveness, 280
  exposure-based, 265, 270
Transfer effect score, 293, 298

Unconditioned stimulus revaluation,
  180–182

Unconscious processes
  evaluative conditioning, 177, 213
  learning, 198–199
Unit formation, 184, 185

Verbal reports, 170–171
Visceral cues, 239
Visual stimuli, 217, 218, 246

www.ingramcontent.com/pod-product-compliance
Ingram Content Group UK Ltd.
Pitfield, Milton Keynes, MK11 3LW, UK
UKHW020348010325
455677UK00021B/355